ISBN: 978129010173

Published by:
HardPress Publishing
8345 NW 66TH ST #2561
MIAMI FL 33166-2626

Email: info@hardpress.net
Web: http://www.hardpress.net

THE GERMANS IN ENGLAND

THE GERMANS IN ENGLAND

1066-1598

BY

IAN D. COLVIN

WITH MAP OF HANSEATIC LEAGUE

LONDON

"THE NATIONAL REVIEW" OFFICE

14 TAVISTOCK STREET, COVENT GARDEN, W.C.

1915

TO THE MEMORY OF MY FRIEND AND COLLEAGUE,
CAPTAIN GERALD MOYNA OF THE ROYAL SCOTS
FUSILIERS, WHO DIED FIGHTING IN FLANDERS, THE
26TH SEPTEMBER 1915, I DEDICATE THIS BOOK

PREFACE

THIS book must bear the stamp of a haste which only the urgency of war can justify. It was written in a few months in the intervals of my daily work, and if it has any merits, it is as a rough sketch and outline of its subject. As usual, I found the British Museum unfailing in its courtesy and in its resources. I have to thank Mr. Ferdinand de Mera for his invaluable assistance in translating German authorities and investigating crucial points in the *Hanse Recesse* and other German archives, and for his map of the roads, towns, and *Kontors* of the Hanseatic League. To Miss Thompson I am indebted for transcripts from Tudor manuscripts at the British Museum, to Mr. Claud Mullins for researches in the London Guildhall Library, and to Mr. J. S. Sandars for a revision of my proofs. The head of Queen Elizabeth, who expelled the Germans from England, was reproduced by the courtesy of the Medal Department of the British Museum.

CONTENTS

INTRODUCTION

WHEN these present hostilities began, there was a prevailing belief that our relations with Germany had always been of the friendliest order, and many people were even surprised to find how bitterly the Germans hated England. Some of the newspapers described the naval engagement off Heligoland as our first fight with our "cousins" on the sea, and the German newspapers were full of talk about the *Stammverwandt* which we were said to have betrayed. And yet, as I have written this little book to show, our sailors were fighting the Germans all through the Middle Ages, and these sea-fights were not mere piracies and accidents, as some historians suppose, but the symptoms, as I might call them, of the long, fierce, and irregular conflict which was waged between Germany and England for sea-power and commercial supremacy.

Unless we understand this conflict, the history of England, from the time of the Angevins to the time of the Tudors, is mere sound and fury, signifying nothing. It is like a jigsaw puzzle which cannot be made into a picture because half the pieces are missing. But when we come to understand that the Germans were always interfering in English policy for their own ends, when we find them bribing a Chancellor, financing an invasion, and raising or pulling down a dynasty, then much that was formerly obscure becomes clear. We begin to see the hidden springs and inner motives of what was before a mere orgy of civil and foreign wars.

As I hope to show, there were two main motives of German interference in English policy, the one political and the other commercial. The main motive on the political side was to secure the assistance of England in the constant wars between France and the Empire, and also in the conflicts between the Empire and the Pope and between the Empire and Venice. Those wars with France, in which we reaped so much glory and shed so much blood for ends so barren and unprofitable, were fought less in our own interests than in the interests of Germany, which promoted and fomented them. The Germans came to look upon English assistance so much as a matter of course that when an English king was found who refused to assist them, an aggrieved King of the Romans set about to finance an English Pretender more amenable to German influence. Thus Perkin Warbeck wrote to the King of the Romans in January or February of 1496 : " Were the Duke of York (*i.e.* Perkin) to obtain the Crown, the King of the Romans and the League (the Holy League) might avail themselves of England against the King of France as if the island were their own."

But we should not understand the political motive of German policy unless we realised the commercial motive. And here we come at once to that strange and obscure power in mediæval Europe vaguely known to English readers as the Hanseatic League. Now I have seen it said that this League of cities was not native to Germany, but I do not think that this objection will be sustained upon a review of the evidence. The League certainly had its origin in Germany, and as certainly its ruling city was Lübeck. It was always the policy of the League to keep secret its extent and its membership ; but of all the cities which are known to have belonged to the League, it is difficult to find one which could not be described as German. The stock exception is Dinant; but it is doubtful if Dinant was in the full sense a Hanseatic city. As will be seen from the notes on the point at the end of my book, there is evidence that Dinant was regarded by the cities as an outsider, and its share in Hanseatic privileges was probably given in order to obtain for Germany a port of entry into France. Bruges and Bergen were no more Hanseatic cities than London and Novgorod. They were *Kontors* or depôts, the economic serfs and thralls of the League, without either membership or voice in its policy. The League had its house in these *Kontor* cities, and its council of merchants to do its business and represent its interests, just as England has its houses and its merchants in Hong-Kong; but just as Hong-Kong has no seat in our English Parliament, so Bruges had no place in the Hanse Day at Lübeck. The German "merchant" in Bruges might go to Lübeck as our Consul or the chairman of our Chamber of Commerce at Hong-Kong might come to London. He would be heard at the Day, and his opinion on Flemish policy would carry weight; but the town of Bruges itself, its mayor and its aldermen, had no place in the League: Bruges was a foreign city to be wheedled and bullied into subservience, but never to be admitted into partnership.

So with Novgorod, Bergen, Venice, Stockholm, London; the Germans were established more or less firmly in all these towns, and influenced to a greater or less degree their fortunes and their policy; but the towns themselves had no place in the League—there was never any question of admitting them to membership. The case of the Polish towns is different. Dantzig was from the beginning in the inner circle, and enjoyed all the privileges of membership; but Dantzig was by nature and origin a Prussian city : its first Protector was the Grand Master of the Teutonic Knights, and it transferred its allegiance to Poland late in the day and for its own purposes : in all essentials it remained a Prussian city. And so with the other cities along the Baltic shore as far as Riga and Reval : they were in their origin German trading colonies, outposts of the League, and remained in policy and character foreign to their immediate surroundings. So we may suppose it was with Cracow, and possibly with those Saxon colonies which remain to this day in the south-east of Hungary, a foreign element in the Magyar State. They were the advance guards of a great commercial system which in substance as in origin was German.

And so if we go over the list of Hanseatic cities we shall find that almost all are German—if indeed we can call the Prussian a German. What were the chief Hanseatic cities ?—their names are sufficient answer : Lübeck, Dantzig, Bremen, Hamburg, Brunswick, Cologne. And we should find if we went more into detail that round Lübeck, Dantzig, Brunswick, and Cologne all the minor cities form themselves : they are the four " Thirds " into which the League for some purposes is divided.

The League, then, is accurately described as a federation of German cities. So it was understood in the Middle Ages. In the English charters its house in London is called " Gildhalla Teutonicorum "; and when the King of Poland sent an ambassador to London on behalf of the Hanse, Queen Elizabeth replied that if the League was not Prussian it was nothing.

" Men of the Emperor " and " Easterlings " are names which both described the German merchant before the Hanseatic League could be said to exist, and the two names possibly represented the two great divisions of German trade—the Men of the Emperor being merchants of Cologne and of the Rhine, the Easterlings of Hamburg and the Baltic. However that may be, we shall find that Cologne was settled in England before Lübeck. Tradition dates the Guildhall of the Cologners in London from the Norman Conquest; but, as we shall see, there is evidence that the origin of those extraordinary privileges of the German merchant which are to be the staple of this little book is even further back in our history. The famous letter of Charlemagne to King Offa of Mercia amounts to a treaty of commerce on a basis of reciprocity: " You have also written to us about your merchants. We would have them enjoy our protection and defence within our realm . . . according to the ancient custom in commerce. . . . Show like favour to our merchants. . . ." On both sides the traders are to appeal to the justice of the country they are in. The significance of this letter to us is that Germany has something which is a necessity to England—command of the pilgrim and trade road of the Rhine. Safe conduct on that road was in the hands of the Emperor, and, under the Emperor, of Cologne and the German princes. The Germans have always been a practical people, and it is not to be supposed that English pilgrims were allowed to use this road for nothing. Indeed our whole story teaches that when the German has something that the Englishman lacks, the Englishman has to pay a very heavy price for it.

But the Men of the Emperor and the Easterlings also commanded certain commodities of importance to England. The ancient exchange of Europe rested on the same basis as the exchange of China to-day—weight of silver. The German pound-weight of silver was the standard for all Europe, and "pound sterling" is a corruption of "pound easterling." The ransom of Richard Cœur de Lion was estimated in the Cologne weight of silver, and the measure of Cologne was probably the measure of the Easterlings, the standard of all Germany. Now Germany set the standard in silver because Germany commanded the supply. The silver of "Beame," of which we hear so much in mediæval trade, is silver from the mines of Bohemia.

But besides their command of silver, and therefore of exchange, and of trade routes, the Germans controlled sea-power outside the Mediterranean. And here we come to the secret of the power of the Baltic cities—the head and centre of the Hanseatic League. Hemp for ropes, flax for sails, pitch for caulking and cordage, timber for masts, all these things came from the Baltic, and the cities which commanded these commodities commanded the sea. And if we add to these command of the Baltic corn-supply, command of the salt-fish trade, and the supply of wax, the necessities of light and religion, we shall be able to estimate the "pull" which the Baltic cities had over the rest of Europe in the Middle Ages.

And Germans would not have been Germans if they had not got full value for all these advantages. There was, as we shall see, a time when the German cities could pass a law that English foreign trade was to be carried only in German ships, and this monopoly was at other times so well recognised that an English Government could forbid its subjects to engage in oversea trade. By skilful and usurious use of these manifold sources of power the Germans established themselves like a flourishing mistletoe in the clefts of our English apple-tree. The tale of their privileges is staggering to consider. They had their fortified Guildhall with its wharves and store-houses on the riverside; they were free of most, if not all, English taxes, both municipal and national, and paid less in customs than native Englishmen; they had not only their own court and aldermen for the government of their own affairs, but had special judges to settle their disputes with natives; they were above English juries and English law; they were exempt especially from that ancient custom of "hosting" which prevailed not only in England but throughout at least Northern Europe; they held their houses in London and other ports in freehold; they had control of one of the gates of the City of London, and were free to go out and in without paying municipal duties; they dealt not only "in gross" but in retail, in defiance of English custom.

They were thus favoured not only over other foreigners, but over Englishmen. Their advantage over other foreigners was so overwhelming that even the trade of the Venetians with England languished and dwindled almost to nothing, and their advantage over Englishmen was substantial enough to make the determination to end it one of the chief forces in our mediæval politics. Here, then, we come to the main thread of our story—the struggle between the German and the Englishman for English trade. This great struggle, which may be traced from the time of Henry III to the time of Elizabeth, seems to me one of the chief factors in our English history, and yet it has been almost ignored by our English historians. I do not know of a single English historian who has treated the

b

subject as a connected whole. Welsford, over whose early death I shall never cease to mourn, touched upon it in that book of gold, *The Strength of England*, but did not fully realise its importance; Anderson, in his wonderful *Origin of Commerce*, which remains to this day our best economic history, tells the story on its commercial side with his accustomed erudition, but the political side is out of his sphere. The Germans understand its importance; but Lappenberg and Sartorius, the chief historians of the Hanseatic League in England, have not even been translated, and of those who deal with periods, like Schanz, Pauli, and Schulz, none, as far as I know, has been given to the English reader.

The cause of this neglect I do not trouble to investigate. Our English historians have been in general superior to trade; our economists superior to history. Some have marched triumphantly in the wake of our glorious campaigns in France, or those parts of them which are glorious; they have been so dazzled with the fair frontage of our Palace of Fame that they have not spared a glance for its kitchen premises; others have concerned themselves in our civil wars and our wars of union; and most have been preoccupied with certain specific factors in English history—its constitutional and its religious quarrels. To me the one is the fine flower, the other the faint shadow of human affairs. I do not gather from his story that Simon de Montfort concerned himself much in the constitution of the English Parliament: his ends were more practical, he led the anti-foreign, and especially the anti-German, party in England. Matthew Paris understood this well enough, but the modern historian almost leaves it out of account. He learnedly discusses constitutional problems for which Simon probably cared little or nothing, and leaves unexplored the practical questions of protection and patriotism, for which Simon and his party cared a very great deal. And so down to the reign of Elizabeth. Froude has nothing to say of the Germans and whole volumes of the Spaniards. Yet our archives show clearly that the struggle with the Spaniard covered a deeper and more ancient conflict—between the English and the German trader.

When even an English statesman can talk of trade as a sordid bond, it would be foolish to quarrel with English historians for leaving it out of account. And yet, as it seems to me, these trade relations with Germany must be understood if we are to understand our English history. I put the motives of man thus, in order of their strength: (1) Blood, that is race or nationality; (2) patriotism, or love of land and country; (3) interest, or the means by which man lives in trade and commerce; (4) religion, which is the hope and refectory of his soul, but as a motive uncertain and incalculable in its influence, and much used as a colour to disguise interest; and (5) politics, including all constitutional questions, which are merely the means or instruments for attaining these other ends. Now it is the proper business of the historian to understand all these motives and to explain their influence on events, for if the historian deals merely in events alone he signifies nothing. And yet if we read our English histories of the Wars of the Roses, it might be supposed that some at least of these motives were not then in operation. Events, in fact, are not so much explained as narrated. Let us, for example, take what is the crux and centre of these wars, the action of Warwick in transferring his allegiance from York to Lancaster, the flight and return of the King-Maker, the flight and return of Edward IV, and the Battle of Barnet in which Neville died. From the English historian we might suppose that Warwick was merely an unscrupulous noble, who acted through some pique or personal motive, ambition, or mere caprice. But if we apply our German key to these events, we find that Warwick fought Lübeck at sea ; that Edward was made king on the " anti-German ticket " ; that Edward, in the absence of Warwick, came to an understanding with the Hanse ; that Warwick's invading army made an anti-German demonstration in London ; that Edward fled to Flanders and returned in German ships ; and that German influence was thrown into the scale for the defeat of Warwick, just as it had been used for the defeat of de Montfort. If English historians say little or nothing of all this, it is not forgotten by the German historians. Thus Pauli, for example : " When Edward IV was driven out they (the Hanseatic League) had to decide whether Henry VI should keep the throne or lose it again. . . . They helped the Germanic element to victory. If Henry VI had succeeded in retaining the Crown . . . the sea-power wielded by the German merchant would have gone to Rome . . . and the whole development of West European commerce would have been different. Thus the Germans freed themselves from a very serious danger, and at the same time forced the King under an obligation to the Hanse." [1] In the opinion, then, of one of the greatest of German historians, at this crisis in English history an English king was a mere puppet in German hands, and the Wars of the Roses were part of the conflict for German

[1] Pauli, *Die Hansestädte in den Rosenkriegen*, p. 177.

commercial supremacy in England. And the contemporary Dantzig chronicler is just as explicit: "In the year 1469 there was great discord in England amongst the barons, one of the reasons being the (German) merchant."[1] Here then is a motive for the Wars of the Roses, which puts all the chief actors in a new and surprising light. Warwick is a patriot who fights against the German domination on sea and land; Edward betrays the cause of English trade and shipping for German money; Warwick remains true to his principles and drives Edward from the Throne on which he had placed him; Edward is restored by the German power, and replaces the German merchant in his position of privilege.

These motives being known, the Wars of the Roses no longer seem mere feudal anarchy, but take their place in English history as part of the great struggle for economic independence and sea-power, which is the substance of our narrative. As Simon de Montfort, so Warwick the King-Maker—they were both national heroes who died fighting the Germans in the cause of protection. And just as the London merchant was defeated by the German merchant when the King of Germany restored Henry III to the throne, so the cause of English trade was laid in the dust when German ships carried Edward IV from Flanders to the port of Ravenspur. The restoration of Edward IV was followed by the most shameful treaty ever signed by an English king, I mean the Treaty of Utrecht. "German power is more firmly established in England than ever," was the opinion of Lübeck. "We have made an end of the English," said the envoys of Dantzig. In the Treaty of Utrecht we have the spectacle of an English

---

[1] *Dantzig Chronicle to* 1469, p. 5.

king, not only exempting German traders from all the customs paid by Englishmen, not only placing them above the justice of English courts, but making England the instrument for punishing the one German city which had deserted the Hanseatic League and espoused the cause of York. Cologne was deprived of all privileges in England until such time as the Hanseatic ban should be removed.

Henry VII, that wary and politic prince, did not dare to challenge directly the power of the German cities, although he must have been sorely tempted thereto by the intrigues of Germany against his throne. How far these intrigues were the work of the cities and how far the work of the German king, I have found it impossible to determine. But it is certain that the German traders in London were suspected of a connection with the Perkin Warbeck invasion, and Busch admits that they were probably the go-betweens. Maximilian's motive is plainly declared in his correspondence with Perkin, and in the despatches of the Venetian Ambassadors. He found Henry VII slack in the traditional English role of picking the German chestnut out of the French fire. But the cities also had a reasonable motive, for the Tudor policy was founded on the support of the English interest both in trade and manufacture. The English Parliament which welcomed the first Tudor to the throne marked its affection by granting the King a poll-tax on foreigners, and Henry's Navigation Acts, his encouragement of cloth manufacture, his charter to the Merchant Adventurers, and his alliance with Denmark were all indirect blows at the Hanseatic League. Yet the state of English shipping and the insecurity of his throne forbade him to do more than lay the foundations of that great national policy which in the hands of Elizabeth was to shatter in pieces the German power.

We shall not understand the mercantile policy of the Tudors unless we realise that this greatest of English dynasties rested upon the organised power of the Merchant Adventurers, and that the Merchant Adventurers were engaged in a truceless and deadly struggle with the Hanseatic League. Who has sung the praises, who has even told the tale, of the Merchant Adventurers ? To some it may appear " sordid ": those who dare not face the realities of life like to pretend that there is no such thing as trade. To me it is one of the epical subjects of our history, this conflict between the English and the German merchant. Why should we allow the German a superiority in organisation when it is matter of history that English organisation defeated German organisation ? For the Merchant Adventurers were nothing less than the organisation of English trade to fight the Hanseatic League. " The Company of the Merchant Adventurers," says Wheeler, " consisteth of a great number of wealthy and well-experimented merchants dwelling in divers great cities, maritime towns, and other parts of the realm, to wit, London, York, Norwich, Exeter, Ipswich, Newcastle, Hull, &c. These men of old time linked and bound themselves together in company for the exercise of merchandise and seafare, trading in cloth, kersey, and all other . . . commodities vendible abroad." And Wheeler always speaks of the Germans as the inveterate enemies of his Society. It is true that we had great merchants even before they were organised on national lines. In the thirteenth century there were the Thornes, who took part in the Crusades, opened out a trade in the Mediterranean, and under the name of " Spina " settled in Italy and financed the popes. In the fourteenth century there were Richard and William de la Pole, high in the councils of Edward III, and Richard Whittington, our nursery Dick, who owned a cat and heard the bells of Bow singing " Turn again, Whittington," from Highgate Hill. He was, in fact, a great English merchant, and his praises are worthily sung in the Libell of English Policy. Then in the fifteenth century there were such merchants as Geoffrey Boleyn, the great-great-grandfather of Queen Elizabeth ; Barantyn, Cotton, Thomas Smith, Thomas Terry and Thomas Baker, of London ; Roger Thornton, of Newcastle ; Taverner of Hull, a pioneer of English trade in Italy and the Levant ; the Jays of Bristol ; and that great Bristol fish merchant, W. Cannyngs, who employed eight hundred sailors and ten ships to trade with Iceland and Prussia in defiance of the Hanse.

Such were a few of the Merchant Adventurers, and if I have treated them rather as a corporation than as individuals, it is not that I forget that they were men as well as merchants. But their chief significance to us is that they organised themselves on national lines to do battle with the German merchant, and carried the commercial war into Flanders and Brabant, into High Germany, into the Baltic, to Iceland, and even into Russia, the jealously guarded trade preserves of the German Hanse. These Merchant Adventurers were from their very nature and purpose in conflict with the Germans : they existed to challenge the supremacy of the League, for they were leagued together to carry English cloth overseas in their own ships and sell it in the mart towns of the Continent. In this they differed from the Merchants of the Staple, who shared their franchises with foreigners and were content to sell our raw material to the Flemish weaver.

But among all these English merchants I give the palm to Thomas Gresham. And his chief title to greatness was not that he founded Gresham College or the Royal Exchange, but that he " practised " with King Edward VI and " my Lord of Northumberland " to break the power of the German merchant in London. The problem before Gresham and his English contemporaries was to induce the Government to resume those privileges which placed the German in a position more favourable than the Englishman—in other words, to secure a reform of the tariff. But the German was strongly entrenched, not only because he had great allies on the Continent, not only because his " scraps of paper " had the sanction of authority and antiquity, but for a more important reason. The Steelyard, as Anderson puts it, served as a sort of bank for the English kings. The English Government was in a chronic state of indebtedness to the German cities, and to destroy the influence of the German it was necessary to secure the financial independence of the Monarchy. And so it came about that in the time of Edward VI and Elizabeth we find Gresham employing all means to induce his fellow-merchants to lend money to the Crown. Thus, for example, old Stow tells us in his *Survey of London :* " King Edward VI borrowed money of Anthony Fugger and his nephews, who were vastly rich German merchants and bankers of Antwerp. And the city was bound with the King for payment. As I find, anno 1551 in the month of April, a recognisance made from the King to Sir Andrew Jud, Lord Maior of the City, and the Commonalty of the same, that the King shall discharge them, their successors, lands, possessions, and goods whatsoever, as well beyond the sea as on this side, from payment of certain sums of money Flemish, which they stood bound for to the said Anthony Fugger and his nephews to be paid at Antwerp." And Stow goes on to tell how Queen Elizabeth "thought of laying aside this custom of taking up money from foreign merchants and bankers, and concluded it better to borrow of her own subjects. . . . This counsel, that famous citizen, Sir Thomas Gresham, her agent, gave her." According to the same authority, Gresham had great difficulty in inducing the Merchant Adventurers "to borrow for the Queen." Not until the Secretary of the Queen's Council (probably Cecil) " wrote to the Merchants to complain of their behaviour " did they lend the Queen money. This transaction of November and December 1569 was made the more necessary because " Duke d'Alva " had closed Antwerp to English trade. Now Stow states as the reason for this change in royal policy "that her own subjects might have the benefit of the interest of the money so lent her rather than strangers "—a very good reason as far as it goes ; but we know from Gresham's letter to Queen Elizabeth, which I quote elsewhere,[1] that Gresham's real object was that the Queen should have no temptation to restore the " usurped privileges " of the Hanseatic League.

Besides lending the Crown money, Gresham " practised against " the Germans in the Courts of Law. I have devoted a whole chapter to the once famous, but long-forgotten, suit of 1551, in which a stout jury of Merchant Adventurers found that the Germans had forfeited their privileges by " colouring " the

---

[1] The letter will be found among the Appendices to Burgon's *Life of Gresham.*

goods of certain " sledded Polacks." [1] It was a curious verdict, for the jury found as part of its true bill that English merchants should have a substantial preference over " all foreign merchants, not native," in the English customs. In other words, the verdict was founded upon sound Protectionist principles. Needless to say, the Germans were shocked at such a court and such a finding—" contrary to laws divine and human and the statutes of this realm and the express words of their ancient privileges." Yet it happened that there were no Germans at that time on the Privy Council, and when the appeal was heard before that august tribunal, it was unanimously decided that substantial justice had been done.

It might have been more heroic if the Germans had been defeated in battle rather than by loans and a suit at law, but it is characteristic of this strange and obscure struggle that the mortal blow should have come in this way. For the blow was mortal. It is true that " bloody Mary," as part of the marriage settlement with Philip, restored, or endeavoured to restore, the German privileges, but Gresham continued to " practise " with the Privy Council, and the German power in England remained effectually broken.

It was for Queen Elizabeth to carry the war into the enemy's country, and for her merchants to fight the Germans in their own markets of Stade, Emden, and Hamburg. I have already told the readers of the *National Review* the story of the last stage of this great conflict, how the Germans supplied Philip with money, munitions, sailors, soldiers, and even ships for his Armada, and how sixty Hanseatic hulks loaded with contraband were captured at one fell swoop by Drake

[1] " He smote the sledded Polacks on the ice."— *Hamlet.*

in the Tagus.   And yet even at this final and desperate
climax of the struggle, Germany and England did not
come to open blows, but fought each other with tariffs
and trade interdicts.   The expulsion of the Germans
from their Steelyard in 1599 was but the final check-
mate in a long game of expulsions, embargoes, tariff
wars, and excommunications of which my last chapter
gives an all too inadequate sketch.

    I have hopes, nevertheless, that my story is neither
sordid nor dull.   If fighting is wanted, I can produce
sea-battles and the sack of cities to prove that German
and Englishman were far enough from living at peace
in the Middle Ages.   The German methods were then
as now : they sank our harmless merchantmen and
drowned our poor fisherfolk.   In the time of Richard
II, and again in the time of Henry III, there was even
open war between England and the German cities.
And why is Wenyngton forgotten, that stout man of
Devon, who, with an inferior force, attacked the Lübeck
fleet and brought it triumphantly into the Solent ?
Most of these battles between English and German
merchants and sailors have been condemned by the
lofty historian as mere acts of piracy unworthy of
chronicle, yet they were part, heroic if obscure, of the
long and stern fight waged by Englishmen for economic
liberty.   And Willoughby and Chancellor also I may
justly call heroes, who circumnavigated the North Cape
to circumvent the German and his ally the Spaniard.
Willoughby, who died in a desolate harbour of Lapland,
and Chancellor, who secured our first alliance with
Russia, are worthy of something more than a grudging
remembrance.   And if we seek the heroic, I boast at
least two figures as illustrious as any in our history,
the first and the last of the barons, the soldier-states-

man Simon de Montfort and the sailor-statesman
Warwick the King-Maker. They both died by German
conspiracy, and they were both remembered as heroes
and patriots by their fellow-Englishmen.

And yet I am willing to concede that the English
protagonists in this struggle were generally men more
of brain than of brawn. Warwick, certainly, if not
Leicester also, was greater as a statesman than as a
warrior ; Gresham won his victories by " practising,"
and so did his good ally, Burghley, the first and by a
long way the greatest of the Cecils. His descendant,
Lord Robert Cecil, is now in the Foreign Office. If
he reads this little book he will find, what he perhaps
does not now realise, that his ancestor defeated the
Germans by giving protection to the English trader.
He might also learn from this story that the Elizabethans
did not deal in half-measures. When they blockaded
Flanders they did not relax the blockade to let Germany do its Christmas trade with Spain. They were
whole-hearted in the struggle, and their design was for
the wealth and strength as well as the honour of England.

I am conscious that there are many faults and
omissions in this book, because it was written in haste
and with an imperfect equipment of knowledge. I have
drawn freely upon secondary authorities when they
were available—to this I make open confession ; but
I may add with a good conscience that, wherever possible, I have tested these authorities by their primary
sources. I have found that Lappenberg is generally
to be trusted where lying does not serve his country,
but that Sartorius is a higher and more equitable court.
Busch, like Lappenberg, takes the German side. Schanz
is great, but only as an economist. Reinhold Pauli
has the style and method of an illustrious historian.

Anderson is fair, like Sartorius. As for the primary sources, there is endless material in the great *Hanse Recesse* (the archives of the League), in Rymer's *Fœdera*, in the Venetian archives edited by Brown, and in our own State papers.

To those English students who may care to trip me up and pursue the subject farther than I have gone, let me say at once that they are sure to find many mistakes in this little book. But in extenuation, at least for my errors of omission, let me say that, if I had allowed myself to be tempted down all the seductive avenues and enchanted glades of this subject, I should never have got to the end of my journey. In particular I had to refuse to go far into the reigns of Richard II and Henry VIII, not because they would have yielded little, but because in my judgment, though important, they were not decisive.[1]

And here let me say a word in guidance as to nomenclature. The Germans in England are at various stages called " Men of the Emperor," " Easterlings,"

---

[1] In particular, I refused to allow myself to enter upon the relations of the Hanseatic League with Scotland, although I found evidence of the great influence of the German cities on Scottish history before the Union of the Crowns. Thus, for example, on 11th October 1297, a month after the battle of Stirling Bridge, Andrew de Moray and William Wallace, " the leaders of the army of the realm of Scotland," wrote to " the Mayors and Commons of Lübeck and Hamburg " that their country had been " recovered by war from the power of the English." Why did the Scottish leaders write to these cities ? Because the Hanse, for purposes of its own, was supplying them with arms, and probably financing them. Mr. Evan Barron, in his *Scottish War of Independence* (pp. 69, 70), quotes this letter, which is preserved in the archives of Lübeck, but fails to explain it. He would add to the value of a fascinating book if he went further into this connection. Scotland's wool was probably carried in German ships to Flemish looms. Had the Germans a *Kontor* in Scotland ? Stirling, at once the head of the navigable Forth and a central and commanding point on the road from North to South, would have suited the German merchant very well. Was Stirling the town of the Easterlings ? Berwick had at one time a " Flemish " garrison. Why ? The Cheviots, like the Ochills at Stirling, would be important to the Flemish weaver. And why did the German cities supply Wallace (and later Bruce) with arms ? Was it merely in the way of trade, or was there the deeper motive of weakening England and getting Scotland into their power ? These, like many other problems no less absorbing, " abide our question."

"Almains," "Flemings," and "Dutchmen"; the Hanseatic League is called the "Steads," the "Towns," the "Hansa," the "Hanse," the "mesne Hanse"; their Guildhall in London is called "Gildhalla Teutonicorum," the Steelyard, and the Stilliard. These various names have confused even such authorities as Lappenberg and the editor of the Acts of the Privy Council. The term "Hanse" was used of any company of merchants : the Merchant Adventurers in the time of Edward VI divided themselves into the "old Hanse" and the "new Hanse," and the index to the Acts of the Privy Council confuses a quarrel between these two with the greater conflict between the Steelyard Merchants and the Merchant Adventurers. As to Germany itself, it is usually called Almaigne, with many variations of spelling, and sometimes Dutchland. In theory the King of the Romans only became Emperor when he was crowned by the Pope; but in later practice at least the custom was more honoured in the breach than in the observance. I have not boggled over all these niceties, but have striven only to give a rough and living outline sketch of the relations between Englishmen and Germans in my period.

And I have set the limits of my period for this reason mainly, that they include the rise and the fall of the German power in England, and all the stages of the first great conflict between England and Germany for supremacy in trade. I hope the story of our first great struggle with the Germans may have its lessons for us who are engaged in the second. For in the first great struggle the Germans were beaten, and they were defeated because England organised herself for victory.

IAN D. COLVIN.

THE GERMANS IN ENGLAND

CHAPTER I

" THE NATURAL ALLY "

THAT redoubtable Hamburger, Dr. Lappenberg,[1] surmises that German traders came to England before the
first German invasion. From our knowledge of German
method, we may regard this as probable ; but we are
upon firmer ground when we reach the letter from
Charlemagne to Offa, King of Mercia, preserved by the
Venerable Bede.[2] The Emperor complains that English traders have been palming themselves off as pilgrims, thereby evading " the fixed tolls in the regular
places." He nevertheless promises security and justice
for English merchants, and asks for reciprocity. When
Eadgythe, daughter of King Athelstan, married the
Emperor Charles the Great, " the German merchants,"
as Lappenberg remarks, " must have found themselves in a very favourable position in England."
Our preferential policy seems to begin with Ethelred,
nicknamed " the Unready," who flourished, if the
term may be used, between 978 and 1016. A document of his time, relating to the institutions of London,
refers to the German merchants as " subjects of the
Emperor (*homines imperatoris*), who arrive in their

---

[1] *Urkundliche Geschichte*, p. 3 et seq.
[2] Bœdæ, *Hist. Ecc.*, I, iv. c. 22.

A

ships." The proclamation testifies that these people are worthy of the same good laws as the Londoners themselves (*bonarum legum digni*), and gives them a preferential status over other foreigners, who are also named—Frenchmen (Ponthieu), Normans, Flemings (Hogge), and people of Liège (Lüttich) and Brabant (Nivelle). The subjects of the Emperor were allowed to buy our chief products, wool and tallow, on board their ships, " whereby probably the payment of certain market duties was avoided." They were not, however, allowed to buy before the citizens—a position to be reversed in later times. The Portreeves were forbidden to put upon them any trading fine, a remark suggesting friction between foreign and municipal policy. On Christmas Eve and at Easter-time the men of the Emperor were to pay a bounty of two pieces of grey and one piece of brown cloth, 10 lb. of pepper, five pairs of men's gloves, and two small barrels of vinegar. To whom these little gifts were made is not clear ; but Lappenberg surmises that they went to the City authorities. And Lappenberg is no doubt right ; for, as we shall find later, the German merchant in mediæval times had a regular scale of these perquisites, ranging from a keg of sturgeon for the Lord Mayor to a dried stockfish for the humble clerk of the customs.

Lappenberg also surmises that as these gifts were made in the winter, when there was no sea-going, the German merchants had already the right to hold property on the banks of the Thames, and lived in London at least through the winter months. But this is to go further than the book : if the Germans wintered in London, we may suppose that they were " hosted " in the houses of the London citizens. All the evidence goes to show that they did not succeed in breaking through this custom before the Norman Conquest.

King Canute further improved the already happy position of the German merchant in our midst by arranging a marriage between his daughter and the son of Conrad II, who became the Emperor Henry III. Freeman, who never grows tired of belauding the Germans and abusing the French, tells us that, in the time of Edward the Confessor, " The German connection was cultivated by the patriotic party as a counterpoise to the French tendencies of the King."[1] German bishops were much in fashion, their promotion being apparently one of the main characteristics of English patriotism in those days. Harold followed the same line of policy : " All the foreigners promoted by Harold, or in the days of his influence, were natives of those kindred Teutonic lands whose sons might still almost be looked upon as fellow-countrymen." Freeman is not, however, quite comfortable about this Germanising of the Church of England : he makes the point that " one whose blood, speech, and manners had not wholly lost the`traces of ancient brotherhood would be more acceptable . . . to England than a mere Frenchman "; but nevertheless " its results were not wholly satisfactory." " I know of no reason to believe," he goes on, " that any of these Lotharingian prelates proved actual traitors to England ; but they certainly did not, as a class, offer the same steady resistance to French influences as the men who had been born in the land. . . . Still something was gained."[2]

---

[1] *Norman Conquest*, vol. ii. p. 57.
[2] *Ibid.*, p. 81. Ealdred, the Archbishop of York, was not a German ; but he had no doubt a " sacred friendship " with the German Emperor, for he spent a whole year at Cologne, and reformed the English Church on " the well-ordered churches of Germany." He surrendered York to William, to the disgust of that staunch English city.

Our excellent Freeman is again a little disturbed by the remarkable circumstance that, although Harold had been in close and constant alliance with Germany, William of Poictiers, the Norman chronicler, boasts that the German Emperor promised William his support in the Conquest. "It is," he says, "utterly impossible to see what interest either the young king or his successive archiepiscopal advisers could have in supporting the claims of William against the claims of Harold."[1] Lappenberg furnishes the answer : "William," he says, "was vigilant and indefatigable in engaging to his interest some of the most influential men at the Imperial Court, for which object the means, irresistible in those times, were supplied him from the wealth of his newly acquired dominion. The chief councillor of the Emperor, Adalbert, Archbishop of Bremen, was by his largesse bribed to intrigue for the security of the munificent conqueror."[2] A German archbishop who takes a bribe from William on the one side, and German bishops who surrender to William on the other—that is not the sort of coincidence which encourages the detached historian to take even Freeman's estimate of the patriotic value of German ecclesiastics.

But when we look for the causes of great events, we shall generally find that there is something more substantial than even a gift or a compliment to an archbishop. William was a great soldier of fortune, and being also a statesman, he understood the sources of power. And the centre of power in his time was the German Empire. The emperors aimed at universal sovereignty : their claim was only disputed by the Popes. The history of the Normans in Italy is too obscure to

[1] Freeman, vol. iii. p. 309.   [2] Lappenberg, *Norman Kings*, p. 115.

afford any certain evidence, but nearer home we find a clue. William diligently sought an alliance with Flanders. Now Flanders was even at that time vital to Germany. It was a main outlet and a main inlet of German commerce : its harbours were crowded with the ships of the Baltic, Genoa, and Spain. The Flemish cities were already wealthy, and with their wealth was bound up the prosperity of Cologne and the Rhineland. " The Flemish Count," says Freeman, quoting William the Chronicler, " was in name a vassal of the Roman Emperor ; in truth he was the stay and glory of his counsels. Rarely did he condescend to visit the Imperial Court ; when he stooped so far, Counts, Marquesses, Dukes, the mighty Primates of the German Church, even Kings themselves, looked on him with wonder and admiration." One of the main routes of pilgrimage and overland commerce passed from the great city of Bruges [1] to Cologne, and so up the Rhine to Mainz, and from there either to Constantinople by way of Budapest, or by Augsburg, Innsbruck, and the Brenner Pass to Venice and the Mediterranean. We shall see later how this great road influenced the commerce and politics of Europe. In the meantime, I only name it to show how Cologne depended on the Netherlands.

William, then, wooed Matilda of Flanders. The Pope opposed this marriage on grounds so obscure that the canonists and historians have been fighting over them ever since. To me as a plain man it seems obvious that the Pope opposed the marriage because it allied the Norman power with the Empire, an alliance dan-

---

[1] Even in Canute's time Bruges was a world market. The *Encomium Emmœ*, written about 1042, says : " Hoc castellum (Bruggense) Flandrensibus incolis incolitur, quod tum frequentia negociatorum, tum affluentia omnium, quæ prima mortales ducunt famosissimum habetur."

gerous both to Italy and Rome.   However that may be, the masterful William had his way : he married the lady, and the Pope's consent was given afterwards. Now, this marriage is important to us for several reasons. It gave William three things necessary to conquest— ships, money, and men.   " The Flemings above all," says Freeman, " the countrymen of Matilda, pressed eagerly to his standard, and they formed an important element in the Conquest and in the settlement which followed it."[1]   William's own ship was a gift from Matilda.   The German Emperor at that time was a mere boy : the power of the Empire lay in the hands of two clerics, one our simoniacal friend, the Archbishop of Bremen, the other the Archbishop of Cologne.   The latter, we may surmise, stood with Flanders ; the former was of special importance to William, because he controlled the trade of the Baltic, from which came ships and all that was necessary to shipping—pitch, hemp, flax, sails, masts, and timber.

But why was Flanders so deeply interested in the conquest of England ?   The romantic historian will reply that Matilda was a loving and dutiful wife.   No doubt she was, although malicious poets of the time suggest that William was practised in the gentle art of wife-beating, and kicked and cudgelled her into the marriage.[2]   But there must have been other reasons.

Now we know that even in the ninth century the Flemish weavers looked on England as their wool- farm, and that England was then to Flanders what the Southern States of America are now to Lancashire.[3] We know also that Italy was a competitor for English

---

[1] Freeman, vol. iii. pp. 312, 381 *et seq.*
[2] *Ibid.*, vol. iii. p. 655.   He anticipated his rights under English Common Law.   See Blackstone, vol. ii. Bk. 3, c. 2.
[3] Welsford, *Strength of England*, p. 27.

wool, and we shall see later the fierceness and wide effects of this competition. So it may be that Flanders hoped by the alliance and the Conquest to confirm her hold on the wool supply, which was vital to her existence.[1] And this would furnish a further explanation for the hostility of the Pope to the Norman-Flemish match.

I lay no great stress on these arguments. The main fact is that William conquered England, and that the Norman and Angevin kings maintained a policy of friendship with Germany and hostility to France. The alliance was both commercial and political. "The merchants of the imperial havens," says Freeman, quoting William of Poictiers, "brought goodly things . . . among their precious wares, and strangers of Teutonic birth had settled in the land to practise the gainful craft of the goldsmith and the moneyer."[2] And again : "The rivalry between France and England which began under Rufus went on under Henry. And thus early in the strife Henry turned to the natural ally of England in such a struggle, to the ally with whom in after days we shared in defeat·at Bouvines and in victory at Waterloo. Close alliance with Germany, the old policy of Æthelstan, Cnut, and Harold, was no less the policy of the first king of the stranger dynasty who had the least claim to be looked on as an Englishman."[3]

The citation of Harold, as we have seen, is unhappy : "the natural ally of England" had refused him help

---

[1] It might be argued that there was also a secret treaty for the supply of mercenaries between William and the Count of Flanders. There was certainly a standing arrangement frequently renewed between the counts and the Norman and Angevin kings, by which the counts received 500 marks a year and undertook to place 1000 mounted men at the king's service when required. Ramsay (*The Angevin Empire*, p. 36) says that these treaties of retainer "came into vogue with the Conquest."

[2] Freeman, iv. p. 85.

[3] *Ibid.*, vol. v. p. 178.

in the hour of need, and had cherished and supported his enemy. Let us now set ourselves to discover how this natural alliance was confirmed by marriage, cemented in free trade, and maintained through some hundreds of years by those Teutonic adepts in the "gainful craft of the moneyer," the merchants of the German cities.

CHAPTER II

THE PRICE OF A KING

WILLIAM OF MALMESBURY tells us that, in the time of Henry I, London was visited by merchants of all countries; but chiefly from Germany, " whose ships also went to York."[1]   This commerce was no doubt strengthened by one of those marriages so much in favour with the practical-minded Lappenberg as being good for German trade.   Adeliza, the daughter of Henry I, was wedded at Mainz on 7th January 1114 to the Emperor Henry V.   The match was made the pretext for a heavy exaction of money from the English taxpayer—an art of which our Henry was a master.   " It is even hinted," says Freeman, " that Henry of Germany took Henry of England as his model of government, and that he specially sought to imitate him in the success with which he contrived to wring money out of his people."[2]   This " first English bride of the Cæsars," as Freeman poetically calls her, returned to England as a widow in 1126, to lead the party in revolt against Stephen. Stephen, we are told, was a good and gentle prince, but he was so unfortunate as to fall out with the Church, and his action in imprisoning several bishops, because they built too many castles, was justly reprobated. Matilda gained the enthusiastic adherence of these persecuted prelates, and was acclaimed Queen on the

---

[1] *De Gestis Pontificorum*, Prolog. I, II, and III.
[2] Freeman, vol. v. p. 184.   Freeman forgets Eadgythe.

distinct understanding that she would never again marry a foreigner—a promise she incontinently broke the following year.[1] The Londoners, who had at that time a strong prejudice against foreign influence, took the side of Stephen. They asked Matilda for the restoration of the laws of Edward,[2] but asked in vain; and the Dowager Empress, after an eight years' struggle, lost all by her arrogance that she had gained by her courage. Her chief claim to memory is that she was the mother of Henry II, first and greatest of the Angevins.

And now we come into a region of our subject in which documentary evidence is more frequent and more definite. And this evidence enables us to read not only forwards but backwards. The first document is a letter written for Henry by Thomas à Becket, his great Chancellor, in 1157, only three years after his (Henry's) coronation. It is addressed to that famous Emperor, Frederic Barbarossa, and was carried to the Imperial Court at Würzburg, along with many costly presents, by a special ambassador. The letter promises German subjects safety of commerce : " Sint inter nos et populos nostros dilectiones et pacis unitas indivisa, commercia tuta." This offer, as Lappenberg surmises, was accompanied by something still more definite—a charter of royal protection for the " house of the Cologne merchants in London," their lives and their goods. The King proclaims that the Cologners are to be treated

---

[1] She married Geoffrey of Anjou, although, in the vulgar phrase, " she was old enough to be his mother."

[2] The old English law forbade foreigners to live in the City except as " paying guests " of the citizens, who received a commission on their sales. Ethelred evaded this law when he gave the Men of the Emperor permission to transact business on shipboard. This custom, for which Londoners stubbornly fought all through the Middle Ages, was called " hosting." (Cf. E. Lipson, Economic History of England, vol. i. pp. 457, 458.)

as his people and his friends, and they are given leave to sell Rhine wine in the London market.[1]

These documents will repay study. They show that Cologne had already a Guildhall in London, and it follows that, although it has not been preserved, there must have been an earlier charter. Such German privileges, as we shall see, were reaffirmed in every reign, and sometimes several times in a single reign. We may assume, then, that Henry II was not granting new privileges to the Cologners, but merely affirming old ; and this is the more likely, as we find in the Brunswick archives a boast of the Cologners of commercial privileges in England, *given in the time of William the Conqueror*, " before all other Germans."

Now we know that Bremen had a price, and that William paid it. Is it possible that he also paid a price for the benevolence of Cologne, and that this price was these commercial charters, which put the merchants of Cologne on a level with the merchants of London, and, in fact, established free trade for the Cologners in England ? These were no ordinary privileges. The people of Cologne were definitely put on a level with the King's subjects ; they were given the

---

[1] " Henricus . . . precipio vobis quod custodiatis et manutenatis et protegatis homines et cives Coloniensis, sicut homines meos et amicos, et omnes res et mercaturas suas et possessiones, ita, quod neque do domo sua London, neque de rebus, neque de mercaturis suis, aut aliquibus aliis ad eos spectantibus, injuriam aliquam vel contumeliam eis faciatis, neque fieri permittatis ; quia et omnia sua sunt in custodia et proteccione mea. Et ideo ferniam pacem habeant faciendo rectas consuetudines suas, et nullas exigatis ab eis novas consuetudines vel rectitudines quas facere non dabeant nec facere solebant. Et si quis super hoc maligno forifecit, plenam eis meam sine dilatione, justiciam fieri faciatis. Testibus ricardo de Luci et Willielmo filio Adelmi, dapifero apud Northampton."

The wine licence reads : " Concedo ut homines Coloniensis vendant vinum suum ad forum, quo venditur vinum francoiginum, scilicet sextarium pro iii denariis." A third charter of Henry II, dated St. John's Eve, 1175, extends the royal protection granted to the citizens, merchants, and men of Cologne to all the dominions of the king in France and England.

Lappenberg, *Urkundliche Geschichte*, pt. II, p. 4.

right to hold property in London, and were not to be affected by new customs. By this last-named provision they were placed in a position more favourable than the English themselves. In course of time, as customs rose, the Germans continued to pay the old rates, German trade was thus given a preference not merely over other foreign trade, but over goods imported by the King's own subjects.

What favour Henry received in return for these grants we do not know ; but it is safe to suppose that the " gainful moneyers " of Cologne financed his wars in Wales and in France at the exorbitant rates of interest then prevailing. Henry II was a firm believer in the " natural " policy of England. His daughter Matilda married Henry of Saxony and Bavaria. To keep the friendship of the Emperor, he took sides with Barbarossa against the Church in the Schism—which was " more than English feeling could support "—and narrowly escaped serious trouble with the Pope. He was a great king, and it was, no doubt, a magnificent policy, but I cannot find that it added much to the wealth or the security of England.

And if England had no cause to thank Henry for his friendship with Barbarossa, still less had she cause to rejoice over Richard's connection with Germany. The tale has been often told : it is the theme of song and legend ; but I confess I do not find it romantic.

The main facts are soon stated. Richard, from 1190 to 1192, was crusading in the Mediterranean and Palestine. The German Empire was using the Crusades to establish its supremacy in the Balkans and the Near East. The Emperor Barbarossa perished in the great march through Hungary, Bulgaria, Macedonia, and Asia Minor. But his son, Henry VI, laid claim to

Sicily ; Isaac, a Greek cousin of Leopold of Austria, had been established in Cyprus ; and Conrad of Montferrat, who was cousin both to the Emperor and the Duke of Austria, had been made King of Palestine.[1] In those days there was a common belief that Englishmen had tails, and Richard had to deny the soft impeachment in the streets of Messina. His method of meeting the insult was to sack the town. Again, at Acre, Conrad was blamed by the soldiers for the execrable provisioning of the army. Richard's soldiers marched to a song with the anti-German refrain of " Curse the Marquis and die."[2] Richard insulted Leopold of Austria and called the Germans contumelious names. In this and other ways, as Ramsay says, " he challenged the hostility of Henry VI and the German party in Palestine."[3] When Conrad was murdered by the assassins of " the Old Man of the Mountain," the Germans affected to believe that Richard was behind the crime. In these circumstances it was unfortunate that our King should have found himself shipwrecked at the head of the Adriatic, and should have elected to go home by the overland route. On 20th December 1192 he was arrested by Duke Leopold in the suburbs of Vienna.

The Duke was not at war with England, and had no legal title to make the King his prisoner. For laying hands on a Crusader he was excommunicated by Celestine III. But the Duke and his suzerain, the Emperor, were firm believers in *real politik*, a science not

[1] A few years later, as part of the same vast project, Count Baldwin of Flanders was made Emperor of Constantinople in defiance of the Pope's commands, Constantinople being then a Christian city.

[2] " Tuno Marchisum detestantur
    Subtracto solamine,
    Per quem escis defraudantur
    In famis discrimine."

[3] *The Angevin Empire*, p. 282 *et seq.*, by Sir J. H. Ramsay.

much affected by the niceties of law. The Duke put his prisoner in the castle of Durrenstein, and held him for ransom. The Emperor gently, but firmly, pointed out to Leopold that, being his overlord, his Cæsarean Majesty had a right to a share in the windfall. On 14th February 1193 a treaty was made at Würzburg by which the ransom was fixed at 100,000 marks, to be shared equally between the Emperor and the Duke. Richard promised, as part of the bargain, to give the hand of his niece, Eleanor of Brittany, to one of the Duke's sons, on whom the Duke's portion was to be settled. In the meantime Savaric, Bishop of Bath, who claimed to be a cousin of the Emperor,[1] was sent by an anxious country to intervene on their King's behalf. He was followed by the Abbots of Boxley and Robertsbridge ; but they interceded in vain. On 23rd March Richard was handed over to the Emperor, and brought before the Diet. " The King," says Ramsay, " was formally charged with having supported Tancred in his usurpation of Sicily, in derogation of the Emperor's rights ; with having unjustly deprived Isaac of his kingdom, and instigated the murder of the Marquis of Montferrat. The insult to the Duke of Austria, and Richard's general behaviour to the Germans in Palestine, formed another count in the indictment. We are assured that he made a spirited defence, at the close of which the Emperor gave him the kiss of peace, saving the ransom, to which Richard agreed.

The total revenue of England at that time is esti-mated by Ramsay at something under £20,000 ; and

---

[1] The learned Stubbs dived deep into Savaric's genealogy but failed to trace the connection, so it may be that Savaric belonged to the genus ecclesi-astical snob, not unknown even in these days. It is certain, however, that he had a sacred friendship with the Emperor, who afterwards made him Chancellor of Burgundy.

100,000 marks he puts at £75,000. So that England and Richard's other territories were faced with a demand that can only be compared with the war indemnity put on France by Germany in 1871. On April 19th, however, the light-hearted King wrote home to Eleanor and the justices that " the terms made with the Emperor are well worth the money."[1] On the same date the Emperor also wrote an exhortation to England to pay, " and thereby show their faith in their King." England responded nobly. Clergy and laity paid a fourth on all rents and movables ; gold and silver plate were melted down, and the host was elevated in pewter. The Cistercians offered their wool. In the meantime the Emperor, evidently an adept in the " gainful craft of the moneyer," had raised the ransom to 150,000 marks, the extra 50,000 being in commutation of military service in Sicily, rashly promised by Richard. In the new treaty of 29th June the Emperor's share has risen to 130,000 marks, and Leopold's has shrunk to 20,000.

In the meantime, also, John and his ally, Philip of France, neither of whom was anxious for the King's return, offered the Emperor a subsidy to keep Richard prisoner. The Emperor had pledged himself to release the King on 17th January 1194, and had received a large part of the money on that condition. But the new offer was too tempting to be refused, and when the 17th January arrived Henry postponed his decision until 2nd February.

The German princes, we are asked to believe, were shocked at such perfidy. Alternatively, they had a quarrel with the Emperor over the murder of the Bishop of Louvain, of which Henry was shrewdly

---

[1] *Roger of Hoveden,* ed. Stubbs, vol. iii. p. 202.

suspected. He now displayed a disturbing tendency to defy them and rely on an alliance with Philip and John. They were consequently anxious to procure Richard's freedom. When, therefore, the Emperor seemed disposed to postpone the release of Richard until the following Michaelmas, the Electors protested. Richard obligingly came to their assistance ; a compromise was patched up ; the affair of the murder was buried in oblivion upon the one side, and upon the other Richard was released. " Thus," says Ramsay, " on Friday the 4th February the King was fairly set free, after more than thirteen months of most unjust detention.[1] But even then he was required to leave hostages for the unpaid balance of his ransom. Nor were the German magnates too proud to accept *douceurs* for their kind offices in the matter."

But this is not the end of the story. The Archbishop of Cologne had been Richard's chief ally and friend in the negotiations. The ransom was fixed in marks " in the weight of Cologne " ; and, according to Lappenberg, Cologne gave Richard assistance—probably by way of credit. When Richard arrived at the city on his way home, the Archbishop preached a moving sermon on a text not altogether complimentary to the Emperor and his subjects : " The Lord hath sent His angel, and hath delivered me out of the hand of Herod, and from all 'the expectation of the people of the Jews " (Acts xii. 11). Cologne also, it was evident, expected its *douceur*. The Archbishop accompanied Richard to Antwerp, and on the way, either in the

---

[1] To reconcile Richard and his people to the ransom, the Emperor had promised to crown him King of Arles. The Emperor having no power over that territory, it seemed an easy thing to grant ; but the promise was nevertheless broken, so that all England got out of the arrangement was the restoration of a picturesque but avaricious and immoral monarch.

town or duchy of Louvain, procured the royal signature to a *freibrief*, or privilege, to "his beloved Cologners, in which he releases them not only from their yearly payment of two English shillings for their Guildhall at London, but also from all other taxes to the King, payable either from persons or goods at London or in any other part of England." [1]

In such auspicious circumstances was made the first recorded grant of complete free trade in England. It will be noted that all restrictions are swept away with a courageous stroke of the pen. Even the rent of their Guildhall is removed, and they are liberated both from customs and poll tax. Their traders are no longer confined to London, they are admitted to every part of the country. And not merely Cologne, for it is surmised by the learned Germans who have studied the subject that Cologne represented in this matter a confederation of German cities, which used its Guildhall and traded under its shadow. The probabilities of this view we shall examine later.

---

[1] Stubbs makes some difficulty about the date of this charter, "Louvain, February 6," and supposes that it must have been granted at Cologne, *cf.* his edition of *Roger of Hoveden*, vol. iii. ; but the document is quite clear on the subject, and may be given here if only because it shows that even at that time the Bernhardi family took a benevolent interest in England :

"Richardus dei gratia rex angliæ, dux normanniæ, aquitaniæ et comes andigauiæ, archiepiscopis, abbatibus, comitibus, baronibus, justiciariis, vicecomitibus, ministris et omnibus Balliuis et fidelibus tocius anglie salutem. Sciatis, quod nos quietos clamasse dilectos nostros ciues de Colonia et mercandisam suam de illis duobus solidis, quos solebant dare de Gildhalla sua London, et de omnibus aliis consuetudinibus et demandis, que pertinent ad nos in London, et per totam terram nostram in anglia. Concessimus eciam eis saluum ire et saluum venire in totam terram nostram et quod libere possint ire ad ferias per totam terram nostram et emere et vendere et in villa London, et alibi. Quare volumus et firmiter precipimus, quod predicte ciues de Colonia prenominatas libertates et liberas consuetudines habeant per totam terram nostram anglie. Testibus H(enrico) Luce de Iouanio. Ganfrido de Sey. Thoma filio Bernardi. Wilhelmo de stagno. Wilhelmo de sancte marie Ecclesia. Datum per manum W(ilhelmi) Elyensis episcopi apostolice sedis legati, cancellarii nostri, apud Louanium, vi. die februarii anno quinto Regni nostri."—*Grosses Priviligienbuch des Stadt Köln*, f. 55, reprinted in *Quellen zur Geschichte der Stadt Köln*, ed. Dr. Leonard Ennen and Dr. Gottfried Eckertz.

B

In the meantime let us pass on to consider the price paid by John for his privilege of sharing with our " natural ally " the defeat of Bouvines.   We have seen already how Henry, attracted by the dazzling prospect of an alliance with the Empire, had supported the anti-pope, to the disgust of his subjects.   John in the same cause fell deeper into the ecclesiastical mire. His alliance with the Empire, necessary to its quarrels with France, brought upon his subjects the spiritual terrors of excommunication, and upon himself disaster and defeat.   But although he was willing to do much for Germany, John hesitated for some time before he confirmed Richard's privileges to Cologne.   London was giving trouble.   We have seen that in 1191 it had asked Matilda for the English laws of Edward, and it was already showing that illiberal hatred of foreigners for which it has been condemned by all our broad-minded historians.   In 1191 it had demanded from John its independence, and promised him its support upon that condition.   Lackland, who was always ready to pay with promises, had then granted municipal self-government.[1]   It was as easy for John, the protector, to grant London a commune as it was for Richard, the absentee king, to grant Cologne free trade.   But when John became king he had to reconcile these two grants, a more difficult business.   On the one hand, Cologne was most helpful to his nephew, Otto, son of Duke Henry the Lion and Matilda of England, and the hope of the family.   It was at Cologne in 1198 that Otto was elected King of the Romans—in other words, King of Germany—and it was the Archbishop of Cologne who crowned him at Aix la Chapelle.   On 4th June 1202 we find John writing a letter of thanks to the citizens

[1] Ramsay, *The Angevin Empire*, pp. 313, 317.

of Cologne for the services they had rendered to his nephew. Two years later he repeated his thanks, and exhorted them, as they had started Otto on his career of good fortune, to help him to the imperial crown, the pinnacle of his ambitions. In the meantime he gave them protection for their goods and possessions, including the Guildhall, but ignored his brother's free-trade charter, and insisted that Cologne should pay taxes in England as heretofore. On 25th December 1205, the imperial crown being still withheld from the nephew, the uncle gives Cologne a letter of protection for their wines and goods in London. But he not only demands payment of the duties, he adds the condition that they remain true to King Otto. Yet the crown still dangled in the future : the party of the Hohenstaufens were active both in Rome and in Germany. John lavished English money and English trade privileges in the great cause. In 1206 we find him granting one Hildebrand of Saxony safe conduct for himself and his goods throughout England.[1] Otto himself had visited England in the same year. In March 1209, Duke Henry of Saxony, Otto's brother, received 1000 marks from the London treasury,[2] and in August 500 marks, as the first instalment of a pension, and on his appeal the merchants of Utrecht were granted safe conduct in England. Such lofty arguments were not used in vain. On 4th October 1209 Otto was crowned in Rome, John paying the expenses of the ceremony.[3] But the glory was transient. Eighteen months later the Hohenstaufens triumphed ; Otto was excommunicated and Frederic elected. Evidently the bribes must be enlarged and repeated. On 24th

[1] Lappenberg, *Urkundliche Geschichte.*
[2] *Fœdera*, vol. i. p. 103. [3] Ramsay, *The Angevin Empire*, p. 435.

July 1213, John at last confirmed all rights to the merchants of Cologne, making only one exception—" saving the rights of London." These, said the King, were beyond his power to dispose. London, evidently, was not enthusiastic about the " natural ally." But Otto's difficulties are pressing, and Philip of France is making headway. Two days after the new grant to Cologne, John commands his civil servants to give safe conduct to the merchants of Bremen. For the first time the great northern town enters our story. There is still a condition. The safe conduct is granted " against payment of dues." We shall presently see how that condition also disappears as the natural alliance grows in strength and power. But the King of England is still in a position to make terms. In 1214 he orders the citizens of Southampton to allow the merchants of the Emperor free passage—as long as they do not trade with the enemy. Nevertheless the people of England are restive. On 7th April the King gives orders for the protection of German merchants " from such ill-treatment as they had been receiving from the men of Taunton."

Thus we see in the reigns of Richard and John the merchants of Germany, north as well as south, firmly established in the ports and capital of England. Englishmen are already hostile; but the Germans are under royal protection. What England gains in return we may briefly note. Otto and John are ignominiously defeated at Bouvines; the people of Cologne desert them both. John and Otto, failures as monarchs and men, die unregretted, nothing left of all their dreams of empire and power. But their debts and their obligations to the German merchants remain.

CHAPTER III

SIMON DE MONTFORT

"This Simon, Earl of Leicester, as numbers asserted, wrought many shining miracles."—*Florence of Worcester*.

AND now we come to the long and lamentable reign of Henry III. He also was a firm believer in the " natural ally," and not only had a sister to make a German marriage, but a brother to make a German Emperor. France is still the enemy, Germany is still the friend. We have seen that Cologne deserted the cause of Otto and John after Bouvines, and we may dimly surmise that trouble between Cologne and London followed. Henry came to the throne in 1219 ; in the fourth year of his reign he either restored or renewed to Cologne its charter to occupy its Guildhall in London.[1] In 1230 he gave the Brunswick merchants a letter of protection to trade in England. On 8th November 1235 he renewed the privileges of the Cologners, not only for its Guildhall, but for the whole of England, with a further letter of protection for the fair of Hoyland in Yorkshire. He also again released them " from the payment of these two shillings which they were wont to pay out of their guildhall in London, and from all other customs and demands which pertain unto us either in London or in any other place in our dominions ; and that they may safely resort unto fairs throughout

[1] " Cives Coloniæ reddunt computum de xxx marcis pro habenda saisina de Gildhalla sua in Londonia, in thesauro liberaverunt et quieti sunt—Magnus Rotulus anno regni 4 Henrici III.—R. Madox, *History of the Exchequer*, I, i. p. 414.

our whole kingdom and buy and sell in the City of London."[1] In fact, he restored the treaty of Richard.

At this time negotiations are proceeding for the marriage of the King's sister with the Emperor. In 1237 Henry gives special privileges to the Gothlanders, another example of the growing importance of the North. In the mid-year of the century Lübeck sacks and burns Copenhagen, and several London merchants who are robbed and injured appeal to their city for protection. Negotiations follow, and on 1st August 1251 a treaty is concluded between London and Lübeck. The treaty is a curious document, for it is witnessed, among others, by Arnold, an Englishman yet " Alderman of the Alemaynes," a merchant of Ghent, a merchant of Bremen, and seven Cologne merchants. The Germans at this time, it is plain, are acting together ; they have their own alderman in London, a citizen of London, but paid to look after their interests. Of this arrangement more later. In the meantime, it is to be noted that the arrangements having been concluded, the City of London cordially invites the City of Lübeck to send their merchants and their merchandise to London and other places in England.

Considering the treatment Copenhagen and the London merchants had just received, the invitation might seem a little rash ; but again " considerations of higher policy," as Lappenberg says, were influencing events. The King's brother, Richard, Count of Cornwall, was all-powerful in London. His tin-mines not only made him enormously rich, but brought him into close contact with the merchants of Germany, who then as now controlled the metal market. That patriotic chronicler, Matthew Paris, tells us that the Earl made a " shameful

---

[1] Hakluyt's trs., vol. i. p. 323.

profit " out of a monopoly on exchange, having the power to levy a tax on any business transaction, however small, as well as on anyone undertaking a journey.[1] Richard was, in fact, an adept in the " gainful craft of the moneyer." He was also ambitious, and as he had wealth and power, even the imperial crown did not seem beyond his reach. Owing to certain loan transactions, to which Paris refers,[2] his weaker brother was, so to speak, in his pocket, and it was easy to use the policy of England for the furtherance of his aims in Germany. Hence, it is surmised, the invitation to Lübeck. In the spring of 1257, Richard's sagacious policy was rewarded: he was elected King of the Romans by the German princes assembled at Frankfort on Main. " The money cries," wrote a contemporary satirist, " it is for my sake that Cornwall is married to Rome." " When the Earl took his departure from England," says Paris mournfully, " there was carried away with him, never to return, seven hundred thousand pounds, blood-stained by many crimes, besides his daily increasing revenues in England, which also followed him. By such means was England robbed and reduced to pitiful want, whilst foreigners gloried in her shame."

But Paris did not know, or does not state, all that was going on behind the scenes. Richard left Yarmouth on 27th April, and was crowned by the Archbishop of Mayence at Aix la Chapelle on 17th May. Between election and coronation Henry granted a royal charter to Lübeck [3] for a period of seven years. But

---

[1] Matthew Paris (Rolls Series), vol. iii. p. 230.   [2] *Ibid.*, p. 115.

[3] Hakluyt translates it thus (vol. i. p. 325) : " Know ye that at the instant request of our well-beloved and trusty brother, Richard, Earl of Cornwall, being of late elected King of the Romans, we have received under our protection and defence, and under our safe and secure conduct, the citizens of Lübeck in Alemain (Germany), with all their goods and wares, which they

the Lübeckers were not yet squared. They were, in fact, trifling with the claims of Alfonso, King of Castile, and weighing trade in Spain against trade in England. The Bishop of Lübeck, however, had a most satisfactory interview with Richard on the 6th of October at Speyer, and the matter was arranged to their mutual satisfaction. Richard visited England shortly afterwards, and returned with an edict from his brother (given on 15th June 1260), assuring " the merchants of the Alemannic Empire, who possess at London the house commonly called the Guildhall of the Teutons, of royal protection for all those liberties and customs which they enjoyed in his time and the times of his ancestors." Thus there was satisfaction on both sides : the Germans were secure in England, and Richard was secure in Germany. The camel had got fairly into the tent. It was now not only Cologne that had its Guildhall in London, but " the merchants of the Alemannic Empire." The exact measure of their privileges does not appear in this document. What they were we shall see in good time ; for the present we must follow our story.

And now appears, " in shining armour," that austere and terrible yet benignant figure, Simon de Montfort. It is strange that he should have led a movement against foreigners, since he was by birth a Norman ; and yet it will be remembered that Normans in those days still regarded Normandy and England as one country. And although he was an aristocrat, he was yet a friend of the commons. As early as 1249 we find him writing to the King from Gascony : " I am hated

shall bring or cause to be brought into our kingdom. We have also granted unto them that of all their goods and merchandise nothing shall be seized unto the use of ourselves or of any other without their own consent, but that they may freely sell and exercise traffic therewith, according as they shall think expedient."

by the great people of the land because I protect your rights and those of the poor people against them." As Simon married the King's sister, both Richard of Cornwall and the Emperor Frederick II were his brothers-in-law. Nevertheless we find him, on his return to England, taking the side of the Barons and the common people, who were for the moment united against both the Imperial and Roman policy. To examine this policy would take us deep into the great quarrel between the Popes and the Hohenstaufens then dividing Europe.[1] Sufficient to say that Rome tempted Henry with the crown of Germany for his brother, and of Sicily for his son. Both were expensive; for the privilege of fighting the Hohenstaufens in Sicily Henry promised Alexander 135,541 marks. Over and above this sum his debts—largely to his brother Richard, and therefore to Germany—ran to 350,000 marks.[2] He extorted illegal amercements from London; he stole his sister's jointure, and when Simon protested, aspersed her honour to excuse his fraud. He repudiated his debt to Montfort for the wars in Gascony. By turns he stormed at and fawned upon his brother-in-law. " I have great dread of thunder and lightning," the King once said to the Earl, " but, by God's head, I fear thee more than all the storms in the world." And he had reason. The Earl placed himself at the head of barons, knights, and commons in a campaign against the foreigners, who were eating up the country. By the provisions of Oxford of 1258, " both Poitevin and Savoyard were banished the realm of England. After their expulsion the crooked and extortionate dealings

---

[1] See Appendix I.
[2] In a single year (1244) Rome drew from England 60,000 marks, equal to £720,000 now in point of expense of living.—Adam Anderson's *Origin of Commerce.*

before mentioned gradually came to an end."[1]   And Matthew Paris describes how the nobles guarded the seaports, re-enacted Magna Carta, demanded equal laws for rich and poor, and made the King promise to consult them on national affairs.   After the Parliament they met in the house of the Preacher Brethren at Oxford.[2] "There," says Matthew Paris, these Mediæval Diehards "renewed their oath and confirmed their determination, that they would not allow themselves for life or death, or for their possessions, for hatred or love, or for any reason whatever, to be beat from or weakened in their design of purifying from ignoble foreigners the kingdom which gave birth to themselves and their ancestors, and of regaining proper and commendable laws." We are not surprised to hear that Henry, son of Richard, King of Germany, "wavered and said that he would on no account take such an oath without the advice and permission of his father."   "Whereupon," continues the chronicler, "he was told plainly and publicly that, even if his father himself would not agree to the plan of the Barons, he should not keep possession of one furrow of land in England."

It is plain that things were becoming uncomfortable for the foreigner. The Oxford Parliament did not confine itself to the interests of the nobles. On the contrary, it passed several resolutions favouring the Londoners at the expense of the foreign commercial interest. The citizens of London detested the "Guildhall of the Teutons," because it defrauded them of their ancient civic rights. By the age-old custom of the

---

[1] *Florence of Worcester*, ed. Forester, p. 331 *et seq.*
[2] Grossteste, the patriot Bishop of Lincoln, Chancellor of Oxford and head of the Franciscans, was Simon's devoted friend and wise counsellor. His Preacher Brethren, the Salvation Army of those days, kept the Earl in touch with popular feeling.

City, foreign merchants lived in the houses of the citizens, who acted as their agents and took a commission on their sales. The foreigners, although permitted to trade, were thus kept under control; but when the Germans got their Guildhall, this custom, and all that it meant to the English guilds, was set at naught. Hence the demand of the Londoners for " the laws of Edward" and of Magna Charta (ch. xli), for equal treatment for all foreign merchants and " for buying and selling by the ancient and right customs."

Not only so, but the Oxford Parliament of 1258 was Protectionist. One of its resolutions decreed " that the wool of the country should be worked up in England and should not be sold to foreigners, and that everyone should use woollen cloth made within the country and not seek over-precious raiment." [1]

Here, then, begins the Parliamentary protective policy in England, as far as we have knowledge, with Simon de Montfort, Bishop Grossteste, and the Barons at Oxford. Taken all in all, we may call it a national policy—England for the English, no foreigners in control, the rights of the cities over their own trade, protection for English weavers, support of home industry, justice and constitutional government. Was it Simon de Montfort, or was it Grossteste, or was it Adam Marsh, the Franciscan friar, who looked into the future and saw an ideal England—its people united in agriculture and industry, enjoying their own wealth, protected by their customs, independent of the foreigner, with a government enthroned on the national will? Perhaps it was all three who lived three hundred years before their time.

[1] Walter Hemingburgh, ed. 1848, i. 306, quoted by Welsford and Macpherson.

It is plain that the Provisions of Oxford and West-minster were most alarming to Germany. If they struck at the Guildhall of the Teutons, they also struck at the trade on which it lived ; for, as we shall see, the German trader carried the English wool to Flemish looms, and sold the finished article in England and elsewhere. The Provisions of Oxford struck at the whole system.

In 1259, as we have seen, the King of Germany was back in England, an unloved and suspected guest. Matthew Paris says, that before he was allowed to enter he was forced by the Barons to swear not to interfere in English affairs. " The people wondered much," he goes on, " that the Germans should give him liberty to go to England with his son and Queen, the objects most dear to him, and had not retained at least one of them as a sort of hostage. . . . For their object was, as they had in great measure done, to drain him of all the rest of his money."

Paris is right in substance, but wrong in fact. The Germans sent Richard to England to re-establish their Guildhall and check the anti-foreign and protective policy of the Earl of Leicester. This is clear from the edict to which we have already referred, secured by Richard on the eve of his return. It is also clear from the unpopularity of Richard in London, as shown by Paris and that strange old ballad :

> " The Kyng of Alemaigne bi mi leauté
> Thritti thousand pounds asked he
> For to make the pees in the countrie." [1]

Richard posed as a pacificator : he was recognised by Englishmen as an enemy. In 1260 the Pope gave

---

[1] *Wright's Political Poems* (Camden Society).

Henry a Bull to absolve him from the Provisions of Oxford, and there followed open war between the King and the foreigners on one side, and Montfort and his Norman-English party on the other. The Pope and his ally, Richard, used the two allied weapons of boycott and interdict. The National Party was excommunicated; commerce with England was forbidden. Montfort replied by stopping the export of English wool, organising a fleet, and exhorting Englishmen to wear English cloth. " Great," says Pauli, " was the lamentation of the commercial classes on both sides of the water when the nimble guardships of the Cinque ports began to search foreign vessels for goods of all kinds as well ds for papal mandates and contraband of war."[1]

Montfort, it is plain, relied on national feeling and the weaving interest for his support; but he went too fast in prohibiting the wool export. There had been cloth woven in England from before the Conquest, but it was coarse and undyed. The patriot wore this cloth as the badge of his party, and Montfort exhorted the nation " to live comfortably of their own without foreign cloth."[2] A handle was given to the enemy when Montfort appointed his son, Henry, Warden of Dover. It was Henry's duty to stop the export of wool in accordance with the protective policy; and he was accused by the exporters of diverting the wool to his own use. The charge is repeated by Thomas Wykes, a Royalist chronicler, who calls Henry " Lanarius," or woolmerchant. Pauli regards the charge as " unsupported and extremely doubtful "; but Professor Prothero, who has forgotten both the papal interdict on trade

---

[1] *Simon de Montfort*, by Reinhold Pauli, Eng. trs., 1876, p. 173 *et seq.*
[2] *Cf.* Welsford, *Strength of England*, quoting Thomas Wykes (a chronicler hostile to Montfort).

and the counter-embargo on wool, accepts the slander.[1]
To the plain man the whole affair is as clear as noonday.
The English looms were unable to absorb the wool-
crop ; smuggling must have been carried on wholesale.
Simon appointed his son as a man he could trust, and
the disappointed wool-broker set the scandal going.

But here lay the danger of the Montfort policy : it
alienated the wool magnates, who depended for good
prices on the looms of Flanders and Lombardy. Moreover, foreign trade was in foreign hands : wax, which
came in German ships from the Baltic ; wine from
Cologne and Bordeaux ; pepper from the Mediterranean
—such things were stopped, and rose in price. The
foreign shippers joined with the great wool magnates
against Montfort. Their united forces were too strong
for him. Prince Edward, the greatest soldier of his day,
and the King of Germany led ·the royalist army. In
August 1265 the Earl of Leicester found himself sur-
rounded at Evesham. " By the arm of St. James ! "
he exclaimed, " they attack wisely ; not of themselves
but from me have they learned that method ; let us
commend our souls to God, since our bodies are theirs."

" And thus ended," says Paris, " the labours of that
noble man, who gave up not only his property, but
also his person, to defend the poor from oppression,
and for the maintenance of justice and the rights of
the kingdom."

The end is soon told. A Parliament was held at
Windsor in Michaelmas, 1265, to which the citizens of
London were invited. London had been fortified with
barriers and iron chains ; but with smooth words the
King's messengers persuaded her citizens to leave their
defences. When they arrived at Windsor they were

---

[1] Professor Prothero's *Life of De Montfort*, a learned book.

thrown into prison, and as another part of the *coup d'état* a royalist army was thrown into London.[1]

And this dark story has an appropriate sequel. In 1271 Guy, son of Simon de Montfort, found Henry, son of Richard, King of Germany, in the Church of St. Lawrence at Viterbo, and slew him, because the father of Henry had slain the father of Guy.

[1] *Florence of Worcester*, ed. Forester, p. 338.

CHAPTER IV

THE HANSEATIC LEAGUE [1]

WE have now come to a point in our road at which we may take a wider view. It is already clear that "the Guildhall of the Germans in London" stands for something of power in its mediæval world. And when Lappenberg speaks complacently of the "common stronghold won in England" as ,"the weighty result of well-directed efforts and the dexterous use of the election of Richard of Cornwall," we are almost forced to ask by whom these efforts were directed. And this brings us face to face with that great, secret, and formidable organisation known vaguely to most English readers as the Hanseatic League. The German Hanse, then, was a confederation of German cities, of which the exact strength and constitution is even now not quite decided. For no outsider was allowed to know the secrets of the German Hanse ; and when perplexed monarchs asked its ambassadors whom they represented, they were put off with evasive answers. No one ever could say exactly how many and what cities were members of the League. The Russians spoke of it proverbially as " the Seventy Cities," or " the Seventy-

[1] My chief authorities for this chapter are : Georg Sartorius, *Geschichte des Hanseatischen Bundes* (Göttingen, 1808) ; Dr. J. M. Lappenberg, *Urkundliche Geschichte des Hansischen Stahlhofes zu London* (Hamburg, 1851) ; Wilh. Stieda, *Hansisch - Venetianische Handelsbeziehungen im 15ten Jahrhundert* (Rostock, 1894) ; Dr. Dietrich Schäfer, *Die Hanse* (Leipzig, 1903) ; Dr. Arnold Kiesselbach, *Die wirtschaftlichen Grundlagen der deutschen Hanse und die Handelsstelung Hamburgs bis in die zweite Hälfte des 14ten Jahrhunderts* (Berlin, 1907). See also map and Appendix II.

seven." A modern authority [1] puts the number as high as ninety-six. Nor are the scholars united on the origins of the League. Even the name is uncertain. The earliest mention of the *deutsche Hanse* (*dudesche hense*) is in a document of 1358, a trading interdict against Flanders drawn up by Lübeck. But long before the word *hansa* was used in England to describe a civic or a trading federation. I suppose it to be connected with a word used in Scotland to this day—"hansel," which means a gift on the signing of a bargain.[2] It may be that the name came from England, and it is certain that the League generally spoke of itself merely as the *gemeine Städte* (the common cities), and of its merchants as the *gemeiner Kaufmann.*

Perhaps in the purpose of the federation might be found its origin. The cities leagued together to push their foreign trade. Probably their merchants met in foreign cities, and there discovered their common interests. Certain it is that in Flanders, in Russia, in Denmark, in Norway and Sweden, and in England, the League had its organisation in close touch with the parent towns, although these countries had no membership in the League, but were rather its economic vassals or serfs.

And if the unifying force came from outside, the directing force was at the centre. Lübeck stood at the head of the Baltic towns; it was also the seat of government of the whole confederation. As early as 1226 we find it a *freie Reichstädt* (a free Imperial city), treating in sovereign style with the neighbouring Powers of the Baltic. And it is clear from the whole history of

---

[1] *Hansische Geschichtblätter* (Leipzig, 1874), p. xxxi.
[2] "Auncel *quasi* handsal weight, an ancient kind of balance, consisting of scales hanging on hooks fastened on each end of a beam or staff which a man lifts up on his hand or forefinger," &c.—*Chambers's Dictionary.*

the League that the German Baltic towns were the main-stay of its strength. They had on one side a monopoly of the Russian trade ; on the other, control of the Baltic Sound. They thus controlled the chief means of sea-power—timber, both for masts and planks, bowstaves, pitch, hemp, and flax. Not only so, but at Nov-gorod they came into touch with a great route which brought to their *Kontor* the furs and fine wools, the corn, wax, and horses of Russia and Siberia, and the silks and spices of Turkestan and China. On the western side they had a monopoly of the herring fishing then centred in the Baltic ; they produced vast quantities of salted stockfish, a necessity in Catholic Europe ; they were the carriers of the corn trade ; they had control of the iron mines of Scandinavia. It may be that through Russia from China they discovered the secret of villainous saltpetre : their ships are said to have been the first to carry guns in Europe.

The merchants of these Baltic towns were called Easterlings, either because they were supposed to come from a region vaguely known as Eastland, or because they dealt with the East through Novgorod. The freedom to trade at that Hanseatic *Kontor* was the test of the true Hanseatic. On the *Städetag* (city day) at Lübeck in 1366, it is laid down as a fundamental rule that no trader can enter Novgorod if he is not *in jure et hansa Theutonicorum comprensus*. " Others," says Kiesselbach, " may be tolerated in the federa-tion ; but unless they are entitled to do the Russian trade they can never become full-blown members." The Hanse in Gotland was merely the advance guard of the Baltic towns. In the thirteenth century it was ruled by the four towns—Lübeck, Wisby, Dort-mund, and Soest, the same four towns that originally controlled the affairs of the Novgorod Guild. Lübeck and Wisby together managed Novgorod in the first half of the fourteenth century, and in the latter half Riga, originally a colony of Bremen, is admitted to the partnership. When, in 1366, Lübeck proposed to bring certain affairs of Novgorod before a general meeting of the towns, Wisby protested that these affairs were in the hands of Wisby and Lübeck alone, and the towns of the German Netherlands struggled long before they were admitted to the inner circle of the Novgorod trade. Lübeck and the Baltic towns stood, therefore, as a league within the League. In 1259 Lübeck, Wismar, and Rostock unite in a treaty for the protection of sea-routes ; in 1265 they decide to hold annual meetings ; and in 1283 Lübeck, Wismar, Rostock, Stralsund, Greifswald, Stettin, Demmin, and Anklam conclude a treaty on the safety of their land routes and the protection of certain princes.

And with these Baltic cities we must include certain cities of Prussia and Pomerania, closely allied by interest and situation. In 1200 Bremen built a wall round Riga, and must have been deeply pledged to the Russian trade. Hamburg, which was given the sovereign right to coin money early in her history, formed a league with Lübeck in 1241. Dantzig, Elbing, and Königsberg, according to Werdenhagen, are included in a league of twelve Baltic cities as early as 1169. Minor combinations form and reform, according to the interests and policies of the cities. There are, nevertheless, rough divisions, called " thirds " in some documents, to which is later added a " fourth third " by some others. Anderson divides the League into four : the towns of the Baltic shore from Lübeck, and including Hamburg ; Dantzig, with the Prussian and Livonian towns ; Brunswick, with the towns of Saxony and Westphalia ; and Cologne, heading the quarter of the Rhine. These, however, are divisions at some periods, and combinations at others. For some objects also they unite ; for others fall apart. They were bound together by no Zollverein, nor even by a common sovereignty. The Order of Teutonic Knights looked after their interests in Prussia : we find the Grand Master on their behalf negotiating treaties with English kings. The Emperor was their ultimate protector, the Imperial Diet their court of appeal in foreign policy. But Cracow, a Hanseatic town, and later Dantzig, were under the King of Poland.

The towns were often stronger than the princes who gave them protection and the kings who granted them their privileges of foreign trade. Even in Germany it was their custom to hold castles in pledge for loans ; Lübeck had sole control over the fortifications of the Swine to its mouth. We hear vaguely of great battles fought by the Knights with the Wendish "pagans" for the right to trade in Russia. In the Baltic they are said first of all to have combined against the pirates. The story is doubtful. When Waldemar III attacked Wisby, the centre of Baltic piracy, in 1361, the Hanse towns (allying themselves with Sweden) replied by destroying Copenhagen in 1362, and the Danish fleet in 1364. In 1348, when Denmark tried to collect toll from Hanse ships passing through the Sound, the Hanse made war on Denmark, defeated its navy, and took possession of the five provinces of Schoenen for sixteen years by way of indemnity. Other prizes of victory were favourable tolls in the Sound, and special privileges in the herring fishery. A little later they made an ingenious treaty with Denmark and Sweden on the subject of piracy. If a Danish or Swedish castle were taken by the pirates and retaken, it should remain in the custody of the Hanse as security for the expense of the operation. The working out of such an arrangement naturally led to misunderstandings, and Norway, Sweden, and Denmark united under Margaret in revolt against the League. The League defeated all three, took King Albert of Sweden and his son into their custody, and seized Colmar and Stockholm. From this time onwards, for a hundred years, Denmark was in the power of the Hanse, and could not so much as elect a king without the permission of Lübeck.[1] The struggles of the Danes to free themselves from the Hanseatic net are the origin of that ancient friendship with England, which has been so much under-valued and misunderstood in this country.

" In those times," says Anderson, speaking of 1400, " the Hanse towns were so potent that they presumed to deem all other nations navigating the Baltic Sea to be invaders of their rights." They enlarged their dominion over Sweden and Norway. In 1348 German freebooters from the Baltic sacked Bergen and destroyed a small settlement of English traders. The act was repudiated by the Hanse, and some of the " Victualling Brothers " were afterwards hanged at Hamburg ; but, as we have seen, and shall see, the relations between the Hanse and the pirates are close and equivocal. In any event, the practical result was that Bergen passed under Hanse domination, and was for centuries a German *Kontor*.

And now let us look at the position of the League in Flanders, for here we shall find the key to much

---

[1] *Cf.* Paul Friedmann, *Anne Boleyn*, p. 236, for an astonishing account of the grovelling dependency of Denmark on the Hanse, and its spasmodic efforts to shake off this terrible domination.

that is dark and mysterious in the history of Europe. The position of Flanders is much the position of a community that flourishes and thrives on the rich soil of some active volcanic region : it prospers, but is nevertheless unhappy, for great eruptions keep it in terror ; landslides overwhelm it, fissures gape for its destruction, and forces gigantic and overwhelming disturb its peace and threaten its existence. The port of Bruges was the staple and centre of Western Europe : it was to the North Sea what Venice was to the Mediterranean, and was indeed linked with Venice by the overland route of the Rhine and the Brenner, as well as the sea route by way of Gibraltar. To their *Kontor* at Bruges the Hanse ships brought the wools of England and Spain to be made into cloth in the surrounding towns. When the cloth was made, it was again exported by the German merchant, who carried it either oversea or by overland routes throughout Europe.

Those who would know the history of Europe must know its roads. Trade-routes are the key which open most of history's doors. From Flanders the roads of Europe open out like a fan. The French-Flanders-Italy road is the best and most ancient : over it passes the great traffic between the rich agriculture of Champagne and the rich industry of the Netherlands ; but Cologne, the Palatine, Saxony, and Austria are the enemies of this road, and seek to divert its Mediterranean trade through Germany and across the Brenner. The great German road bifurcates, and its eastern branch is the pilgrim's highway along the valleys of the Danube to Constantinople and Palestine. But Rome grows more attractive than the holy places, and Venice acts as middleman to the Near East, so that again the Brenner wins. From the North and the Baltic the Hanseatic commerce moves along the sea, but also by way of Middle German towns like Erfurt and Halle, which stand as links between the Baltic and the Rhine. And so also we find link upon link of Hanseatic towns with Cracow its outpost in Poland. Bruges and, later, Antwerp are the seaports to which all this vast system converges : [1]

> " For Flaundres is staple as men tel me
> To alle nacions of Christiantee."

And so it is not surprising that on Flanders concentrated the whole German trade—from the Steelyard in London, the *Kontors* of Russia, the Schoenen and Bergen, and the German " table " in Venice. And so it came about also that the affairs of the German Guild at Bruges became the centre of interest of all German towns from Livland and Gotland to the Rhine. Very early in our story we see the German towns collaborating in the management of Flemish affairs. In 1252–53 a town councillor of Lübeck and a notary of the Council of Hamburg appear as the spokesmen of the German interests in Flanders. In 1280 Lübeck, as the head of the German towns, punishes Bruges by transferring the *Kontor* to Aadenburg. At the end of the same century we find Lübeck conferring with the Wendish, Saxon, Westphalian, Prussian, and Livlandish towns on the French-Flanders war. The town council of Lübeck again puts the screw on Bruges in 1305 and 1307–9, insists on the setting up of Hanse weights,[2] transfers Hanse trade from Bruges to Dordrecht in 1358, and brings it back in 1360. This transfer of trade, a most powerful weapon, is carried through by

---

[1] *Cf.* F. Rauers, *Geschichte der alten Handelsstrassen* (1907). This eloquent passage on trade-roads is, I must confess, chiefly loot from the enemy.

[2] The Hanse weights at Bergen are still a municipal curiosity ; they are said to be fraudulent, but on that point I have no sufficient evidence.

Lübeck, and the resolution is signed by Goslar, Hamburg, Rostock, Stralsund, Wismar, and Brunswick, " the towns of our third of all merchants of the Roman Empire of Germany of the German Hansa which at Bruges in Flanders resides." The German Hanse in Flanders was, in fact, the microcosm of the parent Hanse in Germany, the agents of its towns and of its commerce, and the servants of its policy. It consults with the parent cities even on such distant questions as the condition of the Novgorod and Bergen *Kontors*, and the Norwegian and Danish disputes of 1367. And not only does the German Guild in Flanders communicate with the parent cities about trade : the Duke of Flanders consults Lübeck as to the policy of Flanders in the Wars of the Roses. Flanders, like Denmark, is in the hands of the Hanse, and finds its only refuge in the division of interests which sometimes divides Cologne and the Baltic cities.

The desperate position of Flanders lies in this, that it is the focus of the rivalries of Germany, France, and England. Its Duke owes allegiance to both France and Germany, and has besides a treaty with England. When England and the Emperor are at war with France, England uses Calais to cut off French wool from Flemish weavers, and Flemish cloth from French buyers ; if the Duke of Flanders sides with France, the Flemish towns are cut off from English wool. French Flanders pulls one way, German Brabant another. But Germany generally decides, for Germany has the biggest pull upon Flemish trade. Germany pulls most of the strings in the Netherlands : that is a fact to be remembered.

" The main artery of Venice," says Stieda, " is its commerce with Germany." Genoa, its old rival, depended chiefly on France, and was beaten in the conflict when the French developed Marseilles. The Germans had the use but not the ownership of a palace in Venice, the famous Fondaco, and there sat at two tables. At the Suavian or Regensburger table were Regensburg, Ulm, Augsburg, Biberach, Ravensburg, Konstanz, Vienna, Enns, Linz, Gmunden, Salzburg, and Laibach ; at the Nuremberger table, Nuremberg, Cologne, Basle, Strassburg, Speier, Worms, Mayence, Frankfort-on-the-Main, and Lübeck. One book-entry will serve to show the ramifications of the trade : in 1420, 2000 lb. of amber rosaries are still unsold at the German house in Venice, and ships from Lübeck via Bruges are bringing more.

And Germany seeks to control Venice not only in trade but in politics. In 1411 the Emperor Sigismund goes to war with the Republic for various reasons, but chiefly to preserve " the best and easiest way into Italy through the same country of Friaul." On 12th February 1412, he prohibits the Hanse cities from all intercourse with Venice. The prohibition is not popular in Germany, but it is liked even less at Venice. After three years of war the Venetians pay the Emperor 200,000 ducats, and give him free passage into Italy. The war breaks out again, and the Emperor recommends his cities to take either the trade-route through Hungary to Constantinople, or to go by Genoa and Milan. These two towns eagerly welcome the Germans, testify to their own honesty, their lower duties and their perfect freedom of sale. But the road by Constance is inconvenient, and the Hanse begs the Emperor to make peace. It is a drawn war, and the Emperor removes the interdict in 1421. At another time we hear of an imperial army pursuing a policy of frightfulness and gouging out the eyes of Venetian subjects.[1]

But my reading of the Venetian archives is that it was less the Emperor than the German cities and the German trade combination that subordinated Venice to German interests. The overland road from Flanders to Venice was, of course, in German hands. We hear sometimes of Cologne, sometimes of the Count Palatine, sometimes of the Emperor seizing Venetian merchants on the road; the object may have been either ransom, as in the case of Richard, or pressure in some commercial quarrel. But when we see an English Government deeply in debt to the Hanseatics, forbidding Venetians to trade east of Southampton, we are able to put two and two together.[2] Venice starts with an independent policy designed to favour her sea-going trade. In 1317 the Flanders galleys, a State-protected venture, made their first voyage, and year by year those rich argosies brought to the English market Venetian glass and cloth, Italian earthenware, currants and preserved fruits, sugar and molasses, coral beads, Maltese cottons, silks and yarns, saltpetre, and the precious merchandise of the Nearer and Farther East. " On reaching our coasts," says Brown,[3] " they generally repaired to Camber before Rye, or the Downs, where they parted company; those destined for England proceeded to Sandwich, Southampton, St. Catherine's Point, or London, creating in our English marts as great a sensation as ever did the arrival of the Indian

---

[1] *Cal. State Papers* (Venetian), vol. ii. p. 164.

[2] Adam Anderson, under date 1378, mentions an English statute permitting the " merchants of the West " to trade with Southampton, paying the usual customs ; but forbidding them to trade with any place in the East except Calais. These Western merchants are specified as of Genoa, Venice, Catalonia, Arragon, in contradistinction to the Easterlings, who were thus given their sphere of monopoly in English trade.

[3] *Cal. State Papers* (Venetian), vol. i, Introduction.

fleet at Calcutta some sixty years ago; while their consorts continued their voyage to Sluys, Middleburg, or Antwerp. On the homeward voyage they reassembled either at Sandwich or Southampton. London was almost deserted by them in the latter half of the fifteenth century."

Brown does not mention the explanation of this decline; but such an edict as that of 1378 helps to explain it. The overland route was in conflict with the sea-route, the Venetian galley with the pack merchant of the Rhine. The Venetians began bravely. In 1331 we have a proclamation of the Senate, often repeated, " in favour of the galleys for the Flanders voyage, to the effect that English and Flemish wool imported into Venice overland do pay 25 per cent. duty until after the return of the said galleys, but thenceforth 3 per cent." But by 1339 we find the Germans already enjoying a preference in the Venetian market :

" All wools imported into Venice; namely, French, Burgundian, and English, to pay *ten* livres gross per thousand weight, namely, such as shall be bought by the drapers manufacturing at Venice. German wool to pay *six* livres."

And if we ask how the Germans came to enjoy this preference over the French, the Flemish, and the English, we can only answer by such methods of force and combination as gave them a preference in the Sound of Denmark and the custom-house of London. They were strong enough to make it so.

And now that we have gone the complete circle, what do we find? That the Hanse is a combination of German towns, from seventy to ninety all told; that its centre of power is Lübeck; that it has a monopoly of the trade with Russia ; that it has Denmark and the Sound in its power ; that it has a monopoly in Iceland ; that it drives the English from Bergen ; that it has command of the sea-carriage of the north, the source of sea-power before steam, and the boundless wealth of its sea-fisheries ; that it influences the commerce and politics of Flanders ; that it has, as we shall see more in detail presently, a favoured position in England, not only over foreigners but over Englishmen ; that it has a preference in Venice ; and that it pushes a trade route through Hungary [1] and the Balkans to Constantinople. " While this federal union was strictly preserved," says Anderson, " the Hanseatics were in a manner actual sovereigns of these northern seas, as well without as within the Baltic ; and their ships being very large, they became the general carriers for a great part of Europe, and their huge vessels were, moreover, often hired by princes in their wars." This is only part of the truth. We shall see the League enthroning and dethroning kings, Danish and English, blockading and boycotting towns and whole countries, holding fortified places, and keeping one of the gates of London, setting afoot invasions and revolutions, standing behind governments and monopolising the trade of nations. And the main theatre of the rise and decline of this great and mysterious power will be England. England raised them high, and England threw them down.

---

[1] There are Saxon colonies in the south-east of Hungary called even to this day Hanseatic.

CHAPTER V

Now it happened, says the Arabian fabulist, that a man was asleep in his tent. A camel which lay outside pushed the tip of its nose between the cloth and the ground. "The night is cold," said the camel; "allow me, I beseech you, to lay only my head under your sheltering roof." The owner, being half sunk in slumber, granted the camel's request. But the camel, having got his head into the tent, pushed quietly forward until his neck, his shoulders, his hump, his hindquarters, and even his tail were within, and the tent being too small for man and camel, the wretched owner was forced out at the other side.

And so we shall find with the Germans in England. Cologne, the nose, was followed by Lübeck, the head; and the head being inside, the whole body of the Seventy German cities were soon comfortably installed in the Guildhall of the Teutons, and not only there, but throughout England. The process is called, in these latter days, pacific penetration.

It is possible not only to trace but to explain this growth in power, especially if we keep in mind the nature of the kings and governments under which the process took place. Henry, as we have seen, was a weak and treacherous king, much under the influence of the Pope and his brother, the elected King of Germany. The Germans helped him to defeat Simon, and two years after the battle of Evesham, in 1267, the Duke of Brunswick prevailed upon him to confirm and define the privileges of Lübeck. This Henry did in the following articles :

" That neither they nor their effects in our Dominions shall be arrested but in certain cases, saving, however, the customary duties to the King.

" As far as in our power they may have and enjoy their corporate and joint privileges (*habeant hansam suam*) yielding 5*s.* for the same in like sort as the burghers and merchants of Cologne enjoy the same and have in times past held and paid for the same."[1]

These rights are to continue as long as Lübeck remains under the protection of the Duke of Brunswick.

But why should the Duke of Brunswick be able to secure such rights for his subjects ? The answer is simple. He had just married a niece of the Queen of England. For such was Henry's nature : he never could give anything to a subject, or refuse anything to a foreigner. " England," says Matthew Paris, " was a vineyard without wall or watchman, open to the pillaging of every vagrant."

And speaking of walls, we find that about this time the Germans were establishing themselves on the walls of London City. How it came about that foreigners should have gained the privilege of holding one of London's gates we can only guess. Probably, when the Londoners took the side of Simon, the Germans in their Guildhall were the secret agents of Henry and Richard. And it was convenient for a king who was at chronic war with the citizens to have foreigners in charge of one of the gates. However that may be, it is nearly certain that they held Bishopsgate in the time of Henry III ; for in 1282, only ten years after

---

[1] For this charter, see also Rymer's *Fœdera*, vol. vi. p. 839.

Edward came to the throne, they are being sued for allowing the gate to fall into disrepair. Edward was not the man to neglect his defences, and his Barons of the Exchequer gave judgment against Gerard Marhod, Alderman of the Hanse, with six other merchants of Cologne, Triers, Trivon, Hamburg, and Munster, for the expense of the repairs. To avoid distraint the Germans paid 210 marks to the City, engaged to uphold the gate in future, and promised also to bear a third part of the charges in money and men to defend it. As part of the bargain they were granted leave to store the corn they imported for forty days before selling it, no doubt to enable the Germans to " hold on for a rise "—although the Lord Mayor reserved the right to prohibit the operation " on account of scarcity or other reasonable cause." In 1305 London gave them a more important concession : " On Tuesday, next after the feast of St. Michael, in the 33rd year of the reign of King Edward (1305), it was awarded and agreed that the Alemains [1] belonging to the Hanse of the merchants of Alemaine shall be free from paying two shillings on going in and out of the gate of Bishopsgate with their goods, seeing that they are charged with the safekeeping and repair of the gate aforesaid." [2] Not only so, but they were relieved from paying *muragium* or wall-tax for the same consideration ; and a little later Hanse merchants were exempted from *muragium*, bridge-tax, and *pavagium* (paving-tax) in every part of England.[3] The Germans thus held Bishopsgate for at least two hundred years.[4] And if we make a balance-

---

[1] Alemains, of course, being Norman-French for German.
[2] Letter-book C, folio lxviii (Guildhall).
[3] Lappenberg, *Stahlhof*, p. 18.
[4] I may here give the sequel of this story of the wall : " On the 5th March 1460, the said merchants (of Alemaine) appeared on summons before the Mayor and Aldermen, and were asked, *as they had often been asked before*, to

sheet of the arrangement, we find it may be stated thus :

On the debit side the Germans agreed to (1) maintain the gate, which they habitually failed to do, and (2) to contribute to the cost of its defence—in ordinary times *nil*.

On the credit side they obtained (1) exemption from wall-tax ; (2) the right to store corn for forty days ; (3) exemption from octroi ; and (4) free lodging for at least one German in the Gatehouse.[1]

Here let me say a word or two of their principal seat of power in England, the famous Steelyard. The word, of course, does not mean a yard in which steel is kept, as Sartorius and Lappenberg suppose, but the steel arm of a weighing-machine. It is used in Scotland, and, I daresay, in some parts of England also, to this day in this sense. In an old Scotch weaving

deliver up the keys, so that the gate which had fallen into decay might be repaired. This they refused to do. . . . Notice being sent to the merchants to attend at the gate, they were asked to deliver up the keys, and on their refusal, the Mayor ordered new keys to be made, took seisin of the gate, and expelled the merchants of Almaine."—Letter-book L, pp. 13–14 (Guildhall).

[1] The history of Bergen might be compared with the history of London : " At the same time (1270) the merchants of many cities of the northern parts of Germany, apparently now acting as a confederated body . . . obtained leave from the King of Norway to fix the staple of their northern trade at the city of Bergen. At first their commerce was restricted to the summer months (from 3rd May to 14th September), and the citizens were not allowed to hire their houses to them for more than six weeks, to which, however, three were added for bringing in their goods, and three more for carrying out their returns. In process of time the vandalic cities of Germany obtained permission to establish a *contoir* in the city ; and in consequence of that indulgence the bridge was covered with twenty-one large houses or factories, each of them capable of accommodating about a hundred merchants or factors, with their servants ; and they were bound to keep their houses and also the bridge in repair, and to perform watch and ward in that quarter of the city wherein they lived."—Macpherson's *Annals*, vol. i. pp. 420–1.

As to the Gatehouse, read the following extract from Calendar of Letterbook E (Guildhall) : " 6 April, 11 Edward II [A.D. 1318] grant by John de Wengrave the Mayor, Stephen de Abyndone . . . Aldermen, to John le Long the Easterling of the upper part of the gate of Bishopesgate together with a certain turret on the east side of the said gate for life, subject, however, to the condition that in times of disturbance the Almaines of the Hanse shall safeguard the upper part of the gate according to the terms of the compensation made thereon with the Mayor and Commonalty."

village I know well there is in the market-place an iron platform, with a beam and weights underneath, on which carts are placed on market-days, and it is called the Steelyard.

The " factory," then, was in Danegard Ward on Thames Street and Windgoose Alley, and was originally called the Guildhall of the Germans (*Guildhalla Teutonicorum*). It had spacious wharves on the river, and consisted of a whole group of buildings strongly fortified. The place grew with the growth of their trade. Thus in the sixth year of Richard II they rented a large neighbouring house belonging to Sir Richard Lyons, who had been killed in a riot—possibly for selling bad meat to the troops. The building actually called the Steelyard was acquired later from one John Rainewell, and the freehold of these and other premises from Edward IV in the Treaty of Utrecht.

The affairs of the Steelyard, both in business and discipline, were managed by a German alderman, assisted by a German Council. Hanse government was strict, and Hanse laws were drastic. When the German merchants first came to England they seem to have lived on the monastic system, which they may possibly have adopted from their friends and protectors, the Teutonic Knights. They slept in monastic cells ; they were not allowed to marry—whoever married or lived with an English woman " lost the Hanse," became, that is to say, an outcast. Even a housekeeper or charwoman was forbidden. The sentence for taking a woman into the place by night or day was a heavy fine, or even loss of merchant rights. Such rules were no doubt designed to keep the Germans attached only to the Fatherland. It was against Hanseatic policy to allow any *Kamerad* (master) or *Geselle* (assistant) to

D

break away from the brotherhood and discover its trade secrets to the strangers on whom they lived.[1]

But these archæological details do not concern our story so much as the practical power which the possession of this fortified port conferred. As a general rule foreigners were not permitted to live on the wharves ; but the Germans were an exception. The Steelyard had the most extensive privileges regarding the handling of wares—" a testimony," says Lappenberg, " to the honesty which the custom authorities found amongst the Germans of the Steelyard." To their fortified wharf, as we shall see later, the Germans denied access even to the custom-house officials, and it was not until the reign of Elizabeth that their use of this privilege to cheat the customs was effectually stopped.

But how did the Germans contrive to obtain such good terms ? We have seen that they bribed the King. Did they also bribe the Corporation ? It is a question which may be answered. In 1282 the Hanse was confirmed in its right to have an alderman who acted as a judge in their disputes with the citizens of London, the only condition being that this alderman should be elected from amongst the aldermen of London. This English alderman had to swear that he would

---

[1] Sartorius, ii. pp. 609–610, gives the best account of the interior government of the Steelyard. As to the observance of these rules, the archives show scandalous breaches in the latter days of the institution. By the sixteenth century the place had become the Ritz or Appenrodt of Tudor London. " Let us goe to the Stilliard and drink Rhenish wine," says Nash. " I come to entreat you," says one of Webster's characters, " to meet him this afternoon at the Rhenish winehouse in the Stillyard. Will you steal forth and taste of Dutch bun and a keg of sturgeon." But this was when the Hanse had fallen into decay, and the merchants were trying to raise the wind by developing the hotel business. Holbein had covered the walls with allegorical pictures, and German waiters ran about serving their customers with Rhine wine, German beer, and *delikatessen*. " Who would let a cit. . . breathe upon her vernish," says Nabbe in his *Bride*, " for the promise of a dry neat's tongue, and a pottle of Rhenish at the Stilliard, when she may command a blade to toss and tumble her." Reference to the archives of London crime in the Middle Ages shows that the mediæval prostitute was Flemish or German.

safeguard the interests of the City; but upon the other side he received from the Germans an annual honorarium of fifteen gold nobles delicately wrapped up in a pair of gloves—"which," says Lappenberg, "seems to have served excellently to gain an influential citizen to represent their interests." By 1344 the Mayor himself (John Hammond) was "Alderman of the Almains," and no doubt acting with that austere regard for the interests of London to be expected from a man subsidised by the Germans.

Nor was this all. The Germans extended their system of bribery to the whole Corporation. It became a system so well recognised that the recipients were not ashamed to put the transaction in writing. Thus in Letter-book K (Guildhall), p. 46, under date 20th February 1426, we find this amazing entry :

"Grant by . . . the Mayor, Aldermen, Sheriffs and Commonalty to the Merchants of the Hanse of Almaine within London to have their Aldermen and all their liberties as formerly granted . . . and further, that the said merchants shall be quit of all custom, &c., payable on merchandise on condition that they pay yearly to the Sheriffs for the time being the sum of 40s., and to the Mayor for the time being two barrels of best herring, one barrel of sturgeon, and a hundredweight of good and clear Polish wax, or their value in money prescribed." And Wheeler in his *Treatise of Commerce* (1604) accuses the Germans of bribing the customs officers of the smaller ports of England with a stockfish or a keg of Rhenish wine.

In those unenlightened days there were no party funds to offer an easy and convenient machinery of corruption ; but it must be admitted that, with such means as they possessed, the mediæval German supported the free trade system as effectively as his latter-day descendants.

The Hanse had many ways of influencing the course of trade. The foundation of its system was the grants it secured from needy kings of preferential rates, not only over other foreigners but over natives. In the earliest charters we often find the condition that such duties as they are to pay are not thereafter to be increased. And this clause gave them a good plea for exemption when old duties were heightened or new duties laid on subsequent to the grants. The Parva Custuma, for example, was part of a great settlement made in 1303 by Edward I with all foreign merchants.[1] On the one hand, he gave them the right to wholesale trade in all the markets of England, " without paying wharfage, pontage, or pannage," and many privileges of denizenship, freedom from arrest, speedy justice and recovery, standard weights, and so forth. In particular he gave them a king's judge in London to try their cases, and ordained that the juries, in all except capital cases, were to consist half of men of the place in which the case was tried, and half of foreign merchants. In return for these privileges he laid down a scale of additional duties to be paid by foreign merchants, called the Parva Custuma. Now, it is evident that the Hanse brought their special charters to bear upon this general law, and so gained preferential rates over other foreigners ; but it is more remarkable that, as time went on, not only did they secure this preference over foreigners, but over English merchants in the ports of England.

Thus the graduated tax on the export of cloth was

---

[1] The *Carta Mercatoria*, called by Hakluyt " the great Charter to all Outlandish Merchants, to wit, of Almaine, France, Spain, &c.," vol. i. p. 327.

levied at three different rates, the lowest rate being on German merchants, the middle on Englishmen, and the highest on foreigners other than Germans. On the ordinary cloth of assize Hanse merchants paid 1s. the piece, natives 1s. 2d., and aliens other than Hanse merchants 2s. 9d.[1] Thus in the cloth export trade the Germans were in a privileged position, not only over foreigners, but over Englishmen. The Antiqua Custuma, which was a hereditary royal tax on the export of wool and leather, treated Englishman and foreigner alike. Parliament in its subsidies sometimes strove to differentiate against the foreigner; but here also the German found ways and means of evading the extra tax. He usually pleaded his " ancient privileges," with complete success. He was an expert, as we see in many cases, both in Venice and London, in the art of false manifests. He knew the price of every customs clerk, and he could obtain entry into the Staple, the great wool guild which handled, under Government supervision, the wool trade with Flanders.

The Hanse was, indeed, so strong upon the sea that it could, and did, at times claim a monopoly of our foreign trade. Its general principle, which it had learnt from the Venetians, is shortly expressed in the formula: Hanse goods on Hanse ships. Richard II tried to imitate this policy, but failed; Edward IV again attempted to enforce it, but was bought by the Germans and allowed it to drop; Henry VII took it up in earnest, and established English shipping. But there were times in which the English Government so completely acquiesced in the German monopoly that it forbade Englishmen to export staple goods. Thus

[1] Cf. Ramsay, Lancaster and York, vol. i. p. 149, and Appendix III to this volume.

a statute of Edward III provided that all staple wares were to be brought to a staple town in England, where custom was to be paid; "and then they shall be exported *by merchant-strangers only*, and not by the King's subjects, who are to take an oath not to hold any staple thereof beyond seas."[1]

But the Germans did not confine their interference to the " Municipalities, the Customs, and the King." They had English justice subordinated to their interests. In the treaty of 1437 between that miserable king, Henry VI, and the Grand-Master of Prussia, the merchants of the German cities were "indulged with the option of having any causes wherein they should be concerned tried with dispatch, and without the bustle and formality of a lawsuit, by two or more judges to be appointed by the King."[2] In the more famous Treaty of Utrecht (1474) there is the same provision: " The Hanseatic merchants in England shall not henceforth be subject to the Lord High Admiral's Court or jurisdiction; but in controversies about maritime affairs, &c., shall have two judges allotted to them by the King for determining the same."[3] As King Edward IV was deeply in debt to the Germans, and, in fact, owed his crown to their assistance, it is easy to imagine with what impartiality these judges were appointed. We may be quite certain that there was always among the lawyers, who hived and swarmed in the Inns of Court, a mediæval Lord Haldane or a Lord Reading, who could be trusted to appreciate the German point of view in a case at law.[4]

[1] Edward III, Statute of the Staple (1353), also John Smith's *Memoirs of Wool*, pp. 30 and 41.
[2] *Fœdera*, vol. x. p. 66.
[3] Anderson, vol. i. p. 501; *Fœdera*, vol. xi. p. 792, &c.
[4] Our present High Court would have suited admirably, for since the outbreak of war it has distinguished itself by throwing over Magna Charta

I may have more to say presently of the English staple towns : in the meantime I mention them only to show the strength of the German position in English trade. As part of Edward's policy eleven English and four Irish towns were given a monopoly of the sale of wool.[1] At all of these towns there were courts for settling questions between buyers and sellers. This court consisted of two Englishmen and four aliens, " whereof two shall be of Germany and two of Lombardy." Thus Englishmen were put in a minority against the foreigner in their own town. The two foreign markets for English wool were, of course, Flanders and Lombardy, but the mention of " Germany " in the statute shows that Flemish wool-buying was in the hands of the Hanseatic League. And as the League had also a strong pull in Italy, it is safe to suppose that the four foreigners worked together under German control against the two Englishmen, when any question between alien and native fell to be decided. Thus both in Courts of Admiralty and in Courts Merchant, the German was in the happy position of having his own judges ; and if there should be an appeal to the King, he was no worse off, for he was the King's banker.

Here, then, are the sources of German influence in England. The Germans commanded the North Sea and the carrying trade, and could starve England

and English Common Law in favour of the Hague Conventions, and deciding (1) That a German registered in this country is a " king's friend," and has the rights of a British subject ; and (2) that a registered company whose capital and shareholders are German is an English company, and has the right to sue in our English Courts. Lord Reading could not have been more " impartial " if he had lived in the time of the Hanseatic League.

[1] For England, Newcastle-on-Tyne, York, Lincoln, Norwich, Westminster, Canterbury, Chichester, Winchester, Exeter, and Bristol. For Wales, Caermarthen. For Ireland, Dublin (then called Deyvlin), Waterford, Cork, and Drogheda, 27 Edw. III. In a later Act (36 Edw. III), gallant little Wales is left out and Hull added to the English list.

either by stopping Baltic corn, when there was a bad English harvest, or by stopping her commerce with Flanders. They financed the English Government and influenced the royal policy. They had a preference in the English customs, overwhelming as against other foreigners, and substantial as against Englishmen.[1] They had freedom from municipal taxation—gate tolls, road taxes, and so forth. The King sometimes compelled them to contribute to his special levies for wars ; but if they paid, it was always under protest and without prejudice to their privileges.[2] They sometimes farmed the English taxes, and must have gained thereby great powers both in finance and trade. And, lastly, being a great organisation, covering Europe as well as the chief centres of trade in England, they had the knowledge, the wealth, and the combination to defeat any mere local competitor. " Always trading in a body," says Anderson, " they easily ruined single traders by underselling them." [3]   And this is true not only of the trade " in gross," but of retail trade in at least some branches. We find them at one time setting up in London as fishmongers, after a desperate fight with the English Guild ; and the archives of London are full of complaints by " the Trade " that the Germans have gone into the liquor business. In such circumstances it is not, after all, surprising that an English party grew up sworn to the expulsion of the foreigners. Of this party, which began in failure with Simon de Montfort, and ended in victory with Sir Thomas Gresham and the Cecils, we shall have more to say as our story develops. But we might call it here the anti-German Party, the Party of Patriotism, the Party of Protection.

[1] See Appendix III.   [2] *Ibid.*   [3] Anderson, vol. i. p. 496, under year 1470.

CHAPTER VI

THE HOUSE OF FAME—BACK VIEW

IF we inquire into the policy of the three Edwards, we shall find the same influences at work as we have seen from the Conquest. The kings want money; the Germans want trading rights; the two come together, and the deal is made. Thus, for example, in November 1280, Edward I is forming a great army for the invasion of Wales, and sending his agents not only through all England, but into the neighbouring countries, to buy munitions of war. Is it a mere coincidence that on the 17th of that month he confirms the merchants of Germany in all their privileges, and promises that " he will not himself do anything nor permit others to do anything to infringe them " ? [1] The union of the British Isles under one crown is a great cause, but it needs money : the customs are even pledged for loans to the foreigner, Italian or German. In 1307 the King is unable to pay his debts to the merchants of Brabant, and he allows them to pay themselves from what is due to them from the Nova Custuma.[2] And so we might find the explanation of the famous *Carta Mercatoria* of 1303. We see the process even more clearly in the reign of that glorious prince, Edward III. In the year 1335 he is paying the Emperor Lewis of Bavaria a subsidy of 300,000 florins ; the Electors of Cologne, Palatine, and Brandenburg are his pensionaries ;

---

[1] *Fœdera*, vol. ii. p. 161.   [2] Ryley, *Plac. Parl.*, p. 327.

to the Duke of Brabant he pays 60,000 pounds sterling—
all to help him against the King of France.[1] And in
the same year, at York, he passes an Act protecting
"merchant-strangers" against the "grievous damages" done to them by "some people of his cities,
burghs, ports of the sea, and other places," who refuse
to allow these merchant-strangers to sell their "wines
and other things . . . to any others but to themselves." It is therefore enacted "that all merchant-
strangers, as well as denizens, may freely buy and sell
corn, wine, flesh, fish, and all other provisions ; wools,
cloth, and all other vendible wares from whencesoever
they come, as well in cities, burghs, towns, ports, fairs,
and markets, having franchises, as in all other places."
The only reservation which the "judicious prince"
allows himself to make in this free trade charter to the
foreigner is "that no merchant-stranger shall carry
any wines out of this realm." As for the franchises and
exclusive charters of the English cities, "they are
herein declared to be of no force."[2]

Truly a judicious prince. And when we look at his
exploits in war we cannot sufficiently admire him. In
1359 he transports 100,000 men to Calais in no less
than 1100 ships. What if his grudging Commons
complain that he has destroyed English shipping by
keeping all his merchantmen mobilised for six months ?
His victories are immortal in English history ; his
defeats are immortal in the histories of France. But
glory has its seamy side. The Palace of Fame is fair
to see ; but the broker's man is generally to be found
somewhere in the back premises—the obscure but real
occupier. All those German princes and the German
ships in which the invading armies are conveyed cost

[1] *Fœdera*, vol. iv. p. 777.   [2] *Statutes*, i. 270.

money. Edward III pawns his jewels, he pawns his crown, his second-best crown, his Queen's crown, his Queen, his infant son, and two of his earls.

In 1339 he pawns his crowns to Cologne and Trier, and borrows 54,000 florins from three burghers of Mechlin. He enters into a close alliance with the cities of Brabant, and spends a regal Christmas at Antwerp. When he proposes to depart, his creditors remind him that his debts amount to £30,000. He therefore leaves his Queen, his child, and the Earls of Derby and Salisbury as pledges against his return. A little later Cologne threatens to foreclose on the crowns, as the time in the bond has elapsed. On 14th February 1342 Edward writes to the Council of Cologne begging for an extension, and promising early payment through a Flemish money-lender with the strangely familiar name of Montefiore. In the meantime (1338) he has granted to Cologne confirmation of all their trading privileges in England.

Another of his accommodating friends is the Hanseatic, Tidemann von Lymbergh. To him and to John von Wolde he pawns, on 14th February 1343, half of the duty of 40s. per sack of wool which the merchants had agreed to pay to the King. In 1344 he pawns the great royal crown with two German merchants called Clippink, and two others called Ativolde. About Easter, 1346, he gives Tidemann his second crown, which the said Tidemann keeps for three years and returns on 17th February 1349. On 18th April 1346 Tidemann von Lymbergh, the four Clyppingen, Johan von Bek, and Tidemann Spisenhagel receive on behalf of the German Guild a special copy of the Hanseatic privileges, probably because for the moment there was nothing left to pawn. In 1347 the King pledges with Lymbergh several golden jugs and cups and gem-encrusted ornaments. On August 25th of the same year he confirms an agreement between Lymbergh and the Black Prince, by which the tin mines of Cornwall are pledged to the German for three years. In 1348 the King sets up this mediæval Rothschild as a landed proprietor, with manors on a thousand years' lease in Somerset, Wilts, Southampton, Bucks, Northampton, Cambridge, Suffolk, and Normandy.[1] A little later the invaluable Tidemann is again renting the wool-tax (*subsidium lanarium*) from the King. And we may be certain that where Tidemann had his finger, it was not merely Tidemann, but the other German merchants of the Hanse behind him.

It will not, perhaps, surprise my English readers if I say that at this time feeling is running high against the Germans. It is aggravated when English mer-chants are turned out of Flanders. The Hanse is blamed for the eviction, and the King has to bow before the anti-German storm. On 30th July 1351 he issues an order confiscating German goods in England. It sounds like a policy of thorough, but does not bear inspection. The goods of Tidemann and Oliver von Reule are declared to be exempt. And a little later we find further evidence of the King's real attitude. On 15th November a writ is issued to the sheriffs, " notifying that the King had taken under his pro-tection Hildebrand Sudermann, who had been charged with procuring the death of Richard Curteys, a Bristol

---

[1] *Calendarium Rotulorum Patentium* (Edw. III, p. 157, Tertia Pars., 13) : " Rex confirmavit Tidemanno Lymbergh pro mille annis quamplur' maneria viz. de Norton in Somers' de Connoke in Wilts de Rannuberidge in Southton de Mershe in Buck de Grafton in Northon de Derneforde in Cantabr' de Cretinge et Milkelfield in Suff' parcell' Priorat' de Wilmington quæ fuit Cella Abbathiæ de Greston in Normania."

Also p. 159, Prima Pars. 3 and 10 : " Pro Tidemanno de Lymbergh de quamplur' manerijs, prout antea.

merchant, . . . and of insulting the English nation ;
and commanding proclamation to be made against
inflicting any injury upon the said Hildebrand or
other merchants of the Hanse of Almaine." [1]   And a
little later the situation is entirely cleared up.   On
20th August 1352 the King issues a writ to the sheriffs
" to make proclamation to the effect that, notwithstanding a recent order of the King for the arrest of
merchants of the Hanse of Almaine and their goods, the
said merchants were to be allowed free intercourse
with England, with the exception of Hildebrand Sudermann." [2]   In other words, Sudermann has been banished
as a scapegoat, the storm has blown over a little, and
the King thinks it safe to revoke his temporising order.

Nor was Tidemann von Lymbergh the only German
to rise to greatness in the reign of this judicious prince.
A certain Hanseatic called James or Jacob Doseyn
provided ships and munitions for the siege of Calais,
and found so much favour in the eyes of the King that
popular rumour in England made him the source of
all the privileges of the Easterlings.   Then there was
the redoubtable John, the Iron Count of Holstein, whose
doughty deeds gained for him the thanks, and probably something more substantial than the thanks, of a
grateful monarch. [3]

Altogether Edward's reign was a glorious but expensive example of Freeman's policy of the " natural
alliance."   With all his victories this judicious prince
ended by losing everything in France save Calais.   In
spite of all his gifts and charters, the Emperor and

---

[1] Letter-book F (Guildhall), p. 236.   [2] *Ibid.*, p. 248.
[3] For this little sketch of Edward's financial policy I am chiefly indebted
to Anderson and Lappenberg.   Their original authorities, to whom I have
occasionally referred, are Rymer's *Fœdera, Kalendars of the Exchequer, Kalen-
darium Rotulorum Patentium,* and *Abbravatio Rotulorum Originaliam ;* Fabyan's
Chronicle and *Presbyteri Bremensis Chronica Holsaticæ.*

the subsidised German princes failed him in his hour
of need. He reduced France to a coinage of leather ;
but he himself died in a poverty no less desperate,
leaving a kingdom without a navy, with an oversea
trade almost monopolised by the Hanseatic League.
Yet there are several things which reconcile us to this
judicious prince. He encouraged the cloth industry
in England, if for no better reason than to force Flanders
into an alliance against France. And when he went
to Coblentz to beg the Emperor to allow the princes
(whom he had already paid) to fight against France,
he yet refused to kiss the Imperial toe.

CHAPTER VII

THE GERMANS RULE THE SEA

WHILE the Germans were thus establishing themselves in England, they were also making themselves masters of the sea. The Baltic was their base of operations, ideal because supplied with all things necessary to sea-power in those days; Denmark their tributary; the Sound their fortified gate. When English ships sought to trade in the Baltic, they found all the forces of the Hanse arrayed against them. With English pertinacity they maintained a trading settlement at Danzig, but held it on an insecure tenure, which was constantly being interrupted. At Lübeck, in 1286, the towns actually debated whether the English should not be altogether prohibited from sailing in the Baltic.[1] The majority of the towns thought the measure impolitic, but found ways and means of making things impossible for English traders. Not only so, but they proceeded to drive the English out of Norway and to enforce a monopoly of the trade to Iceland. Now the trade with Norway was vital to the east coast of England, because Norway was the only source outside the Baltic from which the shipowners of Hull, Boston, and Lynne could get their equipment. English traders dated their settlement at Bergen from a grant secured to them a few years after the Conquest; and they fought the Germans through centuries for their right to remain

---

[1] *Lübecker Urkundenbuch*, Part I, Nos. 485, 486.

there. Repeatedly expelled by German force and in-. trigue, they always returned; and as Norway even then feared and hated German influence, they were always welcomed by the Norwegians. But the Norwegians were helpless to protect their friends against their enemies. In the thirteenth century the Germans had been given the right of permanent residence, and free export and import in Bergen, and the English expelled. They returned, and King Eric II " favoured them in their disputes with the Germans."[1] Yet they were again expelled in 1312. How it is done is explained clearly enough in a letter of 1312 from Edward II to the King of Norway.[2] The English King complains that Haquin has suffered several English merchants to be imprisoned and their goods to be seized, to the value of £310, at the instigation of certain Eastland merchants, " who," says our King, " by all possible means strive to obstruct the advantages of the said English merchants." " Those Easterlings," as Anderson explains, " were the Hanse towns on the south shore of the Baltic Sea, who in those times were in great naval power, from Lübeck up to Narva, and seem on many occasions to have acted so arbitrarily, as if none but themselves had a right to trade to the adjacent countries of Norway, Denmark, Poland, and Sweden." And this is only one of many such outrages.

Another cause of complaint is the help Germans are giving to Scotland. In 1297 we find William Wallace appealing to Lübeck for assistance against Edward I, and a little later Edward I complains that Flanders is supplying Robert the Bruce with arms.

---

[1] Lappenberg, *Stahlhof.*
[2] *Fœdera*, vol. iii. p. 449, quoted by Anderson, vol. i. p. 281.

Then Edward II writes to the Earl of Flanders and the magistrates of Bruges that certain Easterlings had used the port of Swen as a base for operations against "his people of Scotland and elsewhere."[1] The Germans even come into the eastern ports of England and cure their herring, in defiance of local custom. They listen to no protest, and obey no injunction. The King of Norway urges the King of England to take measures ;[2] but the King of England is helpless. The King of England urges the King of Norway to take strong steps, but the King of Norway can do nothing.

Things come to a head in the reign of Richard II, the Londoners' King, as he is contemptuously called. Richard depended on the support of the democracy. He was a freeman of the Taylors Company ; he gave the Fishmongers a charter to protect them in their own markets ; he was even suspected of supporting a rising of the peasants in Norfolk. Unfortunately, however, he is not quite his own master : in the first year of his reign he pawns his three crowns for 10,000 crowns. The Londoners come to him with their complaints : " Their grievous clamours against the liberty allowed to foreigners to be housekeepers in that city or to be brokers ; and to buy and sell all manner of wares, by retail as well as by wholesale. . . . By which grievances the merchants of London are greatly impoverished, the Navy impaired, and the secrets of the land discovered to our enemies by those strangers, and by other stranger spies received into their houses." Richard complies with these " unreasonable and impolitic remonstrances of the Londoners."[3] They lend him money ; he redeems his crowns, grants foreign

---

[1] *Fœdera*, iii. p. 131.   [2] *Ibid.*, i. p. 654.
[3] Anderson, vol. i. p. 366.

E

merchants all their former privileges, and rebukes his
unreasonable subjects, " who will not suffer merchant
strangers " to sell their goods, " whereby they are
sold much dearer than if those foreigners were permitted to sell them." We need not blame Richard
altogether : he was not strong enough to carry out the
national policy of his supporters, and his whole reign
is a see-saw between Free Trade and Protection, according as the King or the Germans had the upper
hand.[1] We can almost see the poor King, with the
foreigner pulling at one sleeve and the Englishman at
the other. In 1381 he passes the first Navigation
Act : " That for increasing the shipping of England of
late much diminished none of the King's subjects shall
hereafter ship any kind of merchandise, either outward
or homeward, but only of ships of the King's subjects,
on forfeiture of ships and merchandise, in which ships
also the great part of the crews shall be the King's
subjects." In the following year the Act is practically
annulled : " Where no ships were to be had merchants
might export or import in foreign ships." In 1381,
the very year of his Navigation Act, he grants " unlimited liberty both to aliens and denizens to export
wool and wool-fels, as well as leather, to any country
whatever except France "; and in 1382 he grants
liberty to all merchant strangers " to come into the
realm as well within franchise as without . . . without
the obstruction of any whatever."

The patriotic party had " Reciprocity in Germany "

---

[1] Since writing this chapter I have read the admirable first volume of
Mr. E. Lipson's *Economic History of England*, hot from the press. " It is
impossible," he says on p. 454, " not to connect the struggle of the London
gilds with the measures carried out by Parliament during Richard's reign.
The victualling gilds were adherents of the king, while the non-victuallers,
who were free-traders, were associated with the opposition of John of Gaunt."
John of Gaunt was, of course, John of Ghent.

as one of the principal planks in their platform.[1] And Richard did his feeble best to support them in their claim of equal treatment in the Baltic. The result was war—one of the most disastrous ever fought by England. It began in an irregular fashion, characteristic of all our troubles with the irregular power of the Hanse. In 1387, according to the German version, English sailors had looted six Prussian ships in the port of Swen, in Flanders.[2] The Master-General of Prussia, one of the protectors of the Hanse, thereupon seized English merchants and their goods in the ports of Elburg and Dantzig. According to English reports —which, of course, the Germans said were false—the English prisoners were barbarously treated, " cast into lothsom prisons, drenched in myre and water up to ye neck, restrained from al conference and company of men, and also that their meat was thrown into them, as a bone to a dog, with many other enormities." [3] Naturally, there was fierce indignation in England, and King Richard seized some Prussian merchants at Lynne.

[1] " In 1390 a petition was presented urging that merchant strangers repairing to England should be treated as English merchants were treated abroad. This was to be the watchword of the anti-alien party throughout the fifteenth century. For the moment the reply was unfavourable; merchant strangers were to be " well and courteously and rightfully used," so that they might have the greater courage to repair to England. However, in 1393, the King felt himself strong enough to reverse the proceedings in favour of aliens, and once more re-impose the old disabilities upon them."—Lipson, *Economic History of England*, p. 455.

[2] The port of Swen (or Swin) was, of course, Sluys, and was, by the way, the centre of the Hanseatic contraband trade in arms with Scotland. It is noteworthy that the articles looted were chiefly " armour and weapons."

[3] Chaucer about this time wrote a little poem to one Bukton, advising him not to marry (according to Tyrwhitt, Peter de Bukton was the King's escheator for Yorkshire in 1397), and he pointed the moral by a reference to the German treatment of prisoners :

> " Experience shall thee teache ; so may hap
> That thee were lever to be taken in Frise,
> Than eft to fall of wedding in the trap."

The Germans are marvellously true to type. In the sixteenth century an Englishman described the Hamburgers as " uncivil in manners and without all mercy where they are masters," and we know how they treat prisoners to-day.

The result of this fracas was a Prussian embassy to England and an English embassy to Prussia, with a treaty of mutual indemnity and privileges.[1] This hopeful treaty was concluded in the year 1390, and seems to have made exactly no difference in the policy of the Hanse and the private war between German and English sailors. What England suffered in this war we are told in painful detail by the documents of the negotiations which followed.[2] Most serious was the sack of Bergen, where the merchants of Lynne had their ancient settlement.[3] Whether or not the Hanse was concerned in this affair is in some doubt. The German version lays all the blame on the notorious Victualling Brothers, who are alleged to have destroyed Hanse as well as English property.[4] Lappenberg adds that the pirates of whom the English complained were hanged in Hamburg in 1402. On the other hand, it is certain that the Victualling Brothers belonged to the Hanse towns of Wismer and Rostok, by whom they

---

[1] The most important article provides: " That all lawful merchants of England whosoever shall have free licence and authority, with all kinds of ships, goods, and merchandises, to resort unto every port of the land of Prussia, and also to transport all such goods and merchandises up further into any other place in the said land of Prussia, and there with all kinds of persons freely to bargain and make sale, as heretofore it hath from ancient time been accustomed. Which privilege is granted in all things and by all circumstances unto the Prussians in England."—Hakluyt, vol. ii. p. 23.

[2] Hakluyt, vol. ii. p. 55 *et seq.*

[3] " Item pitifully complaining the marchants of Lenne doe avouch, verifie, and affirm that about the feast of S. George the Martyr, in the year of our Lord 1394, sundry malefactors and robbers of Wismer and Rostok and others of the Hans, with a great multitude of ships arrived at the town of Norbern (North Bergen) in Norway, and took the said town by strong assault, and also wickedly and unjustly took al the marchants of Lenne there residing with their goods and cattels, and burnt their houses and mansions in the same place, and put their persons into great ransoms : Even as by the letters of safe conduct delivered unto the said merchants it may more evidently appear, to the great damage and impoverishment of the merchants of Lenne : namely, imprimis they burnt there 21 houses belonging unto the said marchants, to the value of 440 nobles. Item they took from Edmund Belgetere, Thomas Hunt, John Brandon and from other marchants of Lenne, to the value of 1815 pounds."

[4] *Cf.* Albertus Krantzius, quoted by Hakluyt, vol. ii. p. 68.

were first employed. It is also certain that when the Scandinavian Powers attacked these pirates, the Hanse towns protected them. And I shall show later that the Hanse habitually used the freebooters as allies, who could be repudiated when found inconvenient, and even hanged when policy demanded it. But Lappenberg admits that the Hanse was actively hostile to the English settlement in Bergen ; so, without committing myself too far on this obscure controversy, I may at least say that, if the merchants of Lynne thought that the Hanse merchants had something to do with the affair, they had in the circumstances some excuse for their suspicions.

And, after all, the sack of Bergen was only one of the many grievances set forth by the English ambassadors. The list runs into several pages of Hakluyt, and gives abundant cause to show that " frightfulness " was as well understood by the Germans in those days as in these. I shall not weary my readers with more than a mere summary of the outrages charged against the " malefactors of Wismer and Rostok and others being of the societie of the Hanse," in the space of five years. We begin them with the ship *Godezere* (200 tons) of Newcastle-on-Tyne, with a cargo of cloth. She is taken in 1394, and two of her company killed. The ship is valued at £400, and the cargo at 200 marks. In the same year they take two ships of Hull, the *Cogge* and the *Trinitie*, the one with cloth worth £200, and the other with a mixed cargo of " oyle waxe and werke," worth £300. In 1401 they capture a Zeland ship chartered by John Hughson of Yarmouth, with hides, butter, masts, spars, &c., and in 1405 a small Yarmouth ship. In 1395 and 1396 they seize five fishing vessels belonging to Cley, " and one of the said master's mates they maliciously drowned." In 1395 they capture a whole fleet of six fishing vessels from Wiveton, belonging to one Simon Durham. The chief of them, called the *Dogger*, must have been a vessel of some size, for it had a master and twenty-five mariners, all of whom the Germans "maliciously slewe." They treated the crew of another of these Wiveton boats in the same manner, and those of a third they "beate and wounded." But the chief loss was suffered by Lynne :

"Item pitifully complaining that upon the 14th day after the feast of St. George (1394) as four ships of Lenne, laden with cloth, wine and other marchandises were sailing upon the maine sea, with all the goods and wares contained in them, for Prussia, sundry malefactors of Wismer and Rostok, with others of the Hanse, being in divers ships, came upon them, and by force of armes and strong hand took the said ships, with the goods and merchandises contained in them ; and some of the people which were in the said four ships, they slew, some they spoiled, and others they put into extreme ransomes. And carrying away with them those four ships with the commodities and marchandises therin, they parted stakes therewith, as these listed, to the great impoverishment and losse of the said merchants of Lenne, namely in cloth of William Sileden, Tho. Waterden, Joh. Brandon, Joh. Wesentra and other merchants of Lenne to the value of £3623, 5s. 11d."

With these and other losses the poor town of Lynne must have been almost ruined. Nor was this the sum of the English injuries. There is a long list of merchants of Hull, York, London, Colchester, Norwich, Yarmouth, and Lynne who were travelling, apparently in German ships, and were seized and robbed and put up to ransom.

Such outrages drove the feeble Richard into a feeble war. Margaret of Norway, Sweden, and Denmark was then in revolt against Hanseatic domination, and Richard sent to her aid an expeditionary force of three ships of Lynne, described as "large and warlike," but all too few for the purpose in hand. Margaret was defeated, and the Hanse, with its ally and protector, the Grand-Master of Prussia, set about bringing England to terms. The process was one of blockade. In 1398 the Grand-Master denounced the Commercial Treaty of 1388, withdrew Prussian merchants from England, and turned all English merchants out of Prussia. The boycott that followed was well calculated to bring England to her knees.

In the midst of these troubles and confusions, Henry of Lancaster, son of John of Gaunt, and a good friend of our "natural ally," succeeded in deposing the King. We may say of Richard what Chaucer said to him : "All is lost for lack of steadfastness."[1] He had a national policy, he was a good patriot in intention ; but he either lacked the means or the strength of mind to carry it through. Probably the German and Free Trade party, led by John of Ghent, was too strong for him.

---

[1] " A Ballad sent to King Richard." Chaucer, as Comptroller of Customs, must have had a great deal to do with the Germans, but does not refer to them often. His knight had gone to the wars in Prusse to fight the Lithuanians, whom the Germans, for their own purposes, represented as pagans, and we have seen his reference to the hardships of the prisons of Frisia. His Merchant was plainly a Merchant Adventurer, and an anti-German :

" He would the sea were kept for anything
Betwixte Middleburg and Orewell."

CHAPTER VIII

HENRY IV begins his reign with the usual homage to the anti-German party. In the first year of his reign he takes up the cry of Reciprocity in Germany : " That whereas the privileges and freedom of commerce granted to the German merchants in England were on condition that the English should enjoy the like in Germany, wherefore the said Master-General and the said Hanse towns are thereby summoned, either personally or by deputies, to answer before this King and his Council for the said injuries, and to make due satisfaction for the same." And he goes on to bring against the Hanse that charge of " colouring," which in the end is to prove fatal to their privileges : " That the said merchants of the Hanse towns shall not, under pretence of their own privileges in England, shelter the merchants of other foreign parts, whereby the King might suffer in his customs ; otherwise the King in Council declares that, in case of such practices or colourings, he will absolutely revoke and annul their said charter of privileges ; which declaration the King directed to be registered in Chancery." [1] The proclamation has a robust ring—and yet it hardly bears scrutiny ; for whereas English merchants had been turned out of Prussia, and Prussian merchants withdrawn from England, the other German towns were still represented

---

[1] Anderson, i. 396–7 (1399).

in the Steelyard, and no doubt carried on such trade for the Prussian towns as Lübeck desired or permitted. Moreover, the Baltic continues its war on English commerce, and by 1403 Henry and his subjects are in a mood for peace. The King writes effusively to the Grand-Master, " wishing with all our heart that the ancient friendship and love . . . may persevere in time to come, and that sweet and acceptable peace . . . be nourished and maintained." In the meantime, while the ambassadors of both countries " intreat about the foresaid injuries," he begs for a truce " until the feast of Easter next ensuing . . . all molestations and injuries which may be offered ceasing on both parts," and also that his subjects may have free passage to Sconia " for the providing of herrings and of other fishes there." In a postscript he reveals the impotence of England at sea : he has been unable hitherto to convoy the German messenger back to Prussia because " of the continual assaults of the Frenchmen and Britons against us and our kingdom."

The great Conradus de Jungingen, Master-General of the Teutonic Knights of the Hospital of the Blessed Virgin of Jerusalem, replies " from our castle of Marienburgh on 16th July, 1404." The letter is suave and pleasant, but firm : " Moreover, whereas your Highness hath further requested us that the prohibition of your subjects' access unto our dominions might, until the feast of Easter next ensuing, be released, we answer (under correction of your Majesty's more deliberate counsel) that it is far more expedient for both parts to have the said prohibition continued than released until such times as satisfaction be performed on both sides unto the parties endangered, not in words only but actually and really in deeds, or by some course of

law or friendly composition." As for the fishing in
Sconia, he had been fighting Margaret—no doubt a
delicate reminder of the three ships—but a truce was
concluded, and " far be it from us also that our subjects being occupied in wars, should in any sort willingly
molest or reproach any strangers, of what lands or
nations soever, not being our professed enemies."

We gather already that the Hanse will have the
best of the negotiations, and we are not disappointed.
The Master-General had begun by presenting a claim
for 19,120½ nobles for moral and material damages.
The English ambassadors, William Esturmy and John
Kingston, go to Prussia and present a counter-claim for
4535 nobles. The Master-General replies with a further
claim for 5100 nobles. The negotiations, which begin
in 1403, are postponed and transferred first to Dordrecht in Holland, and then to the Hague, in order to
get the valuation of " other indifferent merchants of
good credit." By 28th August 1407 the Hanse claim
has grown to 25,934½ nobles, which is to be compromised
for 8957 nobles. The King must give his answer by
16th March following " to the Aldermen of the Merchants of the Hanse residing at Bruges : otherwise
from thenceforth all league of friendship shall be dissolved between the realm of England and the land of
Prussia." A claim made by Dantzig to be settled at
Bruges—it gives some idea of the power of the Hanse
and the difficulty of getting " indifferent merchants " to
adjudicate. Little wonder if the English claim has
been written off at 764 nobles, " which," as the English
ambassadors remark, " will be very hard and extreme
dealing."

By this time there are new complications. English
sailors have taken three Livonian ships, with a cargo

of wax and furs, and have drowned 250 men. The claim against this is naturally high, £8037, 12s. 7d., reduced after haggling to £7498, 13s. 10d.

The Hanse towns present their separate bills for their separate injuries, and they also present a long list of grievances on behalf of the Hanse of Almaine in England. Whereas, under their charters, they are " privileged not to undergo any other burthens or impositions, but only to pay certain customs"; they had been constrained in the time of Simon de Moreden, Mayor of London, to pay " fifteenths, tallages, and other subsidies, contrary to the liberties of their charter." They had appealed successfully to the Privy Council, and had paid without prejudice an hundred marks sterling conditionally on an entire and perpetual deliverance from such payments. Nevertheless, the King's officers had recently demanded " tallages, fifteenths, and other subsidies," and when the Germans refused to pay, had " arrested the goods of those said merchants." They had also been compelled to pay certain customs and subsidies " more than their ancient customs." And especially they complained of changes in the customs on wool. Whereas under their privileges they were bound to pay only the ancient customs plus " xld. more than the home born merchants of England were wont to pay," they were now being compelled to pay " a certain imposition called pence for the town of Calais, namely, for every sack of wool 19d. more than the merchants of England do pay, to their great loss and against the liberty of their charter."

Then, as to customs on imports, by their charter they were only bound to pay an *ad valorem* duty of " 3d. for the worth of every pound of silver," which was to be paid on the amount of their manifests (" the letters of their masters and of their companies ''), or, failing manifests, on " the oath of their attorneys," the English customs officers were now putting their own valuation on the goods, and charging accordingly— " scanning about their fraight and expenses particularly disbursed in regard of the said goods and marchandise, to the great hindrance of the said marchants, and against the tenor of their charter."

In the same way they were being compelled to pay more than they ought on the export of small-cloths and kerseys.

Then there was the pitiful case of Nicholas Crossehaire, a Prussian " of their societies," who brought a cargo of bow-staves and other merchandise to Sandwich, where he paid the customs, and had afterwards transferred a parcel to London, where custom dues were again demanded. Nicholas offered security, but refused to pay until the question was decided. He even got a brief from the King absolving him from payment. Nevertheless the goods were kept on shipboard, to their damage, until the London customs were paid. " Another of their company," Peter Herston, was similarly treated over a cargo of cloth, bought at Bristol for Prussia, when the ship touched at London. Then the officers of the petty customs were making charges for schedules and cockets and the sealing of cloth ; they procrastinated over details, and there were cases of over-charges at Southampton and Newcastle.

Altogether, you will say, the usual grievances of foreign merchants. Yet the document seems to indicate something more—a quiet, persistent hostility of Englishmen, showing itself in a hundred trifles. It comes out clearly in the first complaint : " Of late, those that are free denizens in the cities, boroughs, and villages within the foresaid kingdom, do hinder and restrain all others that be strangers, foreigners, and aliens, that they neither can nor dare buy and sel with the marchants of the Hanse aforesaid, to their great hinderance and losse." Englishmen might be compelled by the " natural alliance " between kings and loans to submit to German privileges; but they resented them nevertheless, and in their own quiet and patient way made their resentment felt.

The English ambassadors put their counter-grievances—a much more formidable list. Whereas German merchants could trade freely in England, " the said common society of marchants (the Hanse) by their publike and deliberate common counsel did appoint and ordaine that no society in any cities, townes, or places, neither yet any particular man of any such society should in any wise admit any marchants of the realme of England resorting unto their cities or other places for marchandise to enjoy intercourse of traffike." This exclusion was fortified by " grievous penalties of money." The boycott had been enforced so strictly that certain English merchants, who had gone with their ships to one of the principal German towns, could not even buy meat and drink, much less sell their cloth. Not only were there " grievous pecuniary mulcts," but the cloth itself was forfeit if the prohibition to trade was infringed. And not only so, but the Hanse, designing " an utter extirpation and overthrow of English merchants," had ordered all Hanseatic merchants to leave England and forbidden all English trade. The boycott had not been confined to Germany and England :

" Item that the said society aforesaid hath approved divers very unreasonable statutes and ordinances made and published by merchants of the same society residing in the kingdoms of Norway and Swedland, to the great prejudice of the kingdom of England, and the marchants thereof : and as yet both covertly and expressly do approve the same, unjustly putting them in daily execution."

Lastly, there was the charge of "colouring." Under their privileges and indulgences the Hanse were not to " avow any man which is not of their company, nor shall not colour his goods and marchandise under their company . . . under the perpetual frustration and revocation of the foresaid privileges." " Yet the contrary unto all these provisoes hath bin every yere, for these twenty yeres or thereabout notoriously practised and committed," both by the General Council and by particular Hanse cities, " to the great diminution of his Majesties custome." The ambassadors therefore demanded to know how many and which were the Hanse towns—a question often put, but never, as far as I know, answered.

By means of these dull and long-protracted negotiations we are now in the year of our Lord 1408. On the 26th March of that year Henry IV offers to settle the matter by paying 8957 nobles to the Prussians, and " 22496 nobles, sixepence, halfe penny, farthing " to the Livonians by three equal payments within three years after Easter. The Prussians and Livonians are asked to pay 766 nobles and 4535 on the English claims within one year. As for the people drowned, " we will cause suffrages of prayers and divers other holsome remedies profitable for the soules of the deceased," on condition that the Grand-Master did the same for the souls of Englishmen.

The Grand-Master replied that any arrangement must be subject to further claims being made against England before the King of the Romans. Otherwise, with a good deal of rigmarole, he accepted on behalf of his Prussians and Livonians the sums mentioned. As for the English claims, the Grand-Master agrees to the payment of 766 nobles, but makes no mention of the second and larger claim, except to say that " other like summes," which are sufficiently proved, will be paid, like the first, by the Treasurer of Dantzig. The reply is dated from " our castle of Marienburgh," 27th September 1408.

King Henry, in a letter which may fairly be described as gushing, accepts the Grand-Master's reply, and proposes a " perpetual league between the two countries." This is preliminary to the formal treaty signed at London on 4th September 1409, on which only a few words remain to be said. The treaty is for mutual trade, subject to " all rights and customs due in regard of their said wares and marchandizes." The Hanse privileges being renewed, it is obvious that this does not mean reciprocity, since English merchants in Germany enjoy no such privileges. There is an intimation that all claims have been settled on both sides by agreement to pay certain unspecified sums ; but " besides the sums due unto the said Master-General " there is a long new list of grievances " against himself and divers other of his subjects of Prussia," which are to be settled separately. These amount in the aggregate to 5353 nobles, of which 2025 nobles are claims on people of Calais and Bayonne, then British possessions, which are to be paid by various Englishmen who are named. Thus Tulburie and Terry of Hull are to pay 82 nobles to Matthewe Ludekensson of Dantzig ; Sir William de Ethingham, knight, " who *was* Vice-Admirall for the Sea," is called sharply to book for 114 nobles to John Halewater, also of Dantzig, and so forth. The inhabitants of " Scardeburgh " are to pay 800 nobles of English money for injuries and robberies to John Gruk of Dantzig ; and people of Blakeney, " Crowmer," Plymouth, Dartmouth, Calais, and Bayonne are all mulcted in various sums. The heirs of Lord Henry de Percie the younger are to pay 838 nobles for corn and grain bought by Lord Henry in 1403 from the great procurator of Marienburgh for the use of the castle of South Berwick.

On the English side, John Marion of Wersingham is to be paid 200 nobles for damages received from a Prussian named Eghard Scoff.

Now, if we make a little sum of this treaty, we find that while the Germans get the enormous sum for those days of 34,781 nobles out of England, England only gets from Germany 966 nobles, and this although upon the record the Germans had done much more harm to Englishmen than Englishmen had done to the Germans. Moreover, the Germans have secured [1] a renewal of certain valuable customs, preferences, and trading privileges, well defined by charter and the courts, whereas the English have only secured the ordinary footing—none too good—of the foreigner in Germany.

There must have been a pull somewhere. Where was it ? In the first place, the Germans had sea-power : they controlled Scandinavia and the Baltic—the main source of sea munitions in those days. In the second place, they controlled the Baltic corn supply, which was necessary to an England largely given up to sheep-

[1] *Cf.* Henry V's embassy of 1415, mentioned above.

farming. In the third place, they controlled Flanders, England's chief market.   But, in the fourth place, they financed ambitious kings, like Henry IV and Henry V, in those glorious wars with France, which yielded so little and cost so much.

CHAPTER IX

THE MERCHANT ADVENTURERS

THE politics of the Middle Ages had their parties much as ours, and were naturally divided upon certain great questions. The foreigner, and all who depended on foreign imports and lived on foreign money, were on the one side; the Englishmen who depended on manufacture, on shipping, on fishing, and on agriculture stood upon the other. On the one side was law, on the other side custom; on the one side English guilds, on the other the cities of the Hanse and of Lombardy. On the one side was wool, on the other side cloth. When wool was the staple export of England, the foreigner prevailed, because those who sell raw material are in a weaker position than those who sell the finished article. And our judicious prince, Edward III, did one great service to England, which must stand to his credit against all his wasteful victories: he protected the English cloth industry against Flanders. If we were to inquire into his motive, I fear we would find it no higher than this—to force the Flemish towns into an alliance with England against France. When he brought his staple from Bruges to Calais, and from Calais to Westminster; when he stopped the export of English wool and gave safe-conducts and bounties to Flemish immigrants, he did it all that Flanders might give free passage and support to his armies, in spite of the allegiance the Count of Flanders owed to France.

But what, after all, is the motive so long as the policy is good? And Edward's policy re-established the English cloth industry. I say re-established, because English cloth was woven before the Conquest, and English weaving was already important in the time of Simon de Montfort. But, as we have seen, in the time of Simon English cloth was a coarse article, which the gentlemen of the patriotic party wore as a mark of patriotism—much as the Duchess of Sutherland set a fashion in Harris tweeds.[1] Simon, we may be certain, wore the cloth himself; but Edward III was not quite of Simon's mettle, as witness his statute: " That none should wear any cloth for the future but such as was made in England, except the King and Queen and their children." Between Simon and Edward there was a notable decline in the cloth industry, as was natural with the triumph of the Free Trade and Foreign Party; but the divine accident of Edward's ambitions revived it.[2] English cloth became a great competitor with the cloth of Flanders, and although Flanders stopped its importation by a long series of prohibitions, from the time of the Angevins to the time of Elizabeth, the industry went on, extending, improving, and refining. For a long time Flanders kept its hold upon the cloth-finishing trade, and fought desperately to stop every English advance from the half-finished to the finished article; but in the process of time English weavers learned every secret of their

---

[1] That Simon's Parliament saw the need for importing weavers from Flanders is shown by the proclamation that " all workers of woollen cloths, male and female, as well of Flanders as of other lands, may safely come into our realm there to make cloths—upon the understanding that those who shall so come and make such cloths shall be quit of toll and tallage and of payment of other customs for their work until the end of five years."—Lipson, p. 396, who quotes *De Antiquis Legibus Liber*, 126, 127, 135–137; Riley, *Chronicles of London*, 132, 141, 142.

[2] His preambles always set forth that the measures were taken " in view of the *decay* of the art of weaving " (*cf.* Lipson, p. 399).

wonderful craft, and even in silks our London weavers rivalled the looms of Cologne and Lyons.

In the beginnings of our story we find the party conflict raging between the exporter of wool and the maker of cloth. Simon fell, it has been surmised, because he alienated the wool magnates by his whole-hogging protection of the weaver. A poem, which is put down to the reign of Edward IV, but might have been written at any time from Henry III to the fifteenth century, shows the clamour of the loom for the prohibition of wool export : [1]

> " Let not our wool be sold for nought
> Neither our cloth for they must be sought,
> And in special restrain straitly the wool
> That the commons of this land may work in full."

If wool must be sold, the poet goes on, let it be the coarsest and the worst. Let there be an ordinance to protect spinners, dyers, weavers, and the allied trades, and to prevent " a strange mene " from robbing the poor artisan of his profit :

> " For in these days there is a usance
> That put the poor people to great hindrance
> By a strange mene (foreign crowd) that is late in the land
> Began and used as ye understand."

After describing the tricks of these foreigners, the poet proceeds :

> " By merchants and cloth-makers for God's sake take keep
> Which maketh the poreylle (poor) to mourn and weep.
> Little they take for their labour but half is merchandise
> Alas ! for ruth it is great pity ! "

Now the wool export trade was in the hands of the

---

[1] Wright, vol. ii. p. 282.   Its title-motto is noteworthy : " Anglia propter tuas naves et lanas omnia regna te salutare deberent."   I have modernised the spelling.

Staple,[1] half guild and half tax-farmer, protected by many royal charters because furnishing the King with most of his revenues. The Merchants of the Staple admitted foreigners to their privileges, and as they were exporters of the raw material and importers of the finished article, they naturally leaned to the Free Trade side. They held their mart, sometimes in Bruges, sometimes in Calais, sometimes in the staple towns of England. They sold wool, wool-fels, hides, lead, and tin, and bought foreign merchandise.

The Merchant Adventurers, on the other hand, sprang direct from the cloth trade. Wheeler [2] says they were originally known as the Brotherhood of St. Thomas of Canterbury—Canterbury, of course, being the traditional cradle of the English weaver, and St. Thomas his patron saint. Moreover, in London, down to 1526, the minutes of the Merchant Adventurers were kept in the same books as those of the Mercers' Company—and the Mercers dealt in silks. If a merchant desired to trade in wool as well as in cloth, he had to be a freeman both of the Staple and the Merchant Adventurers' Company, which shows how closely the two corporations corresponded with the raw material and the finished article.

We may take it, then, that the Merchant Adventurers were formed to organise a foreign market for English cloth in English hands, and their design must at once have brought them into sharp conflict with the Germans. Indeed, I think it would be found, by a com-

---

[1] The derivation of the word is so simple that it has escaped the learned. A staple or hook of steel was used for dragging the bales of wool over the warehouse floor. The traders in wool were therefore called staplers, and the wool trade the staple trade. In course of time the Merchants of the Staple exported a few other commodities, like tin and lead, and imported cloth ; hence the term " staple trade " was gradually extended and the original meaning lost.

[2] Wheeler, *Treatise of Commerce*, p. 10.

parison of the rules and constitution of the two organisations, that the English Company was a copy of the Hanse. Thus, for example, no freeman of the Merchant Adventurers was allowed to marry a woman born out of the realm of England. And the Navigation Laws of Richard II and Henry VII, which, I take it, were inspired by the Merchant Adventurers—what are they but a statutory form of the Hanseatic rule of " Hanse goods in Hanse ships "—which, indeed, the Germans copied from the Venetians ? Then the Company, like the Hanse, was an organisation of towns. London was the chief ; but besides London there were Merchant Adventurers' Guilds in Bristol, York, Norwich, Exeter, Ipswich, Newcastle, Hull, Boston, Devizes, Salisbury, and Yarmouth. According to Wheeler, the Freemen numbered some three thousand, so that they were an organisation of national importance. It was said by their enemies that their whole business was managed by forty or fifty London merchants, and it would seem that London had the chief say in matters of national policy ; but the other towns had a voice in the general management, and some of the towns, like Bristol and Hull, for example, had separate charters. Their business being to find a foreign market for English cloth, they naturally concentrated their directing power at the seat of government—and London may be called the Lübeck of the Merchant Adventurers, without any disrespect to so powerful a port as Bristol. The field of operations covered by their charters was between the Somme in France and the Scawe in Denmark : they were the " mercatores in partibus Hollandie, Selandie, Brabantie, et Flandrie," and their method was to hold fairs in one, or at most two, towns within that area—in other words, they sought to establish

what the Germans called *Kontors*. Their affairs in
these mart towns were administered by a governor, a
deputy, and twenty-four assistants, and with this
governor and court all the English towns corresponded,
on such subjects as price, quantity, quality, means of
shipment, and so forth. Not only so, but the court
had powers under their charters to settle disputes,
either between themselves or with strangers who
accepted their jurisdiction ; and Wheeler tells us that
they had charters not only from the kings of England,
but from the rulers of Flanders.

But it will be asked, If England was the manufacturing rival of Flanders, how did it come about
that its Counts allowed this formidable organisation to
settle in its midst ? Not without a struggle, certainly.
Wheeler tells how Edward III found an opening for
the Adventurers in Calais, and how the trade so created
induced " Lewes, Earl of Flanders," to give them a
charter in 1358. This charter gave them access to
Bruges ; but the Flemings, " through wealth and ful-
nesse of bread," drove them out, and they were fain to
settle in the town of Middleburg. This place, being
" full of salt and filthy ooze, stench and noysome
savours," bred agues, and the English accepted the invitation of Antwerp, then a poor and simple town,
which offered them privileges. There, and at the town
of Bergen-op-Zoom, the Adventurers established themselves, and by the sale of cheap English cloth made
Antwerp the rival of Bruges. The fact is that the
weavers of Flanders were betrayed by the seaports
of Brabant : the Netherlands, having no national
trade policy, were unable to protect themselves against
the treachery of one of their towns. Wheeler boasts
that the Adventurers made Antwerp the " pack-house

of Europe "; but it was at the cost of the Flemish weavers.

Thus the Merchant Adventurers began, and as they attacked new markets, they branched out into new companies, all linked children of the same parent, and acknowledging its authority. Russia, " Eastland," Spain, and Turkey—all these had their branch companies of Merchant Adventurers.

But everywhere the chief enemy was the German Hanse. In England, as Wheeler claims, the Adventurers were " the principal obstacle to the bringing of the trade into strangers' hands only," and he chiefly blames the Germans for the troubles of the Merchant Adventurers in the Netherlands : " The Easterlings continue still in their pride of heart and indurate malice." Without them Antwerp could not have given trouble. And if they fought the English in Antwerp, how much more in Bruges, the chief depot of their trade.

Thus we see that the English took a leaf out of the German book, as the Germans themselves had learnt their trade secrets from the towns of Lombardy. They united the chief ports and cloth centres of England in a National League, or Trust, or Hanse, which fixed prices, controlled output, and opened markets oversea. Like the Germans, they organised themselves for foreign commerce, and we shall find in the struggle between these two organisations the master-key to many secrets in our English history.

Now these merchants were called Adventurers because they adventured oversea with their cargoes of cloth, and they had accordingly a naval policy. We find Chaucer's merchant expressing it in two lines :

> " He wold the see were kept for anything
> Betwixtë Middleburg and Orëwell."

And this policy is set out in detail by another poet, the author of the *Libel of English Policie*.[1] Who the author was we have no knowledge, but he wrote in the reign of Henry VI, after the German Emperor Sigismund visited England in 1416, and before he died in 1438. This we know, because the writer refers to Henry V in the past tense, and tells us that " Sigismund the great Emperour, wich yet reigneth," when he was here on a visit, gave a valuable piece of advice to " King Henry the fift," when he had seen the two towns of Calais and Dover :

> " Keepe these two townes sure, and your Majestee
> As your tweyne eyne, so keepe the narrowe see." [2]

And this is the text of the *Libel* :

> " Cherish Marchandise, keepe the admiraltie
> That wee bee Masters of the Narrowe see."

The poet shows us the trade of Europe passing up and down the English Channel, and centring in Sluys, the port of Bruges. There go the Spaniards, as to their staple fair, with their figs, raisins, wine, wool, iron, goatskins, saffron, and quicksilver.

> " For Spain and Flanders is as eche other brother,
> And neither may well live without other."

The Spaniards sell their merchandise to buy " fine cloth of Ypres that named is better than ours " ; but what, after all, were Flemish cloth without English

---

[1] Reprinted in Wright and Hakluyt.
[2] There is a tradition in South Africa that the Emperor William gave Lord Roberts his plan of campaign, and there is probably as much truth in the one story as in the other. But it is pleasant to believe that a German Emperor showed us how to fight the Germans.

wool ? Neither Spain nor Flanders could live without England :

> "They may not liven to maintain their degrees
> Without our English commodities
> Woolle and tynne : for the woolle of England
> Susteineth the Commons Flemmings I understand."

As for Spanish wool, which was draped in Flanders, it was useless unless our stronger wools were mixed with it.

So with the Portuguese : they depended on the Flemish, and the Flemish depended on them :

> "For Flanders is staple as men tell mee
> To all nations of Christiantie."

So also with the Bretons, who were great sea-rovers, and were always raiding our Norfolk coasts. And so with Scotland, whose wools had to pass by England into Flanders. If the English only kept the sea, they would soon have peace with Scotland :

> "Wee should right soone have peace for all her hosts,
> For they must needs pass by our English costs."

Then the poet proceeds to deal with " the commodities of Pruce and High Dutchmen and Easterlings " :

> "which might not be forborne
> Out of Flanders but it were verely lorne,"

because they brought in " the substance of the beere," and it was well known that two Flemings could drink a " ferkin full of good beerekin " :

> "Now Beere and Bakon bene fro Pruse y brought
> Into Flanders as loved and far y sought :
> Osmond, copper, bow-staves, Steele and Wexe,
> Peltre ware and grey pitch, Terre, Board and flexe,
> And Colleyne threed, Fustian and Cauvas
> Card, Bukeram : of olde time thus it was."

They also brought silver wedges " out of the lands of Beame and Hungarie," and they loaded with woollen cloth. Also they

> " . . . adventure full greatly unto the Bay [1]
> for salt that is needful withouten nay."

And therefore :

> " If they would not our friends bee
> Wee might lightly stoppe hem in the see
> They should not passe our streames withouten leve,
> It would not be, but if we should hem greve."

Having settled with the Germans, the poet passes on to the Genoese, the Venetians, and the Florentines, who came in their carracks and galleys to England and Flanders. The Genoese brought cloth of gold, silk, and pepper, and other good merchandise, and loaded English wool ; the others brought spicery and groceries, sweet wines, and

> " Apes and japes and marmusets tayled
> Nifles and trifles that little have avayled."

For these they got our good cloth, wool, and tin, so that the land was impoverished by their trade.

And then the poet has a fling at foreigners in general —" of such lands and of such nations." They were spies and agents of the enemy ; they spread false rumours :

> " Also they bere the gold out of this land,
> And suck the thrifte away out of our hand
> As the waspe sucketh honie fro the bee."

They played tricks with our exchange, to their profit and our loss : they bought our Cotswold wool on credit, and got cash for it at Bruges. They had " freedom and franchise " to trade over all England—more

[1] See Appendix VI.

freedom than the English could get. They should be given only forty days to unload and forty days to load their ships, and they should

> " Goe to oste, as we there with hem doe
> It were expedient that they did right soe
> As we doe there."

In other words, let us have reciprocity : our merchants have to " host " when they go abroad, they should do the same when they come to England.   Here almost certainly the poet is referring to the Hanse towns,[1] for he goes on to urge a strong Navy, and refers, as a dreadful example, to the evil fate of Denmark :

> " In Denmarke were full noble conquerours
> In time past, full worthy warriours :
> Whiche when they had their marchants destroyed,
> To poverty they fell, thus were they noyed :
> And so they stand at mischiefe at this day.
> This learned I late will writon, this no nay.
> Therefore beware."

Again the poet goes back to the standing grievance :

> " What reason is it that we should goe to oste
> In their countries and in this English coste
> They should not soe ? but have more liberty
> Than we ourselves."

Why, in other words, should they have Protection and we Free Trade.   There was bribery at work :

> " Gifts and fests stopen our policie."

But we were the fools, not they.   We always had the worst of it, therefore we must have reciprocity, either " hosting " in our country or Free Trade in theirs.

Take the position in Brabant.   Englishmen had only

---

[1] " The which Parliament (1440) ordained that all merchant strangers should go to host with Englishmen . . . except the Easterlings."—*Chronicles of London*, ed. Kingsford, pp. 146–147.

fourteen days to unload at their marts, and fourteen days to load; if they remained longer, everything was forfeit.   Yet if Englishmen were to withdraw from these markets they would collapse.

What, then, was our true policy ?   To govern the sea, and suffer none to pass into Flanders without our permission.   Then all nations would be our friends :

> " But we be frayle as glasse and also brittle."

We were backsliders from grace.   We allowed " Lombards and other fained friends " to colour merchandise. They had friends in high places ; but

> " Beware yee men that bere the great in hand
> That they destroy the policie of this land."

It was shameful that there was no law against such practices as colouring.

Then the poet touches on Ireland.   He is all for union, because Irish harbours might be used by the enemy—as, indeed, they were shortly afterwards. Wales also should be kept well in hand.   But the great thing, after all, was the Navy.   King Edgar had been strong on sea, and King Edward III and King Henry V, they knew how to build and maintain a strong fleet.   " The sea well kept," if we did that, other countries would not dare make war upon us.   " The end of battle is peace," and " power causeth peace finally " :

> " Kepe then the sea that is the wall of England :
> And then is England kept by Goddes hand
> That as for any thing that is without
> England were at ease withouten doubt,
> And thus should every lond one with another
> Enter common as brother with his brother."

And here the poem ends with a fine apostrophe to

peace, and the peace of God that passeth understanding, which is to be obtained not through weakness, but only by the strength to maintain it.   As for the man who wrote it, if he was a poor poet he was a great statesman and a good Englishman.   But we may take it that the policy of the *Libel* was not the work of one brain : it was the traditional policy of the Patriot Party in England—the policy of Simon de Montfort ; the policy of Richard II ; the policy of London, of Bristol, of the Merchant Adventurers ; the policy of York ; the policy for which Warwick was to die, and which Edward was to betray.

CHAPTER X

THE SACRED FRIENDSHIP

WHEN that unfortunate monarch, Henry VI, made his first State entry into London, on the 21st February 1431, John Lydgate wrote a courtly poem describing the procession. The Lord Mayor goes past in red velvet, followed by his sheriffs, aldermen, and freemen of the Guilds. Then come the foreigners :

> "And for to remember of other Alyens
> First Jeneueyes, thoughe they were straungeris,
> Florentynes and Venycyens,
> And Esterlings, glad in her maneres,
> Conveyed withe sergeauntes and other officeres
> Estatly horsed, aftyr the Maier riding,
> Passid the subarbis to mete with the Kyng."

The Easterlings had, in fact, very good reason to be "glad in their manners." They were supreme at sea, and on land they were also supreme. On the 10th May following the Privy Council gives these "Merchants Dalmaigne" exemption from an increase on the customs levied upon foreign merchants, the increase being held to be in contravention of the ancient German privileges. "With such conscientiousness," says Lappenberg complacently, "which safeguarded the rights of foreigners and of natives, the happy conditions of the Hanse seemed unlikely ever to be disturbed."[1]

---

[1] "Conscientiousness" is an excellent word, and its operation may be traced throughout this period. In 1418 the sheriffs of London, who had rented from the Treasury the royal subsidii from the town and county of Middlesex, tried to make the Germans pay certain new duties on wine, salt, builders'

There was, in fact, only one circumstance which threatened to disturb these happy conditions, and it was this, that the English people, both on sea and land, found the German domination intolerable, and were determined to make an end of it. Yet it must have seemed a hopeless struggle. Edward III had actually forbidden Englishmen to engage in oversea trade. In 1416 Henry V, after his glorious victory at Agincourt, had sent a brilliant embassy to the honourable society of the German Hanse of the Holy Empire— " honorabilis Societatis Hansæ Teutonicæ sancti Imperii "—in order to renew in solemn state all their old privileges in England. In 1428 the English had again been driven out of Bergen, by the inevitable " freebooter," Bartholomew Voet. They were endeavouring to maintain a precarious hold on the Baltic trade, but found themselves enveloped in endless disputes between the Grand-Master of Prussia and the towns of Dantzig and Elbing. In 1423 the English Navy was sold at one courageous stroke of the pen by order in Council. In 1452 two ships, " rotten and useless, practically constituted the Royal Navy of England." Shortly àfter the death of Henry V, English merchants complained to the English Parliament that their ancient settlement at Dantzig had been forcibly dissolved, and that they had been vilely entreated both there and at Greifswald. The Germans in London took up the case of their countrymen before the Privy Council, but at the same time recommended Dantzig to treat the English with a little more tact. Evidently English feeling was

wood, wax, tar, flax, oakum, and other goods. The Germans successfully resisted the demand on the strength of their " ancient privileges," with the aldermen of London as backers. In 1427 the attempt was repeated in connection with other duties—on rice and similar imports. The Mayor, G. Reynewell, and the rest of the Council supported the Germans in their claim of exemption.

running higher. In 1432 the House of Commons was petitioning the King to make German merchants in London responsible for damages to English merchants in the Baltic. The King had just confirmed all Hanseatic privileges—no doubt for the usual cash consideration—and he conscientiously declined to agree to so barbarous a proposal. At the same time the Prussian Grand-Master was promulgating an order expelling all Englishmen from Germany, and the Hanse towns were prohibiting the importation of English cloth. In 1434 a Hanseatic embassy, consisting of the Mayors of Cologne, Lübeck, Hamburg, and Dantzig came to London, and were quietly settling all grievances with the English Government, when the English merchants riotously intervened with their complaints. The King, to soothe the ruffled feelings of both parties, transferred the negotiations to the Hanseatic stronghold of Bruges, and the Hanse threatened to withdraw altogether from England. In 1435, as an earnest of his good intentions, Henry permitted the Germans to sell their fish in the English markets, in spite of the ancient charters of English fishmongers. Negotiations dragged on until 13th January 1436 with no result, "notwithstanding the good intentions of the King." In the meantime (1434) the Flemish had forbidden the importation of English cloth, and troubles followed which made the negotiations at Bruges impossible. The Hanse had forbidden Gothland to trade in the North Sea, and Holland in the Baltic.[1] The Dutch joined with Scandinavia in revolt against the League, but were signally defeated by 1435.

Negotiations therefore languished at Bruges, and by

---

[1] One of many pleasing illustrations of that glorious principle of "liberty of the seas," for which the German submarines, according to Bethman-Hollweg, are now sinking neutral vessels.

G

1437 the German ambassadors were back in London. That redoubtable Mayor of Dantzig, Heinrich Vorrath, had instructions from his city "to demand much of the English and to concede nothing."[1] On the other hand, the English merchants were clamouring for the abolition of all Hanseatic privileges. Their trade in Iceland had just been stopped by an interdict of Eric VII, acting, as the English believed, at German instigation. They were shut out of the Baltic, out of Germany, out of Flanders. It was not reasonable ; it was not fair.

The King, always weak-minded and sometimes imbecile, might have yielded to the prejudiced clamour of his subjects ; but fortunately for the Germans, sacred friendships stood firm in their support. Cardinal Henry Beaufort, Bishop of Winchester, was President of the Council, and he made an eloquent speech on behalf of the Germans. After describing the ancient and sacred character of the charters on which the Hanse based its claims, and the lack of any precedent for the claims of the English, he ended with a lofty and eloquent peroration addressed to his unreasonable countrymen :   " Give up these new claims," he said, " and do not force this kingdom into a new war with countries and towns without which we cannot get along, and with which our merchants must keep up relations in order to make profit."[2]

The battle was won for Germany. On 22nd March 1437 a treaty favourable to the Hanse at all points

---

[1] Th. Hirsch, *Dantzig's Handelsund Gerverbegeschichte unter der Herrschaft des deutschen Ordens*, p. 110.

[2] *Chronic of Detmar the Franciscan* (a Lübeck chronicler), edited by Grautoff, Part II, p. 75, who makes the cardinal end his speech thus : " Ghevet over de nyen vunde, unde maket unsem ryke neu nyen orleghe myt Landen unde steden, der wy nicht entberen konen und dar unse koep man van noet weghen verkeren moet."

was signed in London, and confirmed by the King on 7th June of the same year.

Now, it is worthy of note that the head of the Commission on the English side was William, Bishop of Lincoln, a sacred friend of the Cardinal and of Germany. On 17th June, ten days after the royal signature had been affixed to the new German charter, the house in Windgoose Lane, next to the German Steelyard, is made over by the German widow, Johanna Bokeland, to Henry, Cardinal of England, and William, Bishop of Lincoln.

"It may not be justifiable," says Lappenberg musingly, "to draw conclusions affecting the honour of the Cardinal and the Bishop."[1]

The treaty of 1437, between King Henry VI on the one side, and Paul Rusdorfe, Master-General of the Teutonic Knights of Prussia, and the pro-consuls and consuls of the communities and cities of the Teutonic Hanse on the other, is described as "a renewal of all the privileges granted by either contracting party for one hundred years backward, in commercial and

---

[1] Yet Lappenberg grants that after all Shakespeare may not have been so far out in that famous death-bed scene in Act iii. of the *Second Part of King Henry VI* :

Cardinal. Bring me unto my trial when you will.
.   .   .   .
O ! torture me no more ; I will confess.—
.   .   .   .   .   .   ‡
Give me some drink ; and bid the apothecary
Bring the strong poison that I bought of him.
    King Henry. O thou eternal mover of the heavens,
Look with a gentle eye upon this wretch !
O, beat away the busy meddling fiend,
That lays strong siege unto this wretch's soul,
And from his bosom purge this black despair !
.   .   .   .
Warwick. So bad a death argues a monstrous life.

It is not, perhaps, extravagant to suppose that the German house in Windgoose Lane may have been one of the trifles which weighed a little on the Cardinal's conscience in those self-revealing moments.

nautical concerns, and of the duties and customs on both sides, now agreed to remain on the ancient footing." It is also a readjustment of the debt : " Nineteen thousand two hundred and seventy-four nobles and a half were agreed to be paid in annual sums of five hundred marks sterling, or one thousand nobles yearly." The Germans are given special judges, to be appointed by the King, and the position of Englishmen in Germany is left much as before.[1]

The unequal struggle continued, the unreasonable Englishmen still demanding full and actual reciprocity. In 1439 the King passes a statute exempting " les merchauntz de Hanse dalmaigne " from certain " grievous restrictions placed upon them in England." Immediately after, Parliament empowers the King to rescind all Hanseatic privileges until the complaints of the English in Prussia and Dantzig have been satisfactorily answered. Yet the royal edicts protecting the Hanse continue to issue in endless succession. On 12th February 1446 the customs officials of Boston are recommended to remember a Hanseatic charter of 1317. The English reply is that at the present time the Germans are turning the English out of the Norwegian trade. Thereupon Henry Spicer of Derby is given certain rights against the Hanse in England for damages done to him in Norway. The German merchants point out that by their charters they are not responsible for the misdeeds of other Germans, and the rights given to Henry Spicer are thereupon revoked.[2] In the same year the Hanseatic League

---

[1] Anderson, vol. i. p. 458 ; *Fœdera*, vol. x. p. 66. I do not go into the details of this instrument, as they may be more profitably considered when we reach the Treaty of Utrecht, an even more complete monument to the ability of our "natural ally."

[2] March 20, 1447.

passes a law that no English goods are to be carried except in Hanseatic ships. This evidently precipitates another storm, and Henry tides over the difficulty by granting the Hanse safe conduct for three years, " provided they pay the customs and other dues."

The German plan is, as before, to prolong and protract negotiations through an endless maze of claim and counter-claim. On 24th July 1448 a royal rescript commands Sir Robert Shottesbroke and Sir John Beck, with the Magister Richard Caunton, Archdeacon of Salisbury, to meet the Hanseatic ambassadors at a convenient place and settle the difficulties.[1] In the following year they are at the " convenient place " of Lübeck ; but the Lübeck Council refuses to negotiate alone. The Hanse is convened, but only the Prussians arrive ; the other German cities stay away. The English envoys are hurt by this slight, but nevertheless proceed with the negotiations. The Hanseatic deputies reply that they are unauthorised to act for the absent towns. After a long diplomatic sparring-match it is agreed to transfer the negotiations to Deventer, and to allow two years' truce for the negotiation of a settlement.

" These hopeful peace overtures," says Lappenberg, " were unexpectedly destroyed by the violently hostile sentiments of the English." As a matter of fact, the Baltic towns and their allies, the freebooters, had been scouring the seas of English shipping, and when the English complained, the Hanse as usual disavowed all liability. In those circumstances, on the 3rd April 1449 the King gave royal letters patent " for the cleansing of the sea, and rebuking of the robbers and pirates thereof," to an illiterate but valiant man of Devon called Robert Wenyngton.[2] On 25th May this

---

[1] Rymer, *Fœdera*, I, xi. p. 217.   [2] *Paston Letters*, No. 68.

sailor reports that he had met with a fleet of a hundred great ships of " Pruse, Lubycke, Campe, Rastocke, Holond, Selond and Flandres " between Guernsey and Portland. " And then," pursues Wenyngton, " I came aboard the Admirell and bade them stryke in the Kyngy's name of Englond ; and they bade me skyte in the Kyngy's name of Englond ; and then I and my felerschyp sayd but (unless) he will streke don the sayle that I wyld oversayle him by the Grace of God, and (if) God will send me wynd and wether. And dey bade me do my wurst because I had so few schyppes and so smale that they scornyd with me."

As a matter of fact, God did send him a good wind, and there was a sharp engagement, in which the Germans " schotte at us a jm: (1000) gownys (guns) and quarell (cross-bow bolts) without number and haue slayne meny of my felyschep and meymyd (maimed) allsoo." The Germans surrendered, and Wenyngton asks for instructions, as he had brought them into the Solent (" within Wight "). He adds that, as they had done him and his fellowship so much harm, he and his company were " avesyd . . . to drowne them and slee them." In the meantime he begs his correspondent to come to Southampton and see the sight, " for I der well sey that I haue her at this tyme all the cheff schyppys of Duchelond, Holond, Selond and Flaundrys, and now hyt were tyme for to trete for a fynell pese as for that partys."

Far from leading to a " fynell pese," this gallant action only led to fresh trouble. By way of reprisal, Lübeck seized a big English ship laden with cloth, and asked King Christian of Denmark to act as umpire for the division of the spoils between the cities. Christian, a young and spirited monarch with a sense of humour, decided that the ship had been taken in his territorial waters, and appropriated both ship and cargo, selling the freight for what it would fetch at Copenhagen. At this the ire of the Lübeckers rose to such a pitch that they not only arrested the English merchants who had come to lay their complaints, but Dr. Caunton, the English ambassador. The Hanseatic towns pretended to intervene on their behalf; they were allowed out on parole, and most of them—including Dr. Caunton, I am ashamed to say—took French leave.[1]

These events were not altogether welcome to the more thoughtful of the Hanse towns, and especially to the *Kontor* in London. They had all the privileges they could hope for in England; and the English, although a patient race, were becoming unmanageable. A terrible enemy had risen up against them, no less a man than Richard Neville, Earl of Warwick, known to history as the King-Maker.

---

[1] For these events, see *Detmar's Chronicle*, edited by Grautoff to 1451.

CHAPTER XI

WE might call Warwick the Simon de Montfort of the fifteenth century. He led the Party of York, and the Party of York was the Party of Protection, the Party of the Merchant Adventurers, the Party of the Mercers and Cloth-makers, the Party of the Iron-founders, the Party of the Sailors—in short, the anti-German Party. The weak-minded Henry, as we have seen, was completely under the control of a Free Trade Party, which had its spiritual home in Germany, and the result was a situation which England found intolerable. The York Party gradually gathered power in Court about the middle of the fifteenth century, and forced upon the King a more robust policy. By skilful diplomacy the town of Cologne was detached from the rest of the League : the South German city was offered all the privileges of the Hanse in England. She accepted the position after vain attempts to bring the Baltic to reason, and made a separate peace. Lübeck was faced by the dreadful position of a divided League, and in 1456 the Baltic cities made a truce with England for eight years.

In 1457 Warwick, already Governor of Calais, was made Admiral of the Fleet. Dantzig, as usual, was breaking the peace by covert attacks on English commerce. Warwick struck back, and he struck hard.

He first showed his mettle in a desperate fight with the Spaniards. This naval battle, the greatest since the time of Edward III, took place on Trinity Sunday, the 29th May 1458, and is described by John Jernyngan in a letter to Margaret Paston.[1] There were twenty-eight sail of Spaniards, among them sixteen " great ships of forecastle." Warwick attacked them with five ships of forecastle, three carvels, and four pinnaces, and after fighting all day the English drew off, " well and truly beat." Lappenberg confuses this heroic action with Warwick's attack on a Lübeck fleet a few weeks later.[2] But the second affair was a much tamer business. The Lübeck fleet was returning from the " Bay "[3] with a cargo of salt, when Warwick came down on it. Like Wenyngton, he ordered the Germans to strike their sails " in the King's name of England," and when they refused he took six of them into Calais.

The Germans were furious, and the action being, to say the least of it, irregular, the Lancaster Party seized upon it as a means to bring about the ruin of the Admiral. The King summoned Warwick to Rochester. On 31st July a commission of the Lancaster Party was appointed to go into the affair.[4] Warwick was ordered by the King—or rather by the Queen—to resign his post. He replied that he would only resign it to Parliament, from whom he had received it. There were hot words, and even blows, and Warwick returned to Calais.[5]

Now this fight with the Germans, while it brought

---

[1] *Paston Letters*, vol. i. p. 428.
[2] *Three Fifteenth Century Chronicles*, p. 71.   [3] See Appendix.
[4] *Fœdera*, vol. xi. pp. 374, 415.
[5] As a solatium to the Germans, the privileges of the Hanse were confirmed on 5th December 1458.

Warwick disgrace at Court, made him the hero of England. Henceforth he was—

> "that noble knight and flower of manhood,
> Richard, Earl of Warwick, shield of our defence."

From that time on there was open war, Warwick fighting with Calais for his base ; and when he returned to England in the following year, Kent, London, Sussex, and Essex flocked to his standard. In the wars which followed, York was slain, and Warwick made York's son, Edward, King of England.

There have been various views of Edward IV. He has been called a great patriot, a great king, a great statesman. And as to Warwick, he is generally represented as an unscrupulous and ambitious noble. Let us see how the facts stand. Edward is put on the throne by the same English interest as made Simon de Montfort supreme two hundred years before. The Yorkist cause is the cause of the people of London, the mercers and the artisans, the cloth-workers of Kent, the iron-workers of Sussex, the agricultural interest of the home counties. It is the protectionist cause. Among the first actions of the King is to deprive the German Hanse of its privileges in England. On 29th April 1463, Parliament passes an Act enforcing upon the Hanse the same duty on wine and wool as paid by Englishmen, and a double duty on tin.[1]

In the same year Parliament passed a whole series of protective measures. It decreed that the importation of cutlery and ironware was forbidden during the King's pleasure, and the importation of wrought

---

[1] *Statutes of the Realm*, vol. ii. p. 392. The Parliamentary duty which before had not been levied on the Germans is not to be confused with the " ancient custom " on wool, which was a royal and hereditary tax.

silk for five years ; the export trade in wool was limited to Englishmen, and the first corn-law was passed—obviously against cheap corn from the Baltic. No corn was to be imported until the price was high enough to allow English farmers a profit. In the following year the importation of woollen cloth was forbidden. Thus the mercers of London, the cloth-workers and iron-workers of Kent and Sussex, and the English farmer, were protected against the cheap products of the German Empire—the corn of the Baltic, the iron-ware of Germany, the cloth of Flanders, and the silk of Cologne.

Nor was the shipping interest forgotten. In the second year of his reign, Edward gave a " large charter " to the English merchants trading in the Netherlands— the Merchant Adventurers, in fact. In 1463 he even passed a Navigation Act to compel English exporters to use English ships.

Here certainly is the patriot programme of a patriot King. And yet, if we look closer into his policy, the needle of the compass is seen to be wavering violently, as if there were two opposite forces in conflict. Even in 1463 there is a temporary renewal of Hanseatic privileges, which may either be a mere move in a diplomatic conflict with Germany, or a partial surrender to German influence. In 1465 envoys from England meet the Council of Lübeck at Hamburg. Lübeck demands a large sum for alleged damages to her shipping, but the English refuse. " They disputed the damage, and said that the present King could not be held responsible for the Acts of his predecessors." [1] There was a deadlock, yet on 4th March 1466 Edward renews all the Hanseatic privileges. " According to the English,"

---

[1] *Detmar's Chronicle*, vol. i. p. 285.

says Lappenberg, " the King had received a consider-able sum of money from the Hanse."[1]

Now, it is to be remembered that in 1465 Warwick had gone on an embassy to secure the friendship of France—a policy directly opposed to the Hanse, with which France was at war. In 1467 Warwick again goes to France on a similar mission, and returns to find that Edward has betrothed his sister to the Duke of Burgundy. In July 1468 the marriage takes place at Bruges, the centre of Hanseatic influence, and Edward is committed to the Burgundian and German combi-nation. When the French ambassadors come over, Edward is openly rude to them, and Warwick tells them privately that the King is governed by traitors. Lübeck all this time is squeezing England. In 1468, at Hanseatic instigation, the Danes capture four Eng-lish ships. There is a storm in England, and many Germans are arrested in London. On 1st May 1469, the Hanse shuts out English cloth from Germany, and recalls the Hanse merchants from England. At the same time the Privy Council condemns the Easterlings to pay £13,520 in their first great case with the Mer-chant Adventurers as compensation for losses sustained at the hands of the Germans at sea. In spite of the King there is a state of war with the Hanse, Cologne excepted. Edward's secret favours to the Hanse have led to trouble with Warwick. By the middle of 1469 there is open rebellion. " In the year 1469," says the *Dantzig Chronicle*,[2] " there was great discord in England

---

[1] " King Edward IV of England calling in question the validity of the powers of the ancient charter of German merchants of the Steelyard in London, they made him a present of a large sum of money for the renewal of that charter."—Anderson, vol. i. p. 488. Anderson is silent as to his authority, and there is naturally no mention of the payment in Rymer and the *Hanse Recesse*.

[2] P. 5 (for 1469).

amongst the lords, one of the reasons being the Merchant (*i.e.* the Hanse). The Cologners had set up for themselves and left the others in the lurch. Also the King of England had made enemies of many great lords, who were the Queen's friends and brothers (*i.e.* the Lancaster Party), and had them or their knights beheaded as traitors. As for Warwick and his friends, who had helped to make him King, he treated them with contempt (*do hild er nichts doruon*). Therefore Warwick hated him greatly, and as for many nobles and the common folk who hated the German merchant (*gemeine Volk die auf den deutschen Koffmann hagerden*)— they went with any lord who did what they wanted. So there came about this discord among the nobles."

This is contemporary evidence, and it shows (1) that the rebellion of 1469 concerned the Hanse, and (2) that Warwick stood with the common people against the Germans and the King.

A confused conflict follows. By the end of 1470 Warwick has fled to France. Now, as we have seen, the party of Lancaster is traditionally the German party in England, and at this time Margaret, the Queen, an exile in France, is promising Lübeck anything and everything for German assistance against Edward. As early as June 1463 Henry VI, at that time hidden in a castle in North Wales, had sent an envoy to the *Kontor* at Bruges. This messenger, William Cosinot, Lord of Montreuil, in Picardy, was advised at Bruges to write to Lübeck, and on 30th June he writes to the great city, begging for threefold help—money, soldiers, and guns. In exchange he promises any security the Hanse may desire—including a bond on the English customs—if they will only help the King against his rebellious subjects. He invites them to negotiations at Bruges, and asks them to forgive the rude Latin of a soldier. In August Queen Margaret herself is in Bruges, obviously on the same errand. But the Hanse temporises : probably they hope to get more out of Edward. By 1469 they have broken with England. On 1st May Lübeck recalls the Hanseatic merchants from the Steelyard, leaving the rebel Cologne in possession. On 31st May 1470, Lübeck takes another step : a Hanseatic decree prohibits English cloth in Germany. In August 1470, the Hanse again discusses the prohibition of English cloth; it is found difficult to enforce, the trade being extremely profitable. But the policy must be enforced, and the Master of Livland, the Grand-Master of Prussia, the Kings of Poland and Denmark, the Dukes of Burgundy, Cleves, and Gueldres, and the Bishops of Bremen, Lüttich, and Utrecht are notified accordingly. The King of England is also to be informed. In short, the whole terrific machinery of the Hanse boycott is set in motion against England. And, further, Cologne is expelled from the League.

Strong measures certainly. But Lübeck is still negotiating not only with Margaret, but with Edward. Margaret is now in France—which is obviously against her chances. From her Duchy of Bar, at St. Michel on the Meuse, she writes a desperate letter to Lübeck on 1st May 1470, urging upon the Hanse a common revenge upon England—that is, upon the cause of York—and proposing a meeting between her councillors and the Hanseatic aldermen at Bruges. Lübeck considers this letter at a full meeting of the Hanse, but postpones a decision till its next meeting, on August 24th, St. Bartholomew's Day. " And also," says the Minute, " the most gracious princess, Margaret, Queen of England, and her son Edward wrote to the envoys of the council and asked for help for England. Upon this nothing was finally resolved but left over for Bartholomew's Day. Letters were written, *mutatis mutandis*, to Madame the Queen, and to the Lord Duke of Burgundy." For the Duke by this time is courting the Hanse on behalf of Edward IV, and it is for this reason that Lübeck postpones its decision. On 25th April 1470 the Duke writes from Lille to the Hanse aldermen at Bruges that he has been appointed by his brother(-in-law), the King of England, as mediator " concerning what had happened between him and you " (*angande den geschillen wesende twischen eine unde juw*), and he admonishes them " to discuss this matter amongst yourselves, and also to let your friends know, so that from your side also we should receive the necessary authorities and credentials."[1]

The merchants at Bruges refer the matter to the Hanse at Lübeck, and the Duke writes to Lübeck from Middleburg, on 26th May, advising the assembled deputies to accept him as intermediary. King Edward, he says, has left the matter entirely in his hands, and has agreed to the truce, so that what remains to be arranged is a meeting between both parties. Lübeck replies, requesting the Duke to keep up his relations with the English, and promising that they would decide the matter on St. Bartholomew's Day, after which they would despatch their own envoys. Again an envoy of Reval, reporting to his town on 28th June, mentions this offer of mediation, and adds that the Kings of France and Scotland also are asking the Hanse for a permanent peace. " All this," he says, in an illuminating sentence, " is the result of the freebooters, otherwise it would have cost a great deal of money

---

[1] A copy of this letter is in the archives of Cologne.

to arrive at this result, which we are now almost certain to secure."[1]

Thus, on the very day[2] that Lübeck considers the petition of Margaret, it also considers the petition of Edward. In particular, there is a letter from the Duke of Burgundy. Charles is very much surprised to hear that they had again sent from sixteen to eighteen war vessels against England, since they had led him to expect that they had suspended the matter until St. Bartholomew's Day. It was most awkward, because his own ships had combined with King Edward's against the common enemy (France and Warwick). Therefore, to avoid unpleasant complications, they really ought to recall their ships and consent to a meeting with the English—that is, with Edward.

Upon this the Hanse decided to empower its agents at Bruges to negotiate with the Duke of Burgundy. The instructions are very clearly defined. First of all, he must know whether the English are prepared to recompense the Hanse towns for the losses they have suffered, and to give full security against a recurrence of their misdoings. Furthermore, as a *conditio sine quâ non*, he must demand restitution of all privileges. The English must have credentials empowering them to make good all damage ; on the other side, the Hanse representative is to commit himself to nothing without reference to the Towns ; the meeting is to be held at Bruges ; the war may be stopped before Candlemas,

---

[1] The exact words are : " Dat maken de ulliggers, it solde anders groet gued kosten, dat id dar to gueme, dar it nu light vol to komon sal." Pauli misconstrues this rather obscure piece of old German, turning it into mere nonsense. He makes the envoy say that they did not dare give a definite reply to both parties, fearing the great expense of the war, and so let the free-booters go on. What the envoy meant was that the freebooters were serving the ends of the Hanse, without any expense to the Hanse itself—a confession that those pirates which the Hanse so often disavowed were in effect their secret allies.

[2] St. Bartholomew's Day, August 1470.

with an extension for ships on the high seas ; and the next Hanse day is to be convoked not before Easter, 1471.

Such, then, was the position when Warwick fled to France. The Germans were negotiating both with Margaret of Lancaster and Edward of York, and they were also forcing matters upon the sea. But it is plain that their policy was already shaped : it was to come to an agreement with Edward through the Duke of Burgundy, and throw Margaret over. For Edward was in England, and Margaret only in France. Obviously the Hanse looks upon Edward as pliable : it is Warwick who is the real enemy. Then comes the flight of Warwick.

" Also," says Weinreich, " in the same Lent Warwick fled from England into France, and the Duke of Burgundy went to sea with great force to get him out of France. Henry von der Neere was Admiral of the Fleet. On St. James's Day Von der Neere sailed against France with all his ships, the Easterlings among them, who served the Duke of Burgundy." In a note to the chronicle we are told that this Flemish-German fleet defeated Warwick on July 2nd, and secured thereby the commerce of the Netherlands.[1]

It is clear, then, that Warwick was still the enemy of the Hanse, and that his alliance with France was directed against the German power. In other words, he remained true to the Yorkist policy.

Warwick was a statesman, and he acted swiftly. He made peace with his old enemy, Margaret, and formed a league with the French King. In fact, he mobilised the exiled cause of Lancaster against the Germans, who had already forsaken that cause. He could have

---

[1] Caspar Weinreich's *Danziger Chronik*, p. 6.

H

had little difficulty in persuading Margaret that she could hope for nothing from Lübeck, for, as we have seen, the Hanse had kept her dangling ever since 1463.

This rearrangement of parties being made, Warwick again invaded England. The English Navy was behind him; the cloth-makers of Kent flocked to his banner. An anonymous London chronicler shows how the invasion was directed against the Germans in England :[1] "And in September (1470) the Duke of Clarence, the Earl of Warwick, the Earl of Pembroke, the Earl of Oxford, with divers gentlemen, landed at Dartmouth, in Devonshire; to whom drew much people of every county; and the people of Kent made an insurrection in Kent, and came to London; where in the suburbs of the City and other places, as Saint Catherines and Radclyf, they robbed and despoiled divers Dowchemen (Germans or Flemings) and their beer-houses. And the said Duke and his company made, as he came into the landward, his proclamations in King Henry's name, who at that time was prisoner in the Tower of London. And when they drew towards King Edward, then being at York, he fearing them, and also had but a small people about him in comparison with the Duke and his company. Wherefore seeing he could not make his party good with them, and also some of his own folk about him were not very fast to him, he with a few horse took the next way over the Wash in Lincolnshire, where some of his company were drowned, and he escaped with great jeopardy." The Queen went into sanctuary at Westminster, and "divers bishops and many others that were King Edward's friends also went into sanctuary places for their safeguard. . . . And then, again, many

[1] *Chronicles of London*, ed. Kingsford; p. 183.

Dutchmen, and also some Englishmen, such as kept beer-houses, were despoiled and robbed, and some also burnt; but the Mayor and the citizens kept them out of the city. And upon the 12th day of October the Tower was given up by appointment. And then King Henry was taken from the place where he was imprisoned and lodged in the King's lodgings." Worcester was beheaded, and King Edward and his brother Gloucester attainted by Parliament as traitors.

In the meantime Edward has fled to Flanders. Commynes,[1] our best authority for the events which follow, says that Edward left Lynne without money or treasure, and with only the clothes and armour he and his men wore, in two Dutch ships and a small English boat. And he adds: " At this time the Easterlings were the enemies of England and of France, and had several ships of war on the sea. They were feared by the English, not without cause, for they were good fighters, and in this very year they had done great damage to England and taken several ships." There were seven or eight of these German ships hanging about Lynne when Edward started out, and they pursued the King's little flotilla. They did not catch him, however. He anchored in the harbour of Alkmar, in Friesland. The bigger German ships lay outside, waiting for high tide. Fortunately for Edward a Flemish nobleman, Herr von Gruthuyse, otherwise Louis de Bruges, happened to be at Alkmar at the time, and forbade the Hanseatic ships to touch the English King. He assisted Edward to land, and convoyed him to the Hague, where he became the guest of Charles the Bold. Now it is clear that Edward had not a penny left. He had come to Flanders in

---

[1] *The Memoirs of Messire Philippe de Commynes*, Book III, chap. v.

his shirt.   Charles the Bold, according to Commynes, publicly announced that he could do nothing for his brother-in-law, yet secretly he lent Edward the substantial sum of 50,000 St. Andrew florins to prepare an expeditionary force.   Just as secretly he chartered fourteen Hanseatic ships (*quatarze navires Ostrelins*), well armed, which promised to serve Edward for the passage to England, and for fifteen days afterwards. It was a great help, says Commynes, considering the times.[1]

With his Flemish money Edward had, besides, chartered several ships of war at the harbour of Veere in Walcheren.   He put out of Flushing on the 2nd March 1471, and landed on the 14th near Ravenspur.   When he landed, according to our London chronicler, he had with him only five hundred " Dutchmen " and as many Englishmen.   But the magnates of Yorkshire rallied to his standard.   He defeated and slew Warwick in the great battle of Barnet, which opened the way to London.   On the very day of the battle Margaret had landed at Weymouth ; she was defeated at Tewkesbury.   Edward, Henry's only son, was executed after the battle.   Warwick's vice-admiral, Fauconbridge, attacked London with his sailors ; he was defeated, retired to make war on the sea, and was in the end captured and beheaded.   The day Edward entered London, Henry VI was murdered in the Tower, and thus Edward was restored to his kingdom.

There were great rejoicings in Flanders over Edward's return.   Bruges, which had given £25 to Herr von Gruthuyse for his expenses in entertaining the King, paid the messenger who brought the glad tidings six

---

[1] Edward Hall's chronicle for this period is merely a free translation of Commynes.

gold florins ; and there is a further bill for a big bonfire in front of the sheriff's house to celebrate the victory. But it was a victory not so much for Flanders as the Hanse. Their merchant in Bruges writes to Dantzig on 26th February 1471, expressing his joy that the soldiers and freebooters now serving the Hanse had been permitted to enter the service of the Duke of Burgundy, and to fight against England and France— that is to say, against Warwick. Here, then, we have the position. The Duke of Burgundy is in close touch on one side with King Edward, and on the other side with Lübeck. The Hanse allows its ships and its men to be used for the invasion of England in the cause of York, although their public and traditional policy is the support of Lancaster. When they restore King Edward, they are, and have been for some years, at open war with the Yorkist government of England. At the same time they turn their hostile forces against both Warwick and Lancaster. There is one plain explanation of the whole business ; it confirms the earlier reports that Edward had sold himself to the Hanse, it explains the rupture between Warwick and Edward, it accords with Edward's traditional character as a spendthrift and a voluptuary. It is that Edward had betrayed all that the cause of York stood for, and had sold himself to Germany. If this explanation be accepted, it is Warwick that is faithful to the cause of York—that is to say, to the cause of English shipping and English industries. Edward is the traitor. There is evidence that Edward contrived to keep at least some of his party in the dark as to his double dealing. Warwick, as we have seen from his remark to the French ambassadors, had no illusions. Thomas Cook, the Mayor of London, understood it also. When

Edward landed he fled, but was captured by Paul Beneke, the Hanseatic admiral.[1]

Pauli, the great German historian, concludes from these events that interest drove the Hanse to make this sudden change in its policy, to throw over Lancaster and accept York. "In a short time," he says, "success proved that they were right. With a dynasty at Westminster depending on the House of Valois neither the Hanse nor Flanders could have lived at peace, and the Hanseatic merchant in London could hardly have recovered his privileges. The trident which he (the German) had carried up till now could never be permitted to fall into the hands of that Romanic Power which enslaved both body and soul. The whole development of West European commerce would have been different if Flemish, Dutch, and Easterlings had not been prepared to put Edward back on his throne, notwithstanding the conflict the latter had to settle with the English Government." And Lappenberg makes the point still more clear. "Justly," he says, "was the Hanse delighted over the return of King Edward. It had furthered this return, because it saw in this event the surest means to re-establish peace and its privileges." The Germans, in fact, put Edward on the throne because Edward was ready to betray England, and the fall of Warwick was the victory of Germany.

---

[1] "And also in the same Lent (1471) Paul Beneke took the *Magdalen* of Dieppe, and the *Swan* of Caen. On this he took prisoner the Mayor of London, whose name was Thomas Cook."—Caspar Weinreich's *Danziger Chronik.*

Robert Fabyan, the chronicler, confirms Weinreich, although he confuses Hanseatic and Flemish : "And in this season also Sir Thomas Cook before-named, avoyed the lande to haue sayled into Fraunce. But he was taken of a shyp of Flaunders and his sone and heyre with him, and so sette there in pryson many days, and lastly was delyveryed unto Kynge Edwarde."

CHAPTER XII

KING EDWARD is on the throne of England, but England
is at the mercy of the Germans. And the Germans
have no mercy. Edward sends two English merchants,
H. Bentley and W. de Bristowe, to make a formal
peace. By order of the towns, Hamburg is proposed
as the meeting-place. Bergen and Bruges act as inter-
mediaries. The peace meeting is representative, but
merely preliminary. "The negotiations," says Lappenberg complacently, "are very favourably influenced
by the damage done to English commerce by Paul
Beneke, the Dantziger. Hamburg and Bremen also
send ships and men to the shores of England to do as
much damage as they can." On 5th May and 10th
December 1472, the King gives credentials to his ambassadors. By 21st May 1473 there is an agreement
that negotiations are to be opened at Utrecht on July
1st; in the meantime a truce is asked for by England,
and granted by Lübeck. By 6th October an Act of
Parliament stops hostilities against the Germans, and
empowers the King to restore all Hanseatic privileges.
The negotiations are renewed in July, and then ad-
journed to December. The King's credentials are not
wide enough. The King enlarges them, and his Parliament renews the Hanseatic privileges. Only on 28th
February 1474 is the treaty concluded at Utrecht.

We are told by Lappenberg that Edward was

" willing to conclude peace from the outset," and that it was only a question of putting the Hanseatic conditions in a form acceptable to England. This is curiously confirmed by the King's instructions to his ambassadors at Utrecht, dated 20th December 1473. The King instructs his ambassadors " to aske of thaym more than was asked before "; but if " they of the Hanse wol willfully remaine in thaire first opynions, there might falle a brache of alle the hole matier, whiche God forbede : therefore the Kinge wolle (wills) that his said oratours rather than brake, put the oratours of the Hanse in comforte and hope, that at thaire comyng into England they shal have the residue of thaire ententis accomplished in such wise as of reason they shal be content." [1]

What could ambassadors do with such instructions ? Nothing save what Lappenberg says they did : " The negotiations were slow—step by step only the English ambassadors receded." The King had betrayed them : if they showed themselves stubborn on any point, there was Beneke of Dantzig in the background with his terrible ships.

Now this treaty, which is the perfect flower, the rare and refreshing fruit, of the " Natural Alliance," will repay a careful examination.[2] Here, then, are the terms of the treaty :

" I. All past injuries and complaints shall be buried in oblivion, and all injuries and violences shall be absolutely foreborne for the future.

---

[1] Cotton MS., Nero, Bk. IX, fo. 68, British Museum.
[2] The original transcript is in the archives of Lübeck. It is given in full in Lappenberg, and in *Fœdera*, vol. xi. p. 792, &c., and it is summarised by Anderson, vol. i. pp. 500–2. To look at the bargain as a whole, we should also include the English Treaty of 1473 with Denmark, in which there is a proviso " that the English shall not resort nor trade to Iceland."—*Fœdera*, vol. xi. p. 735.

" II. For the greater safety of the merchants and people of the Hanse Society, King Edward agrees to grant his charter or obligation, in the strongest terms, and shall also get it confirmed by Act of Parliament, that no kind of damage shall be done to their persons or goods, by reason of any sentence or determination of the said King and his Council, for reprisals, &c., on account of matters done prior to this treaty.

" III. The merchants of England may freely resort and trade to the countries and ports of the Hanse League, as the Hanseatic merchants may to England, with their ships and merchandize freely to sell the same, and purchase others there, without paying in either country any more than the ancient duties and customs on any pretence whatever.

" IV. All the privileges and immunities of the Hanseatics in England are hereby renewed, and shall also be confirmed by Act of Parliament, and the English shall enjoy all their ancient immunities at the Hanse towns as formerly.

" V. The Hanseatic merchants in England shall not henceforth be subject to the Lord High Admiral's Court or jurisdiction, but in controversies about maritime affairs, &c., shall have two judges allotted to them by the King for determining the same.

" VI. That the Steelyard in London, in its utmost extent, shall be confirmed to the said German merchants, as also the Steelyard at Boston, and that a like house be assigned for their use at Lynn, near the Waterside.

" VII. That the ten thousand pounds sterling, liquidated to be due by the King to the said German merchants, shall be paid or deducted out of the customs and duties on their merchandize, till the whole sum be discharged.

" VIII. If any city of the Hanseatics shall hereafter separate itself from the general union, the King of England shall cause all the privileges of that separating city to cease in England, until they be reunited to the League.

" IX. The said German merchants of the Steelyard shall have the possessing and keeping of the Gate of the City of London, called Bishopsgate, as by ancient agreement between that City and them.

" X. The King shall provide that the woollen cloth of England be reformed, both as to the quality of the wool and the length and breadth of the cloth.

" XI. The said Steelyard merchants shall be at liberty to sell their Rhenish wines by retail, as well as by wholesale, according to ancient custom."

Now, there is a fallacious appearance of reciprocity about the first block of four articles which might deceive the unwary. In reality all that the English obtained was a repetition of the terms of the treaty of 1437, which they by experience had found useless. " Although," says Lappenberg, " these articles had in times gone by proved to be of very little value, on account of their muddled wording, over them the whole peace was almost shipwrecked." The English envoys insisted upon them as a minimum ; Dantzig refused to accept them. And Dantzig's argument is illuminating : if they were conceded the English might demand the right to trade with Russia, Poland, and Livland. Dantzig even refused a compromise suggested by the other German towns, the addition of a clause that the

Englishman should rank in his rights behind the citizen. The English were even prepared to declare that Dantzig could interpret the articles according to its former habit.[1] But this also Dantzig refused to accept. Not until two years afterwards did Dantzig accept the treaty —and then with the reservation that Englishmen should be treated like non-Prussian Hanse cities, and should pay customs and duties like all other foreign merchants. In actual practice she did not concede even so much. Englishmen, as they complained long afterwards, were treated in Dantzig worse than all other merchants save Jews; but more of that later. As to Dantzig's refusal to sign in 1474, the truth probably was that she found the freebooting business too profitable to be abandoned, and trusted to get her goods smuggled into England under the false manifests of friends in the other German cities. But she was also nervous about the Russian trade, and Riga, her satellite at that time, was not allowed to sign until 1500.

But the financial terms of the treaty show how hollow was the pretence of equality. Thus the Privy Council, in 1569, had condemned the Germans to pay £13,520 as damages to the English merchants. This claim is wiped out, but the counter-claims of the Germans are liquidated at £10,000. And even this sum, enormous in those days, did not represent the whole advantage, for it had been originally fixed at £15,000, but was reduced on the pledge of the King " to hold free from damage every member of the Hanse who had reason to sue any of his subjects for offence, arrest,

---

[1] " Die Engelschen hadden doch siick des begeven, dat de can Dantsiike sulcke articule solden mogen duden unde interpreteren na erer olden wonheit."—*Hanse Recesse*, ii. 7n. 138, par. 84, also 189 (p. 399). Perhaps the most amazing example of " save face " in the history of diplomacy.

loss of ships, wares, or other goods." In other words, the King pledged the justice of his courts as part of the liquidation.

As to the form of payment, there was a double advantage, for until the amount in full was paid the Germans paid no customs at all, and therefore had a great advantage in business over Englishmen and foreigners alike. The royal rescript by which this article of the treaty is carried into practice informs our customs officers that "concedimus et licentiam damus mercatoribus Hanse theutonice . . . quarum omnium mercandisarum sic adducendarum vel educendarum custume et subsidia juxta earundem ratam et quantitatem custumarum et subsidiorum tantum et non ultra . . . ad, summam decem millium librarum in toto se attingent." Up to this amount the Germans were to hold the customs money in their own hands—" in manibus suis propriis habeant et retineant."[1]

For years this arrangement gave the Germans free trade in England. Both Richard III (on 5th December 1484) and Henry VII (on 29th June 1486) confirmed the edict.

A minor provision of the treaty states that the sum of £484, lent to the King by German merchants released by him from prison, is to be repaid to the Germans, excluding the Cologners. And this brings us to the most fascinating article in the treaty, Article VIII. It covers a miserable story of shame and dishonour, which must now be told.

In the negotiations of Utrecht, the Hanse was represented by deputies from the *Kontors* of Bruges, London, and Bergen, and particularly by envoys from

---

[1] After a Hamburg copy compared by Lappenberg with the King's command to his servants at Boston (3rd June 1475).

Lübeck, Hamburg, Dantzig, Dortmund, Deventer, and Campen. Cologne was conspicuous by its absence. Now Cologne, as we have seen, played a peculiar part in the Wars of the Roses. To get to the beginning of it we must go back at least to 1450. On the Hanse Day of that year there is sharp division between Lübeck and the northern towns on the one side, and Cologne on the other. Cologne, it is clear, does not approve of the piratical policy of the Baltic : she is not interested in sea supremacy, and thinks the attacks on English shipping dangerous to German trade in England. In fact, she is all for peaceful penetration. The position is frankly explained by the historian of the Rhine city. " Denmark and the Wendish towns," says Dr. Ennen, " sought to use the wild troubles of the White and the Red Rose to destroy English commerce in the Baltic. English merchants had for a long time experienced manifold maltreatment on the sea at the hands of Lübeck, Rostock, Dantzig, Wismar, and Stralsund. In 1468 the English ship *Valentine* was held up by 400 armed men, looted and taken to Copenhagen. Six English merchantmen on their way to Prussia were attacked by two big Dantzig ships and a few smaller Hanseatic vessels at a time of complete peace, and overpowered and robbed. The King commanded the aldermen and all members of the Guildhall (the German Steelyard) to come to Westminster. They were all declared prisoners, on the suspicion of having informed the Wendish towns of the departure of the captured merchantmen, and were made responsible for the damage of £20,000. The Cologners succeeded in establishing their innocence, and on condition that they would in no way assist the rest of the Hanse, they were liberated and put in possession of their goods and their rooms in the Steelyard. In return for this exemption they became surety for Edward IV for £20,000, and lent him in cash £1000.[1]

We seem to trace the master-hand of Warwick in a series of skilful negotiations with Cologne, which begin about the time his party is gaining influence in the councils of the King. Thus, on 24th September 1452, the King writes a friendly letter to Cologne, complaining of the misdeeds of Lübeck. Cologne is offered all the privileges of the Hanse if she will only make a separate peace. This she does. The Baltic cities are faced by a divided League, and in 1456 they make the eight years' truce referred to in the last chapter.[2]

Thus Cologne had been the ally of the Yorkist cause against the rest of the Hanse. But when Edward was restored by the Baltic cities he was faced by the necessity of throwing his old friend over. The Hanse put the case bluntly and forcibly : Edward was to choose one or the other—" De Stede seden, wolden de Engelschen de Colner hebben, so mosten se der anderen stede entberen, wente de Colner scholden wyken edder se wolden wyken." [3] In vain the Cologners represented their past services to the King, and even tried to form a party among the cloth-workers in Parliament against the Hanse. The country was helpless : the King had sold himself. At first the King refuses to ratify the decree of excommunication, but he is forced to give way. And the miserable man contents himself with instruct-

[1] *Geschichte der Stadt Köln*, by Dr. Leonard Ennen, Stadt Archivar, vol. iii. p. 708 *et seq.* The following curious list is given of those who intervened with the King on behalf of Cologne : Thomas of Beaufort, Primate and Cardinal of England, Archbishop of Canterbury (a great compromiser, no doubt), part of the Privy Council, the Duke Adolphus of Geldern, the Archbishop Ruprecht of Cologne, and John, Duke of Cleve.

[2] That Warwick was responsible for this policy I infer from the fact that in 1470 he put Cologne in sole possession of the Steelyard, and that in 1470 Cologne was excommunicated by the Hanse.

[3] *Hanse Recesse*, ii. 7, n. 34, § 53.

ing his ambassadors to avoid the specific mention of Cologne in the treaty, as that would hurt his honour.[1] The Hanse graciously concedes the point : the article is framed to cover Cologne without mentioning it, and the King's honour is saved. In a secondary contract, which is mainly a commentary on the application of the articles, it is stated that the Cologners are deprived of Hanseatic privileges from the 1st August.[2]

And now, when we consider the whole treaty—the surrender of English justice ; the surrender of the English customs ; the surrender of all the claims of English shipowners and English merchants ; the surrender of the freeholds at London, Boston, and Lynn ; the surrender of Bishopsgate and the renewal of the municipal privileges in London ; the renewal of everything against which the Yorkists had fought ; the betrayal of Cologne, which had risked everything in the cause of York—when we consider these things, we are fain to admit that the ambassadors of Dantzig were justified in their boast—" We have made an end of the English." [3]

[1] *Hanse Recesse*, ii. 7, n. 107. Cologne crawled back into the Hanse on the Hanse Days at Lübeck (Whitsun, and 8th September 1476).

[2] *Ibid.*, ii. 7, n. 142, § 11 ; 143, § 5.

[3] Letter to Dantzig from the envoys of the Council : " Welck allent to herten nemende, hebben wii eynen ende myt den Engelschen gemaket, des de stede, so uns duncket, na legenheit der sake wal myt eren mogen bekant siin."—*Ibid.*, ii. 7, n. 161, p. 375.

CHAPTER XIII

THE FIRST OF THE TUDORS

" WITH the happy event of the Treaty of Utrecht,"
says Lappenberg, " we have reached the high-water
mark of the Hanseatic, perhaps the German, influence
in England." And he adds that, by " the traditional
wisdom of the English statesmen," this influence lived
on for more than half a century. What he really means
is that the traditional neediness of the English kings
and the power of the Hanseatic navy left England at
the mercy of Germany. Warwick, the only great
statesman that England possessed at this time, died
fighting the Germans. Edward IV was the Charles II
of the Middle Ages : money and pleasure were the two
ends for which he lived. He drew a pension from
France, raised loans from the Germans, and forced
benevolences out of the London merchants—thus con-
triving to do without the Parliament he had betrayed.

As for Richard III, his " traditional wisdom " was
chiefly displayed in the murders of which he made a
fine art. His King, his brother, his two nephews, and
his wife, all fell to the traditional wisdom of this statesman, who improved even in the rude Middle Ages
on the methods of such moderns as a Crippen or a
Smith.

No, the English had been betrayed by their Government, and were fain to trust to their own resources.
The Treaty of Utrecht had hardly been signed before
the sailors of Bristol and Hull were fighting the Germans

in Iceland. The perfidious and piratical people of Hartlepool attacked a Lübeck and Hamburg ship off the English coast, and when the Hanse closed Norway to English trade the English replied by robbing German ships on the high seas. All these German grievances were brought before the King and duly visited, we may be certain, upon the transgressors. In the meantime, under our free trade policy, England had fallen into a bad way. In 1482 Parliament granted £6000 for the relief of decayed towns. In 1484 Richard granted Hull, which had suffered terribly at the hands of the Hanseatics, a partial relief from export duties, " in consideration of its ruin, decay, and poverty." He did not dare to touch the Hanse, but he made at least some concession to the strange English prejudice against foreigners. In 1483 he signed an Act, which began by observing that, " whereas merchant strangers of the nation of Italy, as Venetians, Florentines, Apulians, Sicilians, Lucaners, and Catilians (!) do in great numbers, keep houses in London and other great cities and Burghs, taking warehouses and cellars for the merchandise they import, and where they deceitfully pack, mingle, and keep their said merchandise till their prices greatly advance—and they likewise buy here our native commodities and sell them again at their pleasure ; and do not employ a great part of the money coming thereof upon the commodities of this realm, but take it oversea to divers other countries, to the King's great loss in his customs, and the impoverishment of his subjects . . . and do buy in divers places of this realm great quantities of wool, woollen cloth, and other merchandise of the King's subjects, part of which they sell again here," they were to be prohibited from selling in retail, and were to export all their wool and woollen cloth and other English merchandise beyond sea through the Straits of Morocco. They were to lay out their money in English commodities. They were not to set up as master handicraftsmen in England, they were not to take English apprentices. They could, however, go into the retail book trade. Now, there may be several explanations of this measure against foreigners who were not Germans. It might have been a concession to the Hanse, who were jealous of Italian commerce ; but this is unlikely, as the statute seems to favour the Gibraltar route. Or it might have been a concession to the English Merchant Adventurers and the Protection Party in England, and this is the more likely, because there are other Acts of the same year protecting the cloth trade, and a very large number of other trades. One omnibus measure prohibits the importation of goods produced by " girdlers, pointmakers, pinners, pursers, glovers, joiners, painters, cardmakers, wiremongers, weavers, horners, bottlemakers, and coppersmiths." It is plain that the cause of Protection is not dead.

And there were other signs and portents that must have caused the League, even at the height of its power, a little uneasiness. In 1478 their monopoly at Novgorod was attacked by the Russians. In 1494 the Hanseatic properties at that famous *Kontor* were confiscated. The Russians, like the Danes and the English, were a patient people, but the Hanse had brought them to the limits of their patience. Venice, the great depot of the German Mediterranean trade, had been hit hard by Lisbon, whose great sailors circumnavigated Africa, and diverted the trade of the East from the Mediterranean to the Atlantic. Spain, by the discovery of America, brought about another revolution in the trade of the world, shifting more and more the centre of wealth to the South and West. The sailors of the "upstart towns" of Holland had long been fighting the League in a rough alliance with the sailors of England, and certain Dutch discoveries in the fine art of pickling herrings had deprived Germany of its valuable monopoly in the salt-fish trade. The herrings, too, had shown themselves fickle in their habits, and shifted their ground from the coasts of Germany to the coasts of England. Denmark was in revolt. A Danish trading company had been founded to fight the Hanse, and in 1475, in support of this movement, Christian I dissolved the German Hanse in Denmark. In 1470 the Swedish Regent forbade the election of Germans of the Hanse as Swedish town councillors. These arrogant symptoms of revolt were sternly suppressed by Lübeck, but it was clear that neither Scandinavia nor Russia was as docile as of old.

Worse still, England settled both her wars with France and her Wars of the Roses. In 1485 Henry VII killed Richard on Bosworth Field. In 1486 he married Elizabeth, and ended the long feud between York and Lancaster. France had sheltered him in his exile. He had no reason either to hate the French or to love the Germans. Even before his coronation he announced a truce with France, and promised an Anglo-French commercial alliance. By 17th January 1486 he had concluded a three years' treaty with France, and as France was then at war with Maximilian, this did not promise well for the "natural ally." The English merchants crowded in upon their new King with long complaints of Hanseatic privileges and Hanseatic tyranny. They represented that English traders had been expelled from Bergen, from Iceland, and from

Burgundy, and they complained of the bad treatment received in the towns of the Hanse. But Henry was a wary monarch ; he knew the Hanseatic power and his own weakness. With an empty treasury and without a navy it would have been madness to attack the greatest sea-power in Europe. He called the Hanse merchants before Parliament to answer the accusations, and on 9th March 1486 he confirmed the Hanseatic charters and the Treaty of Utrecht. But the English merchants persisted : when their first accusations were answered they brought more. They asserted that the Hanse had fitted out pirates in the harbours of the Netherlands to raid English commerce, and they accused the *Kontor* at Bruges of being behind the freebooters. The Germans in London replied that the pirates were in the service of the King of Denmark. The English rejoined that the Easterlings changed their nationality to suit their convenience.

The King still temporised. The Steelyard proposed a conference, and in October 1487 the King agreed. The English merchants had before them the dismal prospect of negotiations without end, carried on by the Germans with that slow and devious cunning which had defeated so many English embassies. But the German cards were now in clumsy hands. That indomitable old lady, Margaret, Dowager-Duchess of Burgundy, widow of Charles the Bold and sister of Edward IV, was bent on restoring the fortunes of the House of York. Her nephew, John de la Pole, Earl of Lincoln, and his friends were ready for any desperate adventure. Her stepson, Maximilian, King of the Romans, was chafing because England was no longer a mere tool in his hands against France. Both he and the Hanse failed to realise that the Tudors had come to stay, and they set about to plot for Henry's downfall. " And so in the year 1487," says the Dantzig chronicler,[1] " there was a new discord in England between their King Richmond and the lords of the country, so that some of the lords went from England to Zeeland, and there by the help of Charles of Burgundy's old lady (*olden Frauen*) fitted out a powerful expedition—19 ships full of well-armed men, to sail to Ireland.   The son of the Duke of Clarence, the brother of the before-mentioned old lady, was there, and they wanted to bring him with a great force to England, to drive out Richmond and to be king under his name of George."

Weinreich is not quite accurate.   The pretender was in reality Lambert Simnel, who called himself Edward of Warwick, and pretended to be the son of George, Duke of Clarence.   Now Maximilian—and probably the Hanse—was deep in this conspiracy.   Two thousand German soldiers, under the command of an experienced leader, Martin Schwarz, were placed at the pretender's disposal.   The force landed in Ireland on 5th May 1487.   Lambert was borne in triumph through the streets of Dublin, and crowned King of Ireland with a crown taken from an image of the Virgin.   The German-Irish army crossed over to Lancashire, and was defeated at Stoke on the 16th of June.   The views of Henry on this affair are revealed in a conversation with the Spanish ambassador in 1488 : " Henry enumerated all the ill turns the King of the Romans had done him. . . . The King of the Romans had sent his excuses for all that had happened, and threw the blame on his step-mother.   Henry had replied that he could not accept these excuses." [2]

---

[1] Caspar Weinreich, *Danziger Chronik*, p. 65.
[2] *Berg. Cal. England and Spain*, vol. i. pp. 10, 11.

And this story is fully confirmed by the reply of the English ambassadors to the complaints of Cologne at Antwerp in 1491 : " Martin Schwarz had by force of arms invaded England, &c., for which cause the King had fallen out with the King of the Romans, and had issued a proclamation prohibiting, on pain of confiscation, the merchants of these countries to export." [1]

Now a plot which fails is always inconvenient for the plotters, and Henry, although he moved warily, knew how to strike. Towards the end of 1486, when, as Henry well knew, the conspiracy was being hatched, Henry issued his famous proclamation prohibiting the export of cloth to the Netherlands. The Germans represented that this was done in order to obstruct their commerce,[2] and the learned Schäfer regards it as the English answer to the Danish-German freebooters. The no less learned Schanz holds that it was not directed against the Hanse, but against the King of the Romans and Burgundy.[3] Probably its effect was calculated on all three. Henry did not want to quarrel openly with the whole German power, but he could give them a hint that he was not to be trifled with.

Whatever Henry's intention, the effect of the interdict was felt and resented by the Hanse. The Cologne and West German trade felt it most, and in the Hanseatic archives we find many complaints as to the restriction of their liberties. Henry's reply was what we have seen. If the King of the Romans chose to finance pretenders to the English crown, he could not expect

---

[1] " Martinus Swarts, manu armata invasit regnum Anglie, etc., qua de causa rea habuit dissentionem cum rege Romanorum, unde fecit proclamare, quod merces harum terrarum non deberent adduci sub pena confiscationum."— *Hanse Recesse*, iii. 2 S., 523, footnote c.

[2] *Ibid.*, iii. 2, n. 109.

[3] Dr. Dietrich Schäfer, *Die Hanse* (Leipzig, 1903) ; Dr. Georg Schanz, *Englisches Handelspolitik* (Leipzig, 1881).

English trade for his subjects. The reply of the Hanse was to organise a great contraband trade into the Netherlands by way of Hamburg, and here we touch upon an argument for a national trade policy which finds no place in the learned treatises of the economists. Whereas the Hanse sought by all means to set England's foreign policy at naught, the Merchant Adventurers assisted the King. Thus Francis Bacon, in his history of those times: " The Merchant Adventurers, being a strong company at that time, and well underset with rich men, did hold out bravely, taking off the commodities of the kingdom, though they lay dead upon their hands for want of vent." That is to say, the English merchants with their capital took the strain of the boycott off the cloth-workers, and helped Henry to carry through a daring stroke of policy.

These interdicts of trade between Flanders and England lasted for some years. They were renewed as Margaret and Maximilian dealt stroke after stroke at the English throne. We find Henry writing to Lübeck, in October 1487, that he had removed the prohibition. But the very next year the export to Burgundy is again prohibited, and Hanseatic merchants have to bind themselves not to export any more goods to Flanders. Let us see how the thing works out. Perkin Warbeck, a Fleming of Cologne descent, is adopted by the Germans as the new pretender. In 1493, in the city of Vienna, Albert of Saxony presents Perkin to the King of the Romans, and the young rascal goes in great state to the funeral ceremony of the Emperor Frederick III. " In February 1493," says Busch, " he (Perkin) had already from Flanders entered into relations with confederates at Westminster, and there seems to have been some suspicion that on this occasion the Hanse merchants were prepared to act the part of a go-between." Henry, in reply, stops all commerce with the Netherlands, expels the Flemish from England, and transfers the staple for English cloth, tin, thread, leather, and so forth from Antwerp to Calais. This time Henry's injunction covers subjects to the countries of the King of the Romans, which does not, however, cover the Baltic, and the Hanse merchants remain in London. The Hanse renew their contraband trade. "It brought," says Lappenberg with pride, "the greatest profit to the Hanse, which now became the sole agent for imports and exports." The Londoners are furious ; Merchant Adventurers, mercers, cloth-workers and cloth-sellers, who have lost their work for the national policy, rise in a body against the Germans. In the middle of October the crowd, united by a secret oath, enter the Steelyard and ransack its chambers and packing-rooms. The Germans, after a desperate struggle, throw the invaders into the street ; but the 'prentices and artisans, with clubs and lifting-jacks, hammer at the doors until the Mayor of London arrives with an armed force, quells the riot,[1] and takes eighty of the rioters into custody. The Steelyard is saved—the Mayor, it may be, is not unmindful of his cask of sturgeon ; but the King intervenes, not to the advantage of the Hanse. The Germans have to pay surety of £20,000 against their undertaking not to export any goods into the harbours of the Netherlands. The most they can do is to send their Cologne commerce by the costly and circuitous route via Hamburg.

---

[1] In the Hanse archives the da e of this riot is given as the 15th October 1493. Hall says "the Tuesday before St. Edward's Day" ; but the 15th October was the Tuesday after. *Cf.* Gairdner's *Richard III and Perkin Warbeck*, p. 279; also *Three Fifteenth Century Chronicles.* The London chronicler evidently seeks to minimise the tumult, no doubt fearing trouble for the City.

In vain they implore the King to give them an opening into Flanders by way of Kampen and Gröningen. Not until 1496 does Henry end the interdict with the famous victory of the " Intercursus Magnus."

And here we may finish the lamentable story of Perkin Warbeck. When Maximilian enters the Netherlands in August 1494, Perkin is prominent in his train. He lives in Antwerp, at the "Hôtel des Anglais," in great pomp as Duke of York, with the white rose hung over his door. A mob of angry Englishmen tear it down and have to flee the city.[1] Perkin Warbeck makes Maximilian his heir. In return Maximilian equips Perkin for his invasion of England. The Emperor's reason for supporting Warbeck is revealed very clearly in the correspondence with the Venetian ambassador in Germany. On 9th June 1495, Contarini writes " that the Duke of York (Warbeck) is now attacking the island with 1500 men, independently of mariners. His Majesty the King of the Romans means to send him a reinforcement of 800 men, and the Scotch ambassadors at Worms tell him they hope for certain victory." On July 7th he mentions a report that Warbeck had reached England, " whereat His Majesty rejoiced greatly, as he could dispose of this Duke of York *ad libitum suum.*" On July 19th " his Cæsarean Majesty " unburdens himself as follows : " With regard to the

---

[1] The Hôtel des Anglais was probably the House of the Merchant Adventurers, who had moved to Calais. Molinet (v. 15, 16) gives another version (*cf.* Gairdner, p. 283).

Perkin Warbeck was the son of Jehan Warbeque, described in the *Register de la loi* of Tournai as a " pireman " of Cologne ; his grandfather was Diericq de Werbecque, his cousin was John Stienbeck of Antwerp. Perkin was placed at Middleburg with a merchant called John Strewe, and afterward went to Portugal in the service of the wife of Sir Edward Brampton, an adherent of the House of York. Perkin was probably a German or Flemish Jew, and moved from country to country with the freedom and address of that marvellous race.

Duke of York we entertain great hopes that after obtaining the kingdom of England he will soon attack the King of France ; and to this effect have we received every promise and certainty from the Duke aforesaid."

Again, on 14th February 1496, Contarini writes to the Doge : " Were the Duke of York (Perkin Warbeck) to obtain the crown, the King of the Romans and the League might avail themselves of England against the King of France as if the island were their own." The League here mentioned is, of course, not the Hanseatic League, but the Holy League. But the Hanse as well as the German king was interested in the overthrow of Henry VII. For despite his quiet, moderate, and reasonable way of treating them, his renewals of their privileges and his offers of conferences, there was a subtle and dangerous squeeze in his policy. He was, in fact, slowly but surely making England independent of the foreigner, and laying the foundations for the triumph of Elizabeth. In 1488 he signs a statute prohibiting to all foreigners the export of undressed cloth. This regulation has for its object the encouragement of cloth-making in England. It hits the Germans hard, because they have a great trade with Flanders in the undressed cloths of England, Flanders having fallen at this time in great part from cloth-making to cloth-finishing. The Hanse arrogantly tell Henry that his policy is bad for his country, and that it is directed against the German cities. " This matter," they say, " had been instituted neither for the common good nor for the promotion of the cloth-working industry, but merely to drive the merchants of the Hanse out of this trade in England, in order to satisfy the Londoners, the inventors of the innovation, and to put in their hands the trade that is now being carried on by the Ger-

mans."[1] And they continue : " Although the English
cloths are not fit to be dressed, and the English Government know this well, it takes no measures against the
making of bad cloth, but demands that the Hanse
should export only well-finished cloth."

Further, the Germans assert that the Act is administered severely against Germans and leniently
against Englishmen, so that the Antwerp merchants are
willing to buy undressed cloth from Englishmen, but
refuse to buy it from Germans for fear of getting into
trouble.[2]

In 1487 an Act is passed prohibiting the importation
of silk fabrics—a concession to the silk industry of
London. We find evidence here that at first the protective policy was applied gingerly as far as the Germans
were concerned. " And such silk," says a document
in the *Hanse Recesse* for that year, " comes sometimes
into England, although the Act has not been revoked,
as is only right, having regard to the privileges of the
(Hanse) merchant. Still the merchant has great trouble
with the King's officers on account of this silk."[3]

But by 1489 the " jealousy " of the English merchants has forced the King to bring the Germans into
line. They are even forbidden to import silk from
Cologne. In 1494 we find that city writing to the

[1] " Quod ea res non tam instituta dinoscitur ad communem omnium
profectum, neque ad incrementum generalis officii eorum pannos servantium,
sed potius in occasionem extrudendi mercatores de Ansa ab omni mercatura
in Anglia ut soli Londoniensis hujus novitatis inventores questum exerciant
et soli habeant mercandisas nunc ab Almanis tractatas."—*Hanse Recesse*, ii.
2, n. 506, § 7, and 161, § 4.
    [2] " Quod frequentius fit executio adversus Almanos quam Anglicos similiter
pannos Antwerpiam eocheater, ubi tamen Anglici nullum est discrimen inter
justos et injustos pannos, nam ab Antwerpiensibus dicuntur privelegiati, ut
non teneantur emptoribus de defectibus comparentibus respondere."—*Ibid.*,
iii. 2, n. 506, § 10, also 161, § 4 ; 508, § 20.
    [3] " Unde vowol sullyke syde in Engelant sumwilen kumpt, so nochtant de
acte nicht revoceret en is, alse id sik billich na des kopmans priviligien geborde,
steyt de kopman nochtant in groten varen van den officiers des Konynghes
der syden halven."—*Ibid.*, iii. 2, n. 161, § 10 ; 508, §§ 2, 5, 10, 12.

Hanse : " Also the silk which is prepared here in our town, and which our people always brought into England on the strength of our privileges, is also not to be imported : nay, it is daily confiscated by the King's officers like contraband goods."

Again, in the first year of his reign Henry VII partly re-enacted the Navigation Law of Edward IV. Wines from the South of France and woad from Toulouse are to be imported only in English ships. It is a cautious measure, calculated not to hit the Germans hard enough to give serious trouble. Nevertheless, it hits the Hanse a little, for we find a reference in the Hanse archives to a cargo of Bordeaux wine which is confiscated because the Hanse import it in a non-Hanseatic ship.

It is nearly always the English merchants who are behind these prosecutions. Englishmen seem to have constituted themselves a sort of private police against the Germans. London cloth-dressers, for example, have Hanseatic ships stopped before they sail, in order to have them searched for undressed cloth. When the undressed cloth is found, the German merchants have to deposit a guarantee of £600, to be forfeited if they transgress again. The King is always apologising to the Hanse for the prejudices of his subjects. He is forced to do this and that because he can no longer restrain them. Englishmen are taking affairs into their own hands. Several English towns put municipal limitations on the German free trade charters. The Mayor of London, in spite of his cask of sturgeon, fixes the selling price for salt, wine, and grain, and forces the Germans to offer their staple goods, like wood and herrings, at the London staple—that is to say, at the wholesale market. In Hull they are compelled to sell all imported goods inside the town, and have to buy English goods within the same limits. 'The inhabitants of Hull are indeed so angry with the Hanse, on account of the recent loss of two of their ships, that they declare they will recompense themselves with the first Hanseatic ship that comes into their harbour. The London Steelyard writes to the German towns in some alarm, that at Hull feeling is so strong against the Hanse that the authorities are hardly able to keep back the citizens. To prevent murder and bloodshed the Germans are forbidden to go to Hull. In other towns, too, the Hanse merchants run risks of ill-treatment. In 1490, in the streets of London, several merchants of Cologne are attacked and seriously wounded. The assailants remain unpunished, in spite of the efforts of the Steelyard to bring them to justice.[1]

All the time the Merchant Adventurers are pressing their grievances at Dantzig and the other Hanse towns. The King asks for a peaceful settlement. The cities, on their Hanse Day at Lübeck in 1487, contemptuously decline to send an embassy to London, " inasmuch as things are so bad in that country that people often do not know who happens to be King."[2] They do not realise that at last a King has come to England. Henry, in his quiet, persistent way, keeps pressing the Hanse for a conference. In March 1490 he writes to the towns that he can no longer deny his subjects justice. His sentiments towards the Hanse are the same as ever, but he cannot look on while his merchants suffer heavily day by day. The German Guild in London know the new situation better. They beg the towns to accede to the King's request and send ambassadors, otherwise

---

[1] *Hanse Recesse*, iii. 2, n. 193, 217, 223, 320.
[2] *Ibid.*, iii. 2, n. 160, §§ 270–272.

they will not be able to keep the *Kontor* going in England much longer.[1]

At last Lübeck begins to wake up. It declares itself
prepared to send envoys to Utrecht or Antwerp.
Accordingly a Day is held in Antwerp, in June 1491.
They debate on grievances on both sides. The English
stand firm on their cloth-dressing regulations : " It
cannot be rescinded, because it is in the interest of the
old and honourable Guild of Cloth-shearers." [2]

But they promise to investigate a few other of the
German complaints, and add that it is the will of their
King that Hanseatic privileges be maintained. They
complain, however, that the liberties guaranteed to
English merchants by the reciprocity article in the
Utrecht treaty has not been observed, and they demand
that it be re-enacted in the new treaty under discussion.
Dantzig opposes this demand keenly. If Englishmen
are to be allowed into Dantzig, their status must be
clearly specified. The other Hanse ambassadors take
the English side. It is evident that the open hostility of
Dantzig to England has become inconvenient. Dantzig
gives way, but in a formal protest declares that, despite
the article, the English merchants shall not, in their
town, enjoy any more privileges than the non-Prussian
Hanse merchants who trade there. In common with
all foreigners, they are to be allowed Free Trade only
at the " Dominik " Market in August, and as a concession they are to be allowed access to the " Artus
Court," from which they had recently been excluded.
All these " concessions " had, in fact, been included in
the rights of English merchants in former treaties, so
that Dantzig made no real surrender after all, in spite
of what Dr. Schanz says to the contrary. Neverthe-

---

[1] *Hanse Recesse*, iii. 2, n. 311, 340.   [2] *Ibid.*, iii. 2, p. 526.

less, there was some gain : Dantzig was at least compelled to reaffirm and define the English position.   The
new agreement, in fact, which was concluded on 28th
June, confirmed the Treaty of Utrecht.   It is chiefly
important because it shows a more independent attitude on the part of the English.   If they have yielded
the old privileges, they have not surrendered the new
protection—which, in fact, infringes on these privileges—and they agree to the treaty only until the 1st
of May 1492.   The counter-claims as to damages remain
unsettled.   As to the Baltic, we might perhaps accept
Busch's estimate : " Henry had made an opening,
though that a small one, in the exclusive system of
Prussian trade ; a modest gain certainly, but one which
in connection with his new relations with Denmark
was of some value, as representing the first definite
success of his commercial policy towards the North."
It was hardly a success, yet it was not a surrender, and
it contained just a hint of the new Tudor policy which
was yet to break the Hanse in pieces.

Further meetings are put off from time to time.
Neither side will settle the complaints of the other.
Sometimes the Hanse excuses itself, sometimes England.   The cloth-dressing regulation, leniently enforced
as it seems to have been, is the subject of constant
complaints   through   two   reigns.   The   embargo   on
Cologne silk is no less a grievance.   In June 1499 there
is a new meeting at Bruges.   The Germans demand
the repeal of the Acts of Parliament, which by protecting English industries are alleged to infringe upon
German privileges.   Henry declines to repeal his Acts
of Parliament, and he declines to comply with their
demands for damages.   As the Hanse refuses to accept
his offer for a mutual settlement, he appoints a judge

for the Germans at Calais ; but there must be a judge
for the English at Bruges and at Antwerp.   From this
time on until 1504 there is deadlock. In that year
Henry VII adjourns the meeting *sine die,* " because the
Hanseatic grievances are settled."   In that year Parliament passes an Act which appears to be a surrender to
the Germans.   The Act provides that any statutes
which are at variance with the privileges are not to
be applicable to the Hanse.   The *Kontor* in London is
overjoyed, and reports at once to the towns, and the
King writes to Lübeck that he now hopes he has satis-
fied the Hanse in every way.

How far the Act was a surrender and how far an
evasion is one of the many obscure points in our story.
Henry VII was a wary king, and it would appear that
he signed two copies of the statute, one in Latin for the
Germans, and one in English for his own subjects.
In the English statute there is a provision which does
not appear in the Latin copy preserved in the Hanse
archives.   It is that nothing in the statute shall injure
the interests, liberties, and rights of the town of London.
" We do not know," says Dr. Friedrich Schulz doubt-
fully, " if the Hanse knew about the assurance to
London, and what influence it had on the application
of the Act." [1]   As far as the archives inform us, German
complaints on the subject appear to cease for a time.
We know also that the exemption was renewed by
Henry VIII, and that it was disliked by Parliament.
Nevertheless, the German grievance on the point is
again open in the reign of Henry VIII, although the
Act remains in force.   And if we look at the Act with
a lawyer's eye, we see that there would still remain

[1] *Abhandlungen,* &c.   *Die Hanse und England von Edwards III bis auf
Heinrichs VIII,* von Dr. Friedrich Schulz (Berlin, 1911).

open the question of whether the statutes of which the Hanse complained really did affect its privileges. Over such a bone English and German jurists might well have taken different views.

There is another point over which the authorities quarrel. We know that on 31st October 1493, Henry made the Hanse deposit a surety for £20,000 as a guarantee that they would not export English cloth to the Netherlands. According to Schanz, this money was declared forfeit on 8th July 1508. Schulz, on the other hand, is doubtful. If it were forfeit, how is it that there is no complaint on the subject in the Hanseatic records? Such a stone would certainly have made a splash. Schanz's view of Henry's policy is that, while the King evaded a war with the Hanse, he still brought force to bear upon it; and he sums up that at this time the outlook for Germans in England was rather gloomy. Schulz takes the opposite view. Henry, he says, was the friend of the Hanse, and defended it manfully against his Parliament, and he triumphantly quotes in his support the persistent refusal of Henry to join Denmark in a war upon the towns. Henry's words on this point are preserved in the Hanseatic archives, and are worth quoting. He declines Denmark's proposal " because the German Hanse, of which the town of Lübeck is no small part, has enjoyed in this our Realm for many years its liberties and privileges, and as it now is so it always was, so long as its liberties and immunities last as much united in friendship with ourselves as with our predecessors."

Before attempting to decide between these two scholars it is necessary to look at Henry's policy as a whole. When Henry was crowned on Bosworth Field he looked round on a weak and ruined England. For

K

himself his exchequer was empty, and his crown was held on the insecure tenure of one victory. In Margaret of Flanders he had an implacable enemy, and, as he told the Spanish ambassadors, he regarded Maximilian also as his secret foe. But Flanders was also the enemy of the Merchant Adventurers. It was the enemy of the English cloth trade, and Cologne was the enemy of the English silk manufacture. The wealth of Flanders had rested for centuries on the insecure foundation of making cloth from English wool. When England began to make its own cloth Flanders was apprehensive, but as English cloth was rough and coarse, and Flemish cloth the finest in the world—save only, perhaps, the cloth of Florence—the Flemish consoled themselves with the hope that English cloth would have to be finished in Flanders, that Englishmen would remain their mere journeymen, and that they would always be supreme in the finishing process and in the finer counts. Now, the Hanse, except for the silk manufacture of Cologne, was not directly interested in manufacture. Its interest was trade. It preferred, no doubt, to carry English wool to Bruges, and to sell Flemish cloth in England. There, as an uninterrupted trade process, lay its largest profits. But its case was somewhat complicated by the fact that, whereas English shippers enjoyed a preference in the export of wool, German shippers enjoyed a preference in the export of cloth. Amazing as it may sound, it is none the less true that under the English customs the Hanse in England had a substantial preference, not only over all foreign merchants, but over Englishmen themselves. The amount of this preference can be definitely stated.[1] On every piece of undyed cloth Englishmen paid an

---

[1] See Appendix III.

export duty of 1s. 2d., foreigners 2s. 9d., with an additional *ad valorem* duty of 1s. in the £1, while the Germans of the Hanse only paid 1s. all told—that is to say, they had a preference of twopence against Englishmen, and 1s. 9d. plus the *ad valorem* duty against all other foreigners. On half-dyed cloth their preference over Englishmen was again threepence, their preference over all foreigners was 2s. 5d. plus the *ad valorem* duty as before. On finished cloth they had a preference of 4d. over Englishmen, and 3s. 6d. plus the *ad valorem* duty over all foreigners. Obviously they had an artificial reason for being content to export cloth rather than wool to the Flemish market, and we even find them siding with the English against the Flemish in the endeavour to open the markets of Flanders to the English manufacturer.

Now, if Henry was as clever a man as he is generally supposed to be, he would seek to divide the Germans from the Flemish by this difference of interest. He would allow the Hanse to continue their export trade, but he would quietly force them to export first English cloth instead of English wool, and, secondly, the English finished article instead of the English half-finished article.

Dr. Busch's view is that Henry was afraid of the Hanse : " He did not dare at once to irritate the powerful league of the towns, who might support his enemies, as before they had supported the Yorkist prince, Edward IV." And this is probably true, at least of the first years of his reign. And yet there is no weakness in Henry's policy ; there is even a note of contempt in his treatment of the Hanse at Antwerp.[1] He consistently refuses to allow the Hanse to raise the

---

[1] Busch, *England under the Tudors*, vol. i. p. 75.

blockade of Flanders. And this is true of the last years of his reign. In 1504 he renews the interdict. The Hanse protests, and particularly. Cologne ; but Henry sets his face like flint, and the Hanse trade with Burgundy is stopped until the removal of the interdict in 1506.

And even in the North, where he has gained so little and acquiesces in so much, the alliance with John of Denmark must have been felt by the Hanse as a formidable portent. Henry might reassure them as to his intention, and disclaim all thought of hostility ; but if the alliance with Denmark was not against the Hanse, I should like to know what it was against. It was, in fact, the foundation of a policy designed to open the Baltic to English trade.

The Baltic could wait. English trade and the Royal Exchequer were first to be established. A Spanish marriage would help both. By allying himself with Spain, Henry secured the Straits of Gibraltar for English shipping, and pushed forward to Italy and the Levant. Venice was hostile ; but Henry opened negotiations with Florence, and secured the Italian market for English cloth.

We may say of Henry that, if he left for his successors the actual destruction of the Hanseatic power in England, he at least forged the anvil on which it was to be broken. By his navigation laws and commercial policy he founded an English navy in English shipping, and he placed the strength of the crown in the mercantile interest of England. The foundation of his whole policy was the English cloth trade. He realised that a strong English export of cloth would make England wealthy at home and a power in Europe. It would give him a key by which he could open the doors of every European market. To have a commodity which other people want is to take naturally a strong position. But Henry desired not only to create a cloth industry which should be independent of Flanders, but to create a shipping industry which should be independent of the Hanse.

The fight with Flanders had to come first ; the fight with the Hanse would follow later. In the meantime, he strengthened the Merchant Adventurers' Company by vastly increasing its powers. His charter to the company showed that he regarded it not merely as an instrument of trade, but as a great weapon of foreign policy. He gave it a national foundation, and almost national powers. He helped to make it what the merchants proudly called it—an English Hanse, an organisation which was to grow in strength until it could fight the great League on its own ground.

CHAPTER XIV

THE GERMANS MAKE AN ENEMY

HENRY VII desired chiefly wealth and strength, Henry VIII loved pleasure and glory. Henry VII left a full and overflowing treasury, Henry VIII squandered every penny. Henry VII was always thinking of his London and his merchants, Henry VIII of new wives and new titles. If we look for a key to his foreign policy, we find it now in the desire for a divorce, and again in some vain dream of the imperial crown. He makes no difficulty about renewing Hanseatic privileges, no doubt knowing the colour of Hanseatic money. But his people, and some of his ministers, keep up the fight. Both Wolsey and Cromwell are anti-German in their policy. A riot against the foreigners has almost become an annual May-day festivity. The Town Council of London is petitioned to remove them. A certain Dr. Bale preaches fiery sermons against them. On 1st May 1517 an anti-foreign riot grows so dangerous that the King sends guns and troops from the Tower to quell it. The trade quarrels with the Hanse are unending. In 1514 we find Thomas More, then Under-Sheriff of London, and Cuthbert Tunstall, then Master of the Rolls, negotiating a treaty at Bruges. Only in 1520 are the negotiations concluded. But the end of one dispute begins another. In 1520 Thomas More and John Hewester, the Governor of the Merchant Adventurers, meet twelve members of the Hanse, and agree to a truce until the following year. In the following year the King again prohibits the export of undressed cloth, and the Hanse is again complaining. In the same year there is a prohibition of the export of woollens to Flanders. But Henry is by this time deep in the Reformation, and he is also anxious as to the fate of his brother-in-law, King Christian of Denmark, who has been deprived of his crown by Hanseatic influence. In 1524 two of his Privy Councillors—Dr. Standish, Bishop of St. Asaph, and Sir John Baker—are at Hamburg negotiating with the King of Denmark, the Duke of Holstein, and the Hanse. Henry bestows on Marx Meier the golden chain of knighthood, and delights to honour Wuttenmeher, the Mayor of Lübeck. He flirts with the Lutheran pastors of Lübeck and Hamburg, confirms the Hanseatic privileges, and renews the acknowledgment that they are not to be infringed by Act of Parliament. The Germans accordingly feel themselves strong in the reign of Henry VIII—so strong that they go out of their way to insult Anne Boleyn at her coronation. In Anne Boleyn they recognise an enemy, for she is the great-granddaughter of Geoffrey Boleyn, one of the founders of the Merchant Adventurers, and her family is bound up with the trade of London. On the other side, Catherine of Aragon belongs to the imperial and German interest. No wonder if the merchants of the Steelyard do not like the match. Nevertheless, they are compelled by the Lord Mayor to erect a pageant at Grace Church, not far from the German Guildhall. They choose to represent Mount Parnassus, on which sit Apollo and his Muses. The fountain of Helicon runs with Rhenish wine—even at that time the Germans understood the art of advertisement. When Anne arrives before this pageant, and halts in front, the Muses address her, singing verses in her praise. But in these flatteries lurks an insult. On the very top of Parnassus, which is appropriately adorned with coats of arms, is the great Imperial eagle, bearing on its breast the emblems of Castile and Aragon, the arms of Anne's hated rival. Lower down are the arms of Henry, and lowest of all the coat which the heralds have made out for the Boleyns. Anne is well versed in heraldry, and at once detects the insult. According to Chapuis, the Imperial ambassador, to whom we are indebted for the story, she deeply resents the slight, and on the following day tries to induce the King to punish the obnoxious Germans. A little later she is staying at Greenwich, and a large fleet of German hulks is anchored opposite the palace. The Hanseatic captains invite Chapuis to dine on board their ships. When he arrives they hoist the hateful eagles, fire cannon, beat drums, and make a tremendous din. Chapuis is delighted to learn that Anne was intensely irritated by the demonstration. Again she complains to Henry, and asks him to punish German insolence. But Henry refuses to take any steps. An open quarrel with the Germans would have been too dangerous. All that Anne can do is to leave Greenwich, and to retire to Windsor, beyond the reach of German insults.[1]

Henry was perhaps right in his respectful treatment of the Germans, although they were certainly wrong in making an implacable enemy of a clever woman. The Hanse were at this time giving a most impressive exhibition of their strength. By the Treaty of Nystadt Denmark had conceded to Lübeck the right to veto the election of its kings. A union of Scandinavian powers

---

[1] *Anne Boleyn* (1527–1536), by Paul Friedmann, p. 200 *et seq.* Friedmann takes the story from the despatches of Chapuis, the Imperial ambassador to Charles V, which are preserved in the archives of Vienna.

ventured to set the rule at defiance. They were assisted by the Dutch towns, who were prohibited by the Hanse from trading direct with the Scandinavian ports. Yet Lübeck was strong enough to form a combination which drove out the independent King of Denmark, Christian II, brother-in-law of the Emperor though he was, and placed Frederick of Holstein on the throne. When Christian was safe in the dungeons of Goltorp, Lübeck fitted out a fleet to punish Holland. In August 1533 a detachment of this fleet, consisting of five line-of-battleships and 2200 men, appeared in the English Channel, and captured one Flemish and two Spanish vessels off the Nore. The Lübeck captain, Marcus Meyer, landed at Rye. He was arrested on a charge of piracy and brought to London. Anne wanted to punish him, and to make the Hanseatic merchants responsible for the damage. The Hanse, of course, protested that it had no connection with the affair. Meyer, who was the son of a Hamburg blacksmith, did not lack audacity. He proposed to Henry an alliance of England, Denmark, and Lübeck, strong enough to withstand any enemy, and directed against the Empire. The idea was fantastic, but Henry accepted it with enthusiasm. Marcus was allowed to return, and disappears from our story. The alliance, like all Henry's grandiose projects, ended in smoke.

Henry nevertheless persisted in his aims upon the Empire. In 1543 he sends ambassadors to the Landgrave of Hesse to arrange an alliance with Hesse, Denmark, Holstein, and the Hanse towns of Hamburg, Lübeck, and Bremen. In 1546 he sends John Dymock to Hamburg and Bremen to obtain troops and money. From such a king, with such a policy, it is vain to expect very much. Nevertheless, his reign has its signs and portents. The German Empire is going to pieces. Lübeck has imprisoned a brother-in-law of the Emperor, and has robbed Spanish ships. We may agree with Lappenberg that with Henry VIII the end is in sight. "With the death of this monarch," he says, " the luck of the Hanse fell into its grave."

CHAPTER XV

I THINK I have said enough to show that the Germans were not exactly popular in England at this time. And the English grievances were substantial : (1) that in England Germans were treated better than Englishmen, and (2) that in Germany Englishmen were treated worse than other foreigners. As to Germany, the head and front of the offending was the Baltic town of Dantzig. This great centre of the corn trade had consistently followed a policy first laid down in the time of its celebrated Mayor, Heinrich Vorrath, " to demand much of the English, and to concede nothing."[1] Acting upon these instructions, Vorrath had secured for his group of towns a full third of the German Guildhall in London, with all its privileges of trade and customs, and had given the English nothing of any value in exchange. The Dantzigers, as the English alleged, treated the English " worse than any other foreigners, the Jews only excepted." That Dantzig went too far in the openness of its contempt for English power has already been shown more than once in the course of our story. In the reign of Edward VI its outrages filled the cup of English wrath to overflowing.

We may take up the story in 1547. In September of that year Thomas Hunt and Thomas Stynt made their complaint to the Lord Protector, Edward, Duke

---

[1] Thomas Hirsch, *Danzig's Handelsund*, &o., p. 110.

of Somerset, to the following effect. The Hamburg skipper, Claus Schwarte, on his way to Scotland, attacked and robbed an English ship and took a royal standard. When Schwarte arrived at Dantzig, on the instigation of the Dantzig burgesses, he hung out this flag from the window of his cabin, and some Englishmen, who happened to be in Dantzig, were called to see the show. The Englishmen took a boat, rowed out to the ship, tore down the flag, and took it away. Thereupon Schwarte denounced them before the Mayor for robbing his ship. The Englishmen were imprisoned. Dantzig is advised from London that the Lord Protector is looking into the matter.

On October 15th the Steelyard writes to Dantzig that the King and his Councillors are highly incensed at the way the " rebellious Englishmen " were treated at Dantzig. Exaggerated reports are going about, and Dantzig is advised to send a truthful report to the King and the Protector. Dantzig replies, asking the Steelyard to take up its case and explain its treatment of the " rebels."

How the affair ended we do not know—probably without satisfaction to Englishmen—for just about that time Somerset is financing the Protestant cause in Germany against the Emperor—a new form of " the natural alliance," extremely profitable to the towns. In March he lends 50,000 crowns to the Duke of Saxe, through Lübeck, Hamburg, and Bremen, to be repaid by the cities in the merchandise of these parts, " for the furniture of his Navie, as cables, mastes, ankers, pyche, flaxe and such other," and on 11th December (as from 20th June) 1547 he confirms the privileges of the towns.

Yet the Germans in London are plainly uneasy :

such incidents are bad for trade. Feeling is so aggravated in the North that the Mayor and Corporation of Hull persistently evade the King's commands as to allowing the Germans their privileges in that port. Other towns incline to follow this contumacious example. In April 1551 citizens of London are discovered to be in conspiracy to attack the foreigners on May Day, and hardly has the danger been averted when another plot blows the German Guildhall sky-high.

Upon the surface, what the Germans had to face was merely a law case involving a question of customs that had been disputed between the Steelyard and the collectors for generations. But there were two unfortunate circumstances. There were no Germans on the Privy Council ; and there was in London a certain Thomas Gresham, mercer.

Everyone knows the name of Gresham—the founder of the Royal Exchange and of Gresham College. But few are aware of his greatest benefaction to London—it was Gresham who overthrew the Germans. It may be doubted if the Germans knew it themselves, for Gresham was a discreet gentleman, who worked for great ends in a quiet way. But when Queen Elizabeth came to the throne of England, he disclosed the secret to his royal mistress in a letter which was preserved by Burghley and printed by Burgon.[1] Gresham explains to the Queen how the extravagance of her father and "the great freedom of the Steelyard" had led to a serious depreciation in the exchange. And he proceeds : "Now for the redress of these things, in 1551 . . . your late brother (King Edward VI) called me to be his agent and reposed a more trust in me, as well for

---

[1] *Life of Sir Thomas Gresham*, vol. i, App., xxi. See also p. 197 of this book.

the payment of his debts beyond the seas as for the raising of the exchange—being then at 15s. and 16s. in the pound; and your money current as it is at this present being not in value 10s. *First I practised with the King and my Lord of Northumberland to overthrow the Steelyard,* or else it could not be brought to pass for that they would keep down the exchange by this consideration : whereas your own mere merchants pay outwards 14d. upon a cloth custom, they pay (paid) but 9d., and likewise for all such wares as was brought into your realm your own mere merchants paid 12d. upon the pound, the Steelyard paid but 3d. upon the pound, which is £5 difference upon the hundred. And as they the Germans were men that raine all upon the exchange (query : sell a bear) for the buying of their commodities, what did they pass to give a lower price than your own merchants, when they got £5 in the hundred by your custom, which in process of time would have undone your whole realm and your merchants of the same."

Fortified by this knowledge of the forces working behind—no less than the King, his Prime Minister, and the Merchant Adventurers' Company—let us now proceed to examine the musty old law case, recorded partly in Latin and partly in Tudor script, which brought about the downfall of the Germans in England.[1]

The case was heard in Guildhall before Richard Dobbes, Mayor of the City of London, and a jury of stout Merchant Adventurers, trading in the Baltic, and was decided on 25th November 1551.

We need not go into the evidence very far. It would appear that a certain Andrew Moore was factor

---

[1] Cotton MS., Claudius, E 7, folio 84. Inquisitions, &c., concerning the Hansa, 5 Edward VI.

in London for one Keysiler, a Dantzig merchant. Andrew Moore died, and his brother Adrian saw his papers. Among these papers were letters which seemed to show that Andrew had been passing off goods consigned from non-Hanseatic merchants as goods of the Hanse, and thereby defrauding the customs of the difference between the duties paid by the Hanse and the 'duties paid by other foreigners. Besides this evidence there was the testimony of two Steelyard merchants, Lambert Romane and Michael Tymerman, who had been arrested in the street by Baldwin Smith, an officer of the customs. In addition to these witnesses there were certain letters which had been seized on board a Dantzig ship at Gravesend. The letters do not tell us very much, beyond showing that all the Germans in London were in a terrible state of flutter. One of them begins, " Here is an evil saying ' Come in the wind,' " and goes on to tell how the King's Council have taken up the matter " verie highlie " and " keep counsell togeather apase . . . that they may take awaie our priveleges from us which thinge I yet hope shall not come to passe." And another tells one John Brand of Dantzig how, " through Adrian, brother unto Andrew Moore and an English fellow out of a shereman's (cloth-dresser's) house, the thing is told out and betrayed and brought before the King's Counsell, soe that it is now brought into the light, and the same knave doth declare unto the King's Counsell all that he knoweth of our house and saieth perchance more than the truth. . . . They intend to put us from our whole priveleges whereunto by God's leave they shall not come with right." The writer goes on to protest that the worshipful merchants were innocent : they " would suffer no such thing, for they did punish for it as soon as they know it, and did forbid him the House." Then there is a letter from Brant von Holten to his brother, Reignold of Dantzig : " What belongeth unto Cosselor's and Fensell's handlings I fear that the Danskers shall stand with shame before the King's Majesty and his Counsell, for there is a servant which hath been much with Andrew Moore, the same hath betraid it, and Andrew Moore's brother is taken upon the street viii daies agoe and was holden still that we knew not where he was become : now cometh it out that certain of the King's Counsell caused him to be taken and within this eight days hath bin three times before all the King's Counsell, and what they doe therein and how he is examined and how it will goe, wee shall know in short time. . . . If we scape soe that wee lose not priveleges thereby, God give us that wch belongeth unto salvation."

We can imagine with what impartiality the jury of English merchants examined the evidence and arrived at their verdict. They began in a general way by enunciating a sound protective policy :

" All English merchants subjects of the King of England ought to pay for export of every broadcloth of wool, dyed or not dyed, out of the kingdom fourteen pence, and for subsidy on every species of merchandise from foreign parts discharged in the ports of England according to the value of the merchandise at the rate of twelve pence in the pound of English money ; and all foreign merchants not native ought to pay for every short broadcloth of wool dyed six shillings and three pence, for every white short broadcloth five shillings and nine pence, and for imports of all sorts fifteen pence in the pound according to the worth of the merchandise."

Having made this general finding on the question

of customs, they descend to particulars—particulars
are that, in one case : " Reginald Strusse, at London
aforesaid, in the parish of All Saints the Greater,
Dowgate Ward, being possessed of 1380 short woollen
cloths, dyed and coloured, and 59 white short cloths
of his own goods . . . shipped the said cloths in ships
belonging to Hans Smith, Derek von Ling, Hans Molck,
Maynard Bremer, Bartholomew Long, Christian Winck,
Orte Guise, Anselm Breckfeld, Hans Grippenstraw, and
other foreigners mentioned, and has defrauded the King
of his customs, for the dyed and coloured cloths, £431,
5s. 0d., and for the white cloths, £14, 7s. 6d., amounting
in all to £445, 11s. 6d. of English money." They also
find that two foreigners, Adrian Keysiler and Laurence
Fensel, not being inhabitants of the Steelyard, had con-
spired with " Reginald Strusse, Lambart Romane,
Francis von Nuse, Henry von Syth, John Gardo, Antony
Ellers, Garrard Gufferod, Andrew von Bergen, Michael
Tymerman, and John Kinkell, German merchants, inhabitants of the Steelyard, to defraud the King of his
customs by causing to be entered in the books of the
collector of customs in the port of London in the name
of Michael Tymerman eight bales of cloth, the true
owners Keysiler and Fensel not having been at any
time members of the Steelyard," by which means the
King lost in his customs and subsidy due from foreigners
to the amount of £70, 12s. 6d.

There are also certain frauds connected with the
export of " bell-metal powder," in which a verdict
against the German merchants is duly returned.

These somewhat obscure cases gave the Privy Council
its opportunity. The whole position of the Germans
trading in England was opened up in the form of
arguments between the Hanse on the one side and the

L

Merchant Adventurers on the other. The Merchant Adventurers, who call themselves "the merchants haunting and frequenting the Emperor's base countries of Holland, Zeeland, Brabant and Flanders, as also other chief ports beyond the seas, chiefly the town of Dantzig," complain of being "grievously hindered" by the German merchants of the Hanse, "who have their house in the City of London called the Guildhall of Dutchmen." They had been forced by the German merchants to keep their marte only in the town of Antwerp, which had resulted in exceeding heightening in the price of foreign commodities, much damage to the wool trade, and the decay of the cities and towns of England and of the Navy. They complain also that in the town of Dantzig they are "rigorously handled, that all other nations, Jews only excepted, be suffered more liberty than they." Contrary to their privileges, they are forced to pay tolls and customs, which are altered from time to time by the will of the Dantzig customs. They are only permitted to sell their goods on one day in the week, and that Saturday, and then only to the burgesses of Dantzig, except once a year on their Fair Day. They are prevented from buying the commodities of Prussia at Dantzig, and they are not permitted to deal one Englishman with another. All this they have suffered, although by the privileges of the Hanse in England they should have been treated reciprocally. Moreover, the Easterlings have made a regular practice of "colouring" the goods of foreign merchants who do not belong to the Hanse, to the great loss of "your Majesty's customs." In these circumstances, the privileges of the Germans ought to be withdrawn. The Merchant Adventurers go on to tell how, by their enterprise, they contrived to establish four yearly marts in Brabant and Flanders, at Bergen-op-Zoom, Antwerp, and other market-towns. The Germans, however, dumped such large quantities of English cloth on the Antwerp market that the price had greatly fallen, the market being, in fact, " cloyed " with English goods. When the English merchants had the Flemish market all to themselves, they sold their cloth for treasure, and brought to England large sums, between £15,000 and £30,000. ʻThe effect, however, of the German dumping was that the Flemish buyers would not pay in money, but in foreign commodities, to the great loss of England. Another ill effect of the German interference with English trade was that Englishmen were compelled, owing to the glutting of the market, to wait for weeks in the Flemish market-towns, and some of them had even taken up their abode in Antwerp, so that their money was being spent abroad instead of being spent in England. Another great disadvantage of having so many Germans in England was that they bought their commodities at the houses of the weavers, boarded and lodged with the clothiers, learnt the secrets of weaving, and induced " light and idle " Englishmen to transfer the secrets of their craft to other countries. Thus, for example, a foreigner had recently sent out six English workmen to make kerseys in Brabant. Fortunately these men had been sent back by " your Majesty's subjects," but nevertheless they had taught the Brabant people the art of making kerseys, to the great loss of the English weavers. The Germans might in the same way induce English weavers to go to Germany and set up a weaving industry in competition with England.

Another point on which the Merchant Adventurers insisted was that the Germans had no respect for the quality of the cloth they bought. They would buy any kind of rubbish. They encouraged the weavers to turn out cheap stuff. There had even been cases in which five sundry sorts of wool had been used in one piece, each sort being coarser than the outside part which was shown to the purchaser. Such practices degraded English cloth in the eyes of the world. Again, the Merchant Adventurers supported the English Navy by "fraughting and lading the same, and continuing a great number of your subjects in the mariner's craft." On the other hand, the Germans, "to the intolerable decay thereof, ship their goods both inward and outward continually in foreign bottoms." Thus, for example, the Germans had shipped from London in foreign bottoms no less than 42,897 cloths in one year, whereas in the same year all other strangers coming to London had only shipped 1080 cloths. If English masters and mariners had been employed to carry these cloths, they would have made £2333, besides the freight of the German goods which paid for the cloth, whereas all this money was lost to English sailors. Lastly, and here the Merchant Adventurers use an argument calculated to appeal to kings and governments, the Germans greatly diminished the customs, both with regard to exports and imports, because they paid only "a quarter of what your subjects pay." At the great trade conference with the German merchants at Bruges in 1521, the English ambassadors had forbidden Easterlings to bring into England such fine foreign commodities as cloth of gold, silks, and all sorts of linen, spices, oil, oilwood, madder, and other fine and rich merchandise, for the same small customs as they had been used to pay for their own commodities, which were "grose and gruffe," great in storage and small in value. At that

" Diet " it was calculated that in this way no less than
£100,000 sterling had been lost to his Majesty's customs ;
yet it was notorious that they had persisted in this
practice, and that their imports of these rich foreign
commodities, on which they evaded the payment of
high duties, was now greater than ever before.

The Merchant Adventurers admitted that they were
fairly treated at Lübeck, the head town of the Hanse,
but their treatment at Dantzig was a scandal. Whereas
forty years ago they used to pay 2s. 8d. on a pack containing thirty cloths, now they were charged 6d. on every
cloth, or 15s. the pack. And on exports from Dantzig
the officers were continually increasing the customs.
They went on to tell how, by imprisonment and extreme
penalties, they were prevented from trading in Prussia
outside Dantzig, and had only one Fair Day in the year
besides their Saturday market. They gave details of how
the Danskers had framed their trade arrangements so as
to force Englishmen to buy only from the townspeople
the flax, the pitch, the tar, the ashes and other wares
which came into the town from other parts of Prussia.

As reciprocity was the basis of trade arrangements,
such enormities deserved to be punished by the forfeiture of the German privileges. In any case, the
Germans should not be allowed to sell our English
cloths in Flanders. There was an old Act of Edward
IV by which " no Hanse merchant should unpack,
unfardel or put to sale any woollen cloth on this side the
city of Cologne," and the Hanse had been bound in
£41,000 to observe this custom. From these practical
and business arguments the Merchant Adventurers
plunged into a most profound and learned disquisition
on the text of the charters by which the Germans
claimed their privileges, going back to the reign of

Henry III. The best points they made were that Edward II's charter was conditional, on there being no " colouring " of foreign goods and foreign merchants, and that Edward IV's charter was reciprocal. The Germans had, as a matter of fact, " coloured " goods, as had been shown by recent actions in the law courts, and as for reciprocity, there was the notorious case of Dantzig. Then Henry VII had forbidden them to trade with Flanders, yet they had done so, enjoying on this trade a preference of ninepence in the pound over Englishmen, and twelvepence in the pound over all other foreigners. But the policy of Dantzig, that was the worst grievance. To that the Merchant Adventurers constantly return, and on that chiefly they urge the King to take the " pretended " liberties of the German Guildhall into his hands.

The German reply is a skilful document, although, as we shall see, it has its loopholes. It begins with a disclaimer. The Germans in London are but factors or agents. " The steads of the Hanse " are their superiors. As for their charters, they had rights in England long before Henry III. He merely confirmed them, and they had been confirmed by many Acts of Parliament. Time out of mind they had brought into England all manner of merchandise without impediment, and when suits had been brought against them in the Exchequer they had always been acquitted by virtue of their privileges and their charters. As to their recognisance of £20,000 extorted from certain private merchants of the Hanse by Henry VII in 1493, that was merely a temporary matter due to variance between the King and Maximilian the Emperor, and the Duke of Burgundy. Henry forbade shipping for twenty days until he heard from his ambassadors ; and if they had been bound not to traffic in these parts, so had Englishmen and other strangers. When the matter between the potentates had been settled, the embargo was removed. How came it to be that their trade was injurious to England when it had been confirmed by so many treaties and Acts of Parliament? They were simply carrying on their old custom, trading as their ancient privileges permitted. And here they give an interesting list of the commodities which they have brought into the kingdom—corn, flax, wax, pitch, tar, wainscot, cables, masts, ores, iron, steel, harness, osmondes, soap, ashes, copper, saltpetre, gunpowder, coal, silver, bow-staves, stock-fish, salt-fish, linen, cloths, and other commodities. These goods were a living to many people in the country, because they were sold in gross, and the result was cheapness. As for the wares exported by them, they were chiefly woollen cloths, for the most part of the coarsest sort, such as no other nation used, and this trade gave employment to many of the King's subjects. It was absurd to suggest that his Majesty was deceived by them in his customs, or that the navy of England was damaged by the trade. As to the complaints of the English merchants in Flanders, the Hanse reported that it was the " great multitude and desire " of the English themselves and their covetousness that were really at fault. And now as to the charge of " colouring." The German alder-men and merchants had always sought utterly to ex-tirpate such frauds. The case of Adrian Keysiler had been much misrepresented. Adrian Keysiler was a merchant of Dantzig, who was free of the Hanse. He had sent certain merchandise to his factor in London, one Andrew Moore. This Andrew Moore died last July in London, leaving a younger brother, Adrian

Moore. Now it chanced that, after Andrew's death, certain letters from Keysiler's factor and bookkeeper, Laurence Fensel, had come to the sight of Adrian Moore and the German merchants. These letters led them to suspect that Fensel had shipped to London certain foreign goods besides those of his master. This being contrary to their constitution and damaging to the King, they had immediately sealed up the counting-house door of the said Andrew in the presence of Adrian Moore, his brother, until some one sufficiently empowered to take over Keysiler's goods should arrive. Not long afterwards Michael Tymerman arrived on his own business with a commission from Keysiler to take charge of the goods. He was immediately called before the German aldermen and merchants, and examined as to whether he knew that Fensel had done anything contrary to their privileges. Tymerman replied that he knew nothing about the matter. In the presence of Tymerman and Adrian Moore they had therefore gone into the whole business of Andrew Moore deceased, and had read the suspected letters, but finding them very confused, they had written to the magistrates at Dantzig to inquire, and in the meantime they had charged Michael Tymerman on oath not to defraud the King of his custom.

Now this plausible story has one weak point. It is an admission that they took no steps to communicate their suspicions to the customs authorities. But to proceed. Adrian Moore had told the story to a cloth-worker's servant, and he had told it to Baldwin Smith, Deputy Surveyor of Customs at the port of London. Smith had acted most irregularly. He had apprehended Moore and examined him, and still kept him away from his master and friends. He had not only given information to the Privy Council, but he had, contrary to his commission and the laws of the realm, apprehended a merchant of the Steelyard at " burse time " in Lombard Street, and carried him to his own house, where he had examined him " at his pleasure," without any proper commission. He had also got hold of Tymerman, and detained him two days and nights in a secret chamber. When the German alderman required him to be released, Smith's wife had refused to let him go in the absence of her husband. Then Smith had gone to Gravesend and opened a whole packet of German letters which he found in one of their ships, " disclosing all their secrets, to their great slander." On such grounds and by such means he had laid his informations in the Exchequer. There was the awkward point that the German aldermen and merchants, after their consultation, had entered 210 cloths under Michael Tymerman's name, but it was obvious that these goods were in Tymerman's custody. It was not they who had shipped them, but Fensel, who had shipped them himself at his own venture " and peril of sea, fire, and enemies, being his own proper goods." When he shipped them they were no longer Keysiler's goods, but his own. As to the confessions, they had been extorted by an adversary in an irregular way, and the whole case was rushed through, so that they had not had a fair chance of answering. The Escheator of London, who had arranged the case, was " of the said Smyth's Counsel," and he had procured a jury composed of English merchants trading with Dantzig and Flanders, who were " their very adversaries," so that the whole proceedings were " contrary to laws Divine and human, the statutes of the Realm, and the express words of their ancient privileges." Even if the offence had been committed, it was unfair to impute to all the towns of the Hanse an offence committed by one man, without their knowledge or consent.

The conduct of Dantzig was evidently felt to be rather a weak spot. The Germans " would be right sorry that such ungentleness should be done." Obviously the case could not be defended, but at least it might be said that negotiations had been proceeding in the matter since 1542, and the towns were still ready to discuss the points at issue.

It was now the turn of the Merchant Adventurers. They pointed out a flaw in the German logic. They called themselves factors who had no responsibility, yet a company which enjoyed certain privileges. As to the charters, the Adventurers' lawyer had gone further into the matter, for they produced a number of new points—points which show that then, as now, lawyers enjoyed a quibble. Thus, for example, in the charter of Edward I there was no mention at all of merchants of the Hanse in Almaine, but only of the merchants of Almaine. Then the King had said *concedendas*, not *concedimus* or *concessimus*—that is to say, he had given them a grant in the future tense, which was no grant at all. Again, while the grants were given to merchants of Germany in a certain house in the City of London, there was no proof that the Hanse now occupied that same house. They might be living in quite another house. There were a great many other arguments to the same effect, but the upshot of it all was that the Privy Council found as follows :

" Their pretended liberties are void, because the merchants of the Hanse have no sufficient corporation to receive the same.

" Owing to the uncertainty of what persons or towns should enjoy the said privileges, the Hanse merchants admit to be free with them whom and as many as they list, to the prejudice of the King's customs of nigh £20,000 yearly.

" Even if the pretended grants were good, as by the laws of the realm they are not, they were conditional upon their not colouring or avowing foreign goods, &c., which condition they have broken.

" It appears that, for a hundred years after the grant of their pretended privileges, the merchants of the Hanse exported merchandise out of this realm only to their own countries, and brought into this realm only wares of their own countries, but now they export to Flanders, Brabant, and places adjoining, and import wares of all other countries, to the subversion of the trade of the English merchants, and to the loss of the King's customs.

" Whereas the privileges heretofore granted to the merchants of the Steelyard were reasonably used with profit to themselves and no enormous prejudice to the Royal Estate of the realm, now for the reasons above stated your pretended privileges are grown so prejudicial to the crown the same may not be longer endured.

" In spite of requests from the King's Majesty's father and from himself for redress of the grievances of the English merchants established at Dantzig, no reform hath hitherto ensued.

" In consideration whereof the Lords of the Privy Council in the King's behalf decree that the privileges, liberties, and franchise claimed by the merchants of the Steelyard shall from henceforth be and remain seized and resumed unto the King's hands until the said merchants of the Steelyard shall declare and prove better and more sufficient matter for their claim in the premises, saving and reserving unto the said merchants all such and like liberties of coming into the realm and buying and selling as any other merchant stranger hath or ought to have.

"This decree was made and given at Westminster, 24th February, 6 Edward VI." [1]

It was a signal victory for Gresham and his Merchant Adventurers. At a single blow they had swept away all the privileges and immunities of the Hanse, and had done at a stroke what Simon de Montfort and Warwick the King-maker had failed to do by years of fighting.

But if the victory is a testimony to the skill of Gresham, it also displays a decline in strength on the other side. The Germans were, in fact, divided. The Hanse was in almost open conflict with the Empire. A little while before, Lübeck had driven a brother-in-law of the Emperor from the throne of Denmark. Henry VIII had fomented the revolt of the Lutheran towns against the Catholic power. Edward VI had remarked in his boyish diary with wonder that the Emperor meant to punish Bremen and Hamburg. And in March 1552 we find from another entry that the Privy Council quite understood the opportunities given to England by the situation in Europe. " It was agreed," says the boy king, " that it was most necessary to have a mart in England for the enriching of the same to make it the more famous and to be less in other men's danger, and to make all things better cheap and more plentiful. The time was thought good to have it now, because of the wars between the French King and

---

[1] *Acts of the Privy Council.*

the Emperor." No doubt in this entry too we see the hand of the founder of the Royal Exchange.

But the fight was not over. The decree of the Privy Council had been issued in hot haste in February 24th. On February 29th Dr. John Rudelius and Dr. Francis Pfeil from Hamburg appeared before the King. Evidently it was a neck-and-neck race, and the decision had been procured just in time. On March 2nd the Lord Chancellor, two secretaries, a judge, and four members of the Privy Council were deputed to reply to these Hanseatic envoys. By May 1st of the same year the decree was confirmed, but by May 11th the Germans had got so far as to obtain a commission to go into their case.

The reopening of the case was something of a score ; but the Hanse could hardly have hoped very much from its constitution ; it consisted of the Lord Chancellor and six Privy Councillors, with Dr. Wotton. Cecil, then a rising young politician and a strong anti-German, was secretary. Yet Lappenberg gives the impression that this commission substantially restored the Hanseatic privileges, " although," he adds, " they were hard fought by Sir William Cecil, who wanted to earn the gratitude of his countrymen for having suppressed the foreigners." The Acts of the Privy Council hardly bear out this view. On the contrary, all that the Germans seem to have secured was an extension of the low duties while the matter was in debate, and permission to export on the old terms certain consignments of cloth and lead that had been contracted for before the case. In October the Privy Council issued a decree that their just sentence, which had been suspended in the meantime, should now be enforced. The Germans had gained little but delay.

The fact was that the English merchants were now too strong for them. The astute Gresham was using the credit of the company to do for the Royal Exchequer what had long been done by the Steelyard. " Because," says Sir John Hayward, speaking of the year 1552, " the King was to make payment of £48,000 beyond the seas, and had but £14,000 towards the sum, three hundred of the chief Merchant Adventurers granted to him a loan of £40,000 for three months, to be levied from the cloths which they were then to transport after the rate of 20s. for every cloth." This lesson also the Merchant Adventurers had learnt from the Germans, that to control the policy of a Government it is necessary to supply its purse.

CHAPTER XVI

ALLIANCE WITH RUSSIA

THE merchants had broken the power of the Hanse in London, but they had still to consider the trade of the Baltic. After such an open breach the Sound was likely to be, as the Americans would say, " unhealthy " for Englishmen. Dantzig was certain to retaliate. And now we are to see the real greatness of our Merchant Adventurers. They determined to circumnavigate the North Cape and cut into the trade of the Easterlings by way of the Arctic.

It was a great project, and had been propounded long before by Robert Thorne of Bristol. In 1513 he had laid before the King, and in 1527 at greater length, the idea of a new route to the East. The Spaniards, he said, hold the Western route, by the Straits of Magellan ; the Portuguese the Eastward, by the Cape of Good Hope. The English have left to them but one way to discover, and that is by the North. It would be shorter by two thousand leagues. And we should by the way find lands no less rich of gold and spicery, and also should, " if we may passe under the North, enjoy the navigation of all Tartary, which should be no less profitable to our commodities of cloth than those spiceries to the Emperor and King of Portugale." As for the cold and the ice, he replied, like a true English sailor : " There is no land uninhabitable nor sea unnavigable." [1]

1 Hakluyt.

Thorne, no doubt, had often discussed the matter with the Cabots, and now, when the Privy Council case made the Baltic almost impossible, Sebastian Cabot laid the idea as a practical scheme before the Merchant Adventurers. There had been a time when the London merchants distrusted Cabot as a " foreigner," but that was a long time ago.[1] This time the Merchant Adventurers trusted Cabot. And not only the merchants, but the King, the Marquis of Winchester, and other leading Englishmen backed the adventure.

The little expedition saluted the King at Greenwich on 11th May, leaving behind it an astute Privy Council to dangle with the ambassadors of the German Hanse. In August the three ships were separated by a gale. Sir Hugh Willoughby, with the *Bona Esperanza* and the *Bona Confidentia*, found his way into the river " called Arzina in Lapland, neere unto Kegor," a desolate land. There they wintered, and there they died of starvation or cold. But Chancellor, the pilot of the expedition, made his way alone, in the *Edward Bonaventura*, to the White Sea. He landed in Russia, in the Bay of St. Nicholas, where the town of Archangel now stands. Making his way overland, he reached Moscow, where the Emperor, Ivan Basilowitz, was as glad to see Chancellor as Chancellor was glad to see him. For the Tsar had just turned the Germans out of Russia, and was, no doubt, at a loss how to supply his subjects with cloth. " Next unto Moscow," as Chancellor told Adams, " the Citie of Nougorode is reputed the chiefest of Russia . . . it is the chiefest and greatest Marte Towne of all Moscouie . . . this towne exceeds all the rest in the commodities of flaxe and hempe : it yeelds also hides,

---

[1] See Appendix V.

honie and waxe. The Flemings there sometimes had a house of marchandize ; *but by reason that they used the like ill dealing there, which they did with us, they lost their privileges, a restitution whereof they earnestly sued for at the time that our men were there.* But those Flemings, hearing of the arrival of our men in those parts, wrote their letters to the Emperour against them, accusing them for pirats and rovers, wishing him to detain and imprison them. Which things, when they were knowen of our men, they conceived fear, that they should never have returned home. But the Emperour beleeving rather the King's letters which our men brought [1] than the lying and false suggestions of the Flemings, used no ill intreatie towards them."

The Flemings were, of course, the merchants of the Hanse, and it is surely a very remarkable coincidence that Englishmen and Germans, after their quarrel in London, should continue it in Novgorod, and that Edward VI and Ivan the Terrible should be at the same time turning the Easterlings out of their kingdoms. And not only so, but when we think of it, from that time to this the Germans have stood between Russia and England, slandering Englishman to Russian, and Russian to Englishman. It would be of service to both Empires if they kept in mind this good example of Chancellor and Ivan, who refused to be estranged by " the lying and false suggestions " of the Teuton.

The result of the conference was that Ivan gave Richard a letter to his King, written in most friendly wise : " They shall have their free Marte with all free liberties through my whole dominions with all kinds of wares to come and goe at their pleasure without any

---

[1] Cabot had thoughtfully provided letters in Greek, Latin, Chaldee, and Hebrew as likely to be understood in those parts.

let, damage, or impediment." The intercourse begun thus bravely prospered for a time. Chancellor made a second voyage to the White Sea in the summer of 1555, taking with him George Killingworth, the Company's first agent in Muscovy. In 1556 he made his third voyage, and loaded, in the *Edward Bonaventura*, at the Bay of St. Nicholas, " waxe, trane oyle, tallow, furres, felts, yarne and such like "—in fact, good Dantzig merchandise—to the value of £20,000, with £6000 worth in the *Bona Speranza*. Not only so, but he embarked a Russian ambassador, " Osep Napea," with a train of twenty-six. Most unfortunately the *Edward Bona-ventura* was wrecked on the east coast of Scotland, at " Pettislego Bay," on 7th November 1556, and Richard Chancellor drowned in endeavouring to save the ambassador. " The rude and ravenous people of the country " appropriated the cargo ; but the Ambassador, nothing daunted, made his way to London, where he had a magnificent reception. Twelve miles outside London he was received by " four score merchants with chains of gold and goodly apparel," on horseback, with servants in livery. Four miles from London he was brought to a merchant's house, and presented with gold, velvet, and silk. Next day—Saturday, 28th February 1557—he was escorted by Viscount Montague, on behalf of the Queen, with three hundred " lustie knights, esquiers, gentlemen and yoemen," and one hundred and forty of the " merchants adventuring for Russia," to the City of London, after being shown by the way " the hunting of the fox and such like sport." At " Smithfield barres," " the first limits of the liberties of the Citie of London, the Lord Maior, accompanied with all the Aldermen in their skarlet, did receive him, and so riding through the Citie of London in the middle, between the Lord Maior and Viscount Montague, a great number of merchants and notable personages riding before, and a large troupe of servants and apprentices following, with great admiration and plausibilitie of the people running plentifully on all sides," he was brought to his lodging in " Fant Church Street," where a house had been richly furnished for his stay. " Feasting and banquetting," sightseeing, " a notable supper garnished with musicke, enterludes and bankets," at the Drapers' Hall (on 29th April), occupied his time until he departed from Gravesend, " not without expressing of teares," in the " noble shippe the *Primrose*, Admiral to the Fleete, on the 3rd of May."

Now the Londoners rejoiced because a friendship with Russia was the best possible reply to the hostility of Dantzig and the Easterlings. This is made clear by the trading instructions given to Killingworth for the voyage of 1557. The merchants had sent seven ropemakers to Russia, and " seeing you have great plentie of hempe there, and at a reasonable price, we trust we shal be able to bring as good stuffe from thence, and better cheape than out of Danske : if it be diligently used and have a good overseer." The gravest disadvantage was the dangerous passage and long freight, which made it unprofitable to carry the raw hemp and tar ; but the chief cargo was to be wax, flax, tallow, and train oil, with a special line in furs, and inquiry after steel, copper, and Russian leather. And not only so, but the Emperor of Russia desired " that such commodities as be in his dominions shall not pass to Rie, Revel and Poland as they have done but bee reserved for us ; therefore we must so lay for it that it may not ly upon their hands that have it to sell." Moreover, Leonard Brian, whose "bringing up hath bene most in Danske and hath good understanding in making of ropes and cables," has been sent, and two coopers to make casks for the oil and tallow. Obviously the design is to cut out the Germans from the Russian trade :

"For we must procure to utter good quantitie of wares, especially the commodities of our Realme, although we affoord a good peny worth, to the intent to make other that have traded thither, wearie, and so to bring ourselves and our commodities in estimation and likewise to procure to have the chief commodities of that country in our hands, as waxe and such others, that other nations may be served by us and at our hands. For we doe understand that the greatest quantitie of waxe that commeth to Danske, Lübeck, and Hambourgh, commeth out of Russia. Therefore if we should buy and they also buy, it would raise the price there, and would be litle woorth here. And all such letters of importance and secrecie as you doe send by land for any wares or otherwise you must write them in cyphers."

Obviously, too, there is danger in the undertaking, and the nature and seriousness of the danger is soon made clear. Thomas Alcocke, not, I gather, one of the ten apprentices to the Company who were sent "into the notable cities of the country for understanding and knowledge," but a trusted servant of the Company, undertook a bold journey from Smolensk to Dantzig. The reason of the journey is remarkable. Gray, the Company's agent, had discovered that the season in the North was mild, and the Arctic was not much frozen. He therefore hoped to get the news home to England, through Dantzig, in time for a summer voyage to be undertaken " to discover Cataia "—in other words, to reach China by the North-East Passage. At midnight, 26th February 1558, Alcocke was arrested in a village in Poland, and was brought to a town which he calls " Tirwill." There, " with a payre of fetters clapped on my legges," he languished for some time. On Saint George's Day the Marshal told him that the King had ordered that he should be " delivered out of prison to depart into England, but no way else." He added that " I might thanke God that I escaped with my head, and that if ever there came any more of us through the land, they should not so doe." They took almost everything from him, including his sword, his boots, his money, and " a booke of the Flowres of godly prayers." He was kept five-and-thirty days more, and then taken by the Captain into a great chamber, " to bee examined for letters and of the cause of my comming through the country. In the Captain's companie was one of the Lordes of Danske " (Dantzig). Alcocke told them the reason of his journey, which, he pleaded, would not only be of service to England, but to all Christian lands. He was next questioned as to the wares the English had taken to Russia, and charged with doing a contraband trade in arms : " Then they burdened mee, that wee brought thither thousandes of ordinance, as also of harneis, swordes, with other munitions of warre, artificers, copper, with many other things. I made them answere, that wee had brought thither about one hundred shirtes of mayle, such olde thinges newe scowred as no man in Englande would weare."

All this is written by Alcocke to Richard Gray and Henry Lane, the Company's agents in Russia. How the letter was smuggled through does not appear, but it contains news that must have made Lane and Gray start as they read it :

" At my comming hither heere were Ambassadours from the townes of Danske, Lübeck, Hamburgh, as also out of Liefland [1] to desire this King to be their Captaine and head in their intended voyage, which was to stoppe all such shippes as shoulde goe out of England for Moscovia. Whereunto the King graunted, and immediately they departed to prepare their shippes. So that I am afraide that either these our enemies, or the great warres that we have with France and Scotland, will be an occasion that you shall have no shippes at Colmogro this yeere."

The true inwardness of this story will be understood when it is remembered that Dantzig had, a short time before, cast off its allegiance to the Grand-Masters of Prussia, who were thought to be too complaisant to the English trade, and had transferred its allegiance to the Kings of Poland. Poland rewarded Dantzig by trying to shut Narva to English trade. King Sigismund explains his policy to Queen Elizabeth in a letter dated 6th December 1559, remarkable as containing almost the first printed statement of that campaign of calumny which has been used ever since to estrange England from Russia : " . . . We know and feele of a surety, the Muscovite, enemy to all liberty under the heavens, daily to grow mightier by the increase of such things as be brought to the Narve, while not only wares but also weapons heretofore unknowen to him, and artificers and arts be brought unto him : by means whereof he maketh himself strong to vanquish all others. Which things as long as this voyage to Narve is used cannot

---

[1] John Lucke, another servant of the Company, was imprisoned by the Leifelanders in 1559.

be stopped. And we perfectly know your Majesty cannot be ignorant how great the cruelty is of the said enemy, of what force he is, what tyranny he useth on his subjects, and in what servile sort they be under him. We seemed hitherto to vanquish him onely in this, that he was rude of arts, and ignorant of policies. If so be that this navigation to the Narve continue, what shall be unknowen to him ? Therefore we that know best and border upon him, do admonish other Christian princes in time, that they do not betray their dignity, liberty, and life of them and their subjects to a most barbarous and cruell enemy, as we can no less do by the duty of a Christian Prince."

Here we see the whole policy of the Hanse and of Germany laid bare : Russia is to be kept in ignorance, to be bullied, browbeaten, and cheated, by means of superior weapons, superior knowledge, and superior cunning. Prussia is to fatten on a monopoly of trade with these inhuman barbarians. If England dares to trade with Russia, her merchants are to be imprisoned and her ships are to be sunk. And to enforce this policy the English Government is to be given the impression that Russia is " the enemy of liberty," and the enslaver of her people. When Englishmen hear this story next, let them remember Thomas Alcocke in irons, and the Lords of Dantzig, and let them remember the conspiracy of the Hanseatic cities " to stoppe all such shippes as should goe out of England for Moscovia."

With such enemies it is no matter for wonder if English trade did not prosper in Russia. The Russian revolt against the German Hanse was subdued by bribery. " The Dutch nation are free of this," writes John Hasse from Russia in 1554 ; " notwithstanding for certain offences they had lost their priveledges which they have recovered this summer to their great charge. It was reported to me by a Justice of that country, that they paied for it thirtie thousand rubbles." The dangers and hardships of the White Sea route and Hanseatic competition made the enterprise unprofitable. But the great adventure remains as a heroic chapter in the annals of English commerce. It was a magnificent scheme, well planned and boldly executed. Servants of the Company explored Nova Zembla and the Sea of Kara ; they opened a river and caravan route from Archangel to the Caspian. In 1558 Anthony Jenkinson reached Bokhara in a vain endeavour to get to China by the overland route. The faithful Alcocke was murdered in Persia in 1566. And the friendship then struck up between Russian and Englishman remains traditional to this day, despite the organised hypocrisy of the German and his ally, the German and Russian Jew.[1]

---

[1] The sources of this chapter may be consulted in Hakluyt (vols. ii. and iii.), which contains the reports, letters, instructions and charters of the Russia Company, and correspondence between the Emperor Feodor and Queen Elizabeth, and between Lord Burghley and the Emperor's brother-in-law and "Protector," Boris. The letter from Sigismund II, King of Poland, to Queen Elizabeth will be found in vol. ii. pp. 485-487.

CHAPTER XVII

PHILIP AND MARY

THE fair promise of Edward VI ended in tragedy and conflict. The boy king died, it is said, of consumption.

Northumberland, with whom Gresham had practised for the downfall of the Hanse, attempted to secure a Protestant (and Dudley) succession by putting Lady Jane Grey on the throne. He failed, and he was beheaded. Mary had always boasted of her Spanish blood, and leant upon the Emperor. The Emperor's hand was deep in English politics. He was concerned in the fall of Somerset,[1] and is said to have plotted that business with Warwick. If Warwick—afterwards Northumberland—practised 'with the Emperor, then he must afterwards have practised against him, and the end of practising against Charles V was usually the block. Mary depended on the Emperor. The Emperor had great hopes of Mary. In 1550 he sent a member of his Council, called Seepper, to kidnap Mary and take her to Antwerp ; but this promising scheme failed owing to the vigilance of our fleet. When the practising Northumberland was defeated and Mary was proclaimed Queen in London, the Hanse and the Emperor's Party counted it a victory. Mary was not only a good Catholic, but,

---

[1] Marin Cavalli, Venetian Ambassador with the Emperor, to the Doge and Council of Venice (12th January 1550): " The news of the release of the Protector of England was heard here with no little regret, as it will apparently be the ruin of the Earl of Warwick, with whom his Imperial Majesty has an understanding (*praticha*), and it has been hinted to me on authority, that the arrest of the Protector and these late risings in London had their root in this Court."—*Cal. State Papers* (Ven.), vol. v. p. 298.

it was hoped, a good German, a good " Imperialist."
These hopes may or may not have been heightened
when the Queen made that Vicar of Bray, the Archbishop Stephen Gardiner, her Chancellor, and, as we
should say, Prime Minister. " In the Lord Chancellor," says Lappenberg, " the Hanse found a man
who had been for many years conversant with their
affairs, thanks to his earlier mission to Hamburg and
Lübeck "—the " sacred friendship," in fact[1]—and when
an embassy, consisting of the most prominent councillors of Lübeck, Cologne, Bremen, Hamburg, and
Dantzig, approached the Queen, they were graciously permitted to reopen the question of their privileges. In
November 1553 their privileges were confirmed. At the
same time the English Parliament granted the Queen
a subsidy tonnage and poundage on wines and other
goods, as imported by foreigners, including the Hanse,
and also export duties on cloth, skins, and leather.[2]

By January 1554 the " Ambassador of the Free
Cities of the Hans " procured an edict from the Queen
exempting the Steelyard from duties and taxes not
in accord with their privileges as granted by Henry
VIII. By March 1st the " Aldermen and the Company
of the Steelyard " had secured the abolition of the
restrictions on the export of woollen cloth.[3]

Thus even before the marriage with Philip the
Germans were scoring all along the line, not without murmurs in England. But when the match was

---

[1] Gardiner, however, was unfaithful to his German friends, and seems to
have practised against them in the Privy Council, while pretending to support
them in the Court. Family connections may have had their influence. Gardiner
was "the reputed son of a cloth-worker." Thomas Cromwell, by the way, was
the same, and had been a Merchant Adventurer.

[2] *Statutes of the Realm*, vol. iv, S. 1, p. 218.

[3] Imposed in 1535 and 1536, and in 1541 and 1542. It was these restrictions, no doubt, which prompt the German historians to regard Wolsey and
Cromwell as hostile to the Hanse. They were obviously intended to protect
the English cloth industry.

announced, the murmurs increased to open rebellion. Gardiner, who in the time of Henry VIII had distinguished himself by opposing the divorce, supporting the divorce, and advising " a middle course," was now both supporting the match and practising with the House of Commons against it. " He managed dexterously," says Hume,[1] " to vote an address to the Queen praying her not to marry a foreigner."

The men of Kent saw in the marriage the triumph of their enemies and the final destruction of the cloth industry. When the imperial envoys landed in Kent, in January 1554, a crowd nearly killed Count Egmont, whom they mistook for Philip. When they arrived in London, " the people nothing rejoicing held down their heads sorrowfully," and " the street urchins pelted their retinue with snowballs." At Hampton Court the Queen had to make a public declaration of her patriotism. " Fixing her eyes on the ring that had been placed on her finger at her coronation, she told the envoys to bear in mind that the realm was her first husband." [2]

But by this time the men of Kent had risen, and were being led to London by Sir Thomas Wyatt. By the time he reached Deptford he had 15,000 men. He marched on Southwark, and the City of London seemed on the verge of embracing his cause. But the Queen after all was a Tudor. Just as Wyatt was reaching Southwark she rode to the Guildhall and appealed to the citizens. As for the marriage, she gave her promise that unless Parliament approved of her choice she would not wed.

London was saved, and the rebellion suppressed. " I will not now tell," says Soranzo, " of the great danger which then threatened the City of London, as, had

[1] *Two English Queens and Philip*, p. 36.   [2] Hume, *ibid.*, p. 272.

Wyatt succeeded, the foreigners at least would have been sacked, it being quite certain that the Londoners had an understanding with him ; nor could any better means be devised for keeping them in check, as they had already commenced rioting, than for her Majesty to go in person through the City to the Guildhall," &c.[1]

But the match was important to the Emperor for several reasons. There was, first of all and most important, the prospect of securing the help of England against France. But besides that obvious advantage, there were others. Charles, like most really great men, was in perpetual embarrassment for money. His creditors were continually pressing him. On 7th March 1554, when negotiations for the match were in progress, the Venetian Senate reports that the Emperor had sent an Ambassador to England to hasten on the marriage, that he had summoned a Diet at Augsburg for Easter, and that " in Flanders negotiations were on foot to obtain from the States of these Provinces a considerable sum of money."[2]

On 22nd July 1554 the Venetian Ambassador with the Emperor reports from Brussels that the King of Spain had brought 3,000,000 ducats—300,000 for the Queen of England, 1,000,000 for the merchants, and the rest for the Emperor. A little later (August 13th) the same agent reports that the Fuggers had " made a bargain with the Court " for 150,000 crowns—Brabant, Flanders, and Holland furnishing a certain quota.

---

[1] *Cal. State Papers* (Ven.), vol. v. p. 561. Wriothesley's *Chronicle* gives a fuller account of the affair, and Foxe (*Acts and Monuments*, vol. vi. p. 414) professes to give the actual speech of the Queen. The story of the rising is well told by J. M. Stone in her *History of Mary* (p. 275, *et seq.*); and she quotes these and other authorities to show how extremely critical the situation was when Mary appealed to Guildhall. Mary escaped only by her courage, for it is evident from the story that neither London nor the Court, nor even the Guards, could be relied upon in so unpopular a cause as this German-Spanish match.

[2] *C.S.P.* (Ven.), vol. v. p. 474.

On August 18th he goes more into detail. Flanders is to give 300,000 crowns; Brabant, 200,000; Holland, Zealand, and other provinces make up the total to 1,000,000. And further, "a bargain (*un partito*) now very near conclusion is being treated with German merchants for 500,000 crowns, to be disbursed by them forthwith to the Emperor in Spain, his Majesty repaying it in these provinces at the end of fifteen months without any interest, security to that amount being given on the *giuri* (the funded debt) in Spain. Of the money received from England, 100,000 crowns have been distributed to the Imperial Army on account of arrears without making any inspection."

Now, it is fairly obvious that the English marriage was a "bull point" with the Emperor: it not only brought him money from Spain and from England, but it pleased the German merchants, whose beloved English privileges were trembling in the balance. The first result, says Rapin, of the alliance with the Emperor was the restoration of the German privileges. It was of special importance to placate the Free Cities at this time, not only because they financed the Emperor in his expensive wars, but because of the Lutheran heresy. "Were it not," says the Venetian Ambassador at Vienna, "for the Emperor and this King of the Romans, who do their utmost to preserve what little religion there is in these territories (the Free Towns), *actum esset.*"[1]

Such, then, were the reasons which prompted our "natural ally" to arrange this English marriage. That they were well understood by Englishmen is shown by Wyatt's rebellion, as well as by the stringent terms of the marriage settlement. Philip was to have no direct

[1] *C.S.P.* (Ven.), vol. v. p. 42.

political power in England; Charles had to content himself with Mary's secret promise to Renard, that "notwithstanding the conditions, the will of the Emperor should prevail in England after the marriage."[1]

The marriage can hardly be described as a union of hearts. Egmont, who had received such a rough reception in Kent, did his best to make it popular, but failed. "I should like your Highness to know," he wrote to Philip, "that the Emperor has not provided us with a sou to spend on necessary presents. More can be done here with money than anywhere else in the world."[2] Philip was advised by his friends to put on a coat of mail under his doublet. "I am not going to a marriage feast," he said, "but to a fight." His means of ingratiating himself were perhaps a little awkward. The treasure he brought with him was displayed to all beholders, "in twenty carts containing four score and seventeen chests, a yard and four inches long, and it was estimated that when it was coined it would produce about £50,000 sterling." The Steelyard merchants were, of course, in great feather : their accounts show that they spent no less than £1000 on the wedding festivities. A Dutchman crowed on the top of St. Paul's,[3] and Philip did his clumsy best to obey instructions about "unbending" by pledging his new country in English beer.

Nevertheless, a chill east wind seemed to blow in the face of the Imperial Prince and his German-Spanish train. Although the heads of Wyatt and his brave

---

[1] Hume, *Two English Queens and Philip*, p. 42.
[2] Hume, *ibid.*, p. 45.
[3] "Then was there one Peter, a Dutchman, stood on the weather-cock of Paul's steeple, holding a streamer in his hand of five yards long, and waving thereof stood some time on the one foot and shook the other, and then kneeled on his knees, to the great marvel of all people."—Stow's *Annals*, p. 616. The German "Pageant" was at Gracechurch Corner (*ibid.*).

men of Kent had been taken down from their spikes, their rueful countenances seemed still to mock the marriage feast. And it was not long before the German merchants began to feel that they were not getting value for all the money they had spent in promoting this natural alliance. "The Hanseatic Ambassadors," says Lappenberg, "had hardly left England when the Privy Council, at the instigation of the City Council of London, started again to restrict the import and the export of the German merchants."

The marriage took place on the 25th July 1554. On the 23rd March 1555,[1] the Ambassadors of the Hanse appeared before the Privy Council at Greenwich to complain of the grievous treatment they were receiving from the Lord Mayor and Aldermen of London. The Germans began by demanding to know if they were, or were not, at liberty to buy and sell in London : " Petimus simplici responso." Although they had committed no offence, and in spite of their privileges, " recenter restituta," the cloth bought by their merchants had been seized, and they could get neither restitution nor indemnity. In the third place, the Lord Mayor was forcing them to pay " quotam salis," contrary to their immemorial rights. Fourthly, whereas the German merchants had always been free to pack their own cloth, " per proprios ministros," the City Packer and his officials were now intruding daily upon the Steelyard, contrary to their liberties, and were vexing them unjustly and intolerably with the maximum exactions. Lastly, they pleaded that the suit of their

---

[1] This is the date given in the Acts of the Privy Council, vol. v. p. 252, but may well be a misprint for 1556. If it were so, the correspondence between the Mayor and the Privy Council given in the same volume would fall into its natural place. The Mayor arrests German cloth and refuses to give it up (p. 116). The Hanse Ambassadors therefore appear before the Privy Council.

old enemy, Baldwin Smith, Examiner of Customs, should be quashed " in perpetuum."

The Council answered just a trifle drily. The Mayor was to give order that the merchants should be allowed to buy cloth at the Steelyard, " without the said Mayor or City's interruption or trouble," either to the merchants or to the clothiers. The cloth which had been arrested should be delivered to the German merchants, but the merchants were bound over to restore it if the case went against them. The Mayor was not to demand " quotam salis " of the Germans, but the Packer of the City or his deputy was to be present at all packings of cloth in the Steelyard, " and view such cloth as he suspecteth, and for his paynes shal have for every shorte packe 6*d*., and for every long packe 8*d*." As for the suit of Baldwin Smith, it was to be " suspended as it is "—an equivocal expression. The Mayor was to allow the Germans to import fish, corn, and other victuals without any " imposition or price " ; but these orders were to continue only for a year. And at the same time a reply was made to the Hanse in Latin on the question of general policy. With many expressions of regard and desire for the old friendly relations, the Privy Council reminded the Germans of the misdoings and abuses which had led to the forfeiture of their privileges. Their Majesties would shortly state their intentions on the subject : in the meantime the Hanse was permitted to export a certain amount of cloth. But the Germans were reminded of the privileges of the Merchant Adventurers in Flanders and Brabant, and were warned not to unpack English cloth in Flanders, Brabant, Holland, and Zealand. They must also give English merchants reciprocity in their own territories.

These evidently were not the old privileges. There

might be a representative of the Empire on the throne, but on the Council there were Englishmen who were determined to protect English trade. The Hanseatic Ambassadors, Sudermann and Plonnies, must have returned raging at such a result after all the expenditure and expectations of the Imperial marriage.

And so the fight proceeds. The Mayor sticks to the German cloth : the Council is just a little dilatory in ordering its restoration. On 23rd December 1556, the Privy Council are informed that the Germans are shipping a large quantity of English cloth to Antwerp, with the intention of selling it there, " contrary to the order taken with the Orators or Commissioners of the Hanse by my said Lords of the Council on 23rd March last." The merchants of the Hanse had of late been bound in a sum of £20,000 to abide by this order. They had excused themselves from entering the bond, and had pleaded for latitude to send a little cloth by way of Antwerp, as there was no direct shipping to Hamburg. This permission had been given for a small amount, on a pledge that there would be no " fraud or covin." As fraud was evidently contemplated, the most stringent orders were given to the General Receivers of Revenue to prevent it. On 14th April 1557, the Steelyard merchants approach the Privy Council with a most humble request to be allowed to pack and ship such coloured cloths as they had bought but had not entered in the Customs House before the end of the term of twelve months allowed them. There were not above two thousand pieces, and it would be permitted " for this time only." In April another embassy appears upon the scene, consisting of the Lübeck Syndicus, Dr. von Vechtelde, and the Cologne Town Councillor, Hermann Sudermann. Their instructions

N

are " to recapture privileges in England of which they had been robbed." They make charges against the customs and against the Judge of the Admiralty Court, which are duly answered, and on 7th July the Privy Council " consult upon some convenient answer," which is duly made in ponderous Latin. It gives them no comfort, for it amounts to a recital of that dreadful case in the reign of Edward VI, by which they had forfeited their privileges.

In making its reply the Privy Council had been fortified by a whole armoury of " books and writings," which are returned, on 22nd August, " sealed upp in a bagge," to " Mr. Doctour Wootton," probably the secretary of the Merchant Adventurers' Company. The list begins with a " Defensio mercatorum Anglie contra Hanzianos mense Junij 1558," and ends with " A compendious declaracion of injuryes doone to the merchaunts, owners, maisters and maryners of Englonde by Hans Brandois, Boroughmasters and others naming themselves Lordes of the towne of Dantezick, 1557." [1]

And on the 30th August there is an entry [2] which discloses to us the inner meaning of the whole reign.

" A lettre to Mr. Anthony Hussey, Governour of the Marchauntes Adventurers, that whereas ambassadors of the Stedes, that have been here for the matter of the Stillyarde presently departed hence, he is required in the Quenes Majesties name to use all the best wayes and meanes he can to understande whither they take their journey directly home to their cuntrey orelles (or else) that they goo to the Kinges Majestie, and to signifye the certentye hereof with all spede ; he is also required to write hither from tyme to tyme such occurrentes as he shall understande."

[1] Acts of Privy Council, vol. vi. pp. 378-9.   [2] *Ibid.*, under that date.

The long fight was won. By the end of August Queen Mary had taken to her chamber ; in less than two months she was dead—a poor, lonely, heart-broken monument to the natural alliance. Philip had deserted both her and England. He had failed the Steelyard, and the Germans, who called him a Spaniard, never forgave him.[1]

He had failed also in his policy of using England against France. " I do not know what to make of these people," Feria wrote to his master in despair. Mary made promises, but her subjects defeated them. In March 1558 she sent Gresham to Antwerp to borrow £100,000. Gresham, who never failed to get money when he really wanted it, could only raise £10,000. " He deserves punishment at your Majesty's hands," Feria wrote to the King. London was asked to contribute £80,000, but met the demand with endless evasions.

There was no doing anything with these English. The whole nation, in fact, had set its face like flint against Spain and against the Empire. Although Wyatt's head had fallen, the men of Kent and the Merchant Adventurers had won. Mary might grant privileges, the King might favour the Hanse, but the Council, the Lord Mayor, the Aldermen, the Sheriffs, the Judges were all in a conspiracy with the whole country to make the privileges of no avail.

---

[1] In 1561 the Venetian Ambassador with Philip reports that he was " thoroughly disliked by the Flemings and hated by the Germans." " Moreover, contrary to the custom of the Emperor, he takes no notice of Italians and Flemings, and least of all Germans."—C.S.P. (Ven.), vol. vii. pp. 331-2.

CHAPTER XVIII

A GAME OF CHESS

" OBSERVE, by the way," says Fuller, " how God set up a generation of military men, both by sea and land, which began and expired with the reign of Queen Elizabeth, like a suit of clothes made for her, and worn out with her." And that is true. But her great men were not only warriors; they were statesmen and merchants, poets and dramatists. Her England was a sphere, a perfect round, following its own course in harmony. In the reign of Mary we see a sullen England, working against its Queen, spying on its King. Now we see an England full of a sweet accord, working in unity for great ends. And if we inquire into the reason of this harmony, we must reach the conclusion that it is because at last England has a monarch whom it can trust to the uttermost, whom it knows will always prefer an Englishman over a foreigner, and an English interest over any other interest in the world.

The Queen, let us remember, was a daughter of Anne Boleyn. Anne Boleyn was the descendant of a Merchant Adventurer, and had been insulted by the Germans. She herself had suffered many things from the foreigner. And Queen Elizabeth had this fine quality, that she never forgot and seldom forgave an injury. But apart altogether from her mood and temper, she derived her whole strength from the English Party. Mary had leant upon the Emperor, and was

hated by her subjects.   Elizabeth leaned upon Englishmen, and was hated by foreigners.   Her greatest work,
as it seems to me, was to make England a country for
the people of England ; her eternal fame is that she
defeated the Armada ; but I imagine that in her own
time she was loved even more because she drove out
the Germans.   It is a side of her policy that has been
strangely overlooked by the historian.   Froude has
nothing at all to say on the subject.   But it is nevertheless true that she fought as great and as victorious
a fight with the Germans as with Spain.

When she came to the throne in 1558, she received
some excellent advice from Thomas Gresham.[1]   Here
it is :

(1) To refine her currency.

" (2) Nott to restore the Stillyarde to ther usorpid
privelidges.

" (3) To grant as few licences as you can.[2]

" (4) To come in as small debt as you can beyond seas.

" (5) To keep up your credit, and specially with your
own merchants, for it is they must stand by you at all
events in your necessity."

And it was on the point of the German trade that
Gresham laid his greatest emphasis :

" The great freedom of the Steelyard and granting
of licence for the carrying of your wool and other
commodities out of your realm, which is now one of
the chief points that your Majesty hath to foresee
in this your Commonweal ; that you never restore the
' Steydes called the Stillyarde ' again to their privilege,
which hath been the chiefest point of the undoing of
this your realm, and the merchants of the same."

[1] Burgon, *Life of Gresham*, vol. i. App. xxi.   The letter was preserved
among the Burghley papers.   Cecil shaped his policy on Gresham's advice.
[2] Licences to foreigners to export wool and undressed cloth.

Now it is strange and characteristic that, while Froude, the historian, never mentions Germany, Gresham, the contemporary, does not mention Spain. To Gresham the real enemy of England is the Hanseatic League, the Steelyard, the German towns, and their Free Trade privileges.

And this policy is followed by the Queen steadily, cautiously, relentlessly. The Germans are not so much driven as gradually squeezed out of England. We have seen how, in the reign of Mary, the Privy Council ordained that an official " packer " should watch the German shipments.[1]   In 1564—" Mr. Cecil," by the way, being at that time secretary—the Privy Council decides that " some person of credit besides the Packer, should for the Queen and for the Merchant Adventurers see the packing of all the cloths of the said Merchants of the Steelyard for discerning of the colour of the said cloths," &c. The Privy Council is careful to add that no offence is meant either to the official Packer or to the Germans ; but the object of the precaution is reasonably clear.

The Hanse in the meantime is scheming and plotting desperately either to capture or intimidate Elizabeth. In 1560 Gresham is in Antwerp trying to raise money for the Queen. He finds Antwerp mysteriously tight ; but Count Mansfeld, " a German nobleman of the highest rank and distinction,"[2] offers him £40,000. He accepts the offer with eagerness. The Count employs one Hans Keck, who takes in Gresham so completely that he sends him to the Council in Eng-

---

[1] " Foreigners were not permitted to live in the wharfs, with the exception of the Steelyard, which got the most extended privileges regarding the handling of wares—a testimony to the honesty which the custom authorities found amongst the Germans of the Steelyard."—Lappenberg.

[2] *The Unsuspecting Burgon*, vol. i. p. 337.

land. To Gresham's annoyance, Keck lingers in England, but ultimately returns. In the meantime "the Countie of Mansfylde hath given marvellous interteynment to my factor." Gresham is enthusiastic. "Sir," he writes to Cecil, "doughtless the Count of Mansfild is a joylly gentillman and valliant and marvellus well loved of the nobells and captaynes of Saxony." And he goes on to describe how Clough, the factor, had been overwhelmed with honours: "In the presence of all these nobelmen, there was no remedy but my factor must first waysse (? wash) alone, and fyrst sett at the table being marvelously sumtuously served." Not only so, but the Count offered to give the Queen £75,000 at 10 per cent.—a very low rate in those days. "And then came the County's Chancellor and presented to my factor in his master's name a silver standing-cup of the value of xx lib.; and the Countess sent him by one of her gentillwomen a little feather of gold and silver of the value of x lib. and thanked him for the paynes he took in his journey." Overwhelming, in fact!

The Count sent Gresham a letter; but some things he would not trust to paper, and one of them seems to have been that he would lend the Queen even more than the sum he had named—400,000 dollars more, " provided that the Queen would give him the bond of the Merchants of the Steelyard."

There Gresham drew back, in spite of the silver cup and the 10 per cent. He would not accept the condition, and the negotiations fell through.

Since nothing was to be done by guile, other forms of pressure were brought to bear. In 1563 the Duchess of Parma forbade the importation of English cloth into Flanders. Her pretext was the plague then in England, but her true reason was to force Free Trade upon Elizabeth.[1]

It was a measure most formidable to England, even if it had been taken by Flanders alone, for by that time England was sending to the Netherlands above 200,000 pieces of cloth per annum, to the value of about 5,000,000 crowns, or £1,000,000 sterling.[2] But the Germans were working in concert with the Regent of the Netherlands. If they did not inspire, they lent their strength to the blow. This is shown beyond dispute in a letter from Antwerp to Cecil:[3] " Has received a letter from the merchants at Emden, who are informed that, upon suit from the Low Countries, the Hanse Towns have consented to the banishment of all English cloth out of their countries for six years, as well for the great customs they pay, as also for their privileges." Here indeed was a blow to English trade : at two strokes it was prohibited in its two chief markets, Germany and Flanders. England, in fact, was excommunicated, as she had been in the time of Simon de Montfort, and again in the time of Warwick : the Hanse had launched

[1] *Cal. S. P.* (Foreign), 1564–65, pp. 52–53. Also John Wheeler, *Treatise of Commerce*, p. 51 : " Whenas through the complaint of the Merchants of Antwerp principallie, and of others of the said low Countries, against the raising of the custome of Clothe and of foreign Wares brought into England, and specially against an Act of Parliament made for the setting of her Majesties people on worke, by virtue whereof foreign wares, as Pinnes, Knives, Hattes, Girdles, Ribbin, and such like, were forbidden to be brought in ready wrought, to the intent that Her Highnes' subjects might be employed in making thereof, the said Duchesse of Parma, by proclamation forbadd the carying into England of anie kind of matter or thing, wherewith the said wares might be made, and banished out of the low countries all manufacture or handie-work as Bayes, &c., made in England, clothe and kersye onely excepted, which also shee afterwards forbad to be brought in upon payne of confiscation, under shew or pretence of infection (for that the plague had raigned very sore in London and other places of the realm that sommer) but in verie truth the right cause was, for that shee could not have her will in the above-mentioned pointes," &c. Another grievance was the English shipping laws : Englishmen were now compelled to pay higher custom dues if they used foreign ships. —*Cal. S. P.* (Foreign), 1564, p. 52.

[2] Anderson, vol. ii. p. 127. Giucciardini's description of the Netherlands.

[3] From John Fitzwilliams, the English agent there, dated 21st August 1564. *Cal. S. P.* (Foreign), 1564–65, p. 191.

its heaviest thunderbolt. But this time there is no Free Trade Party in England ready to back the foreigner, and there is a Government with courage to reply blow for blow. Thus we find a decree of the Privy Council, on 8th August 1564, " to call earnestly uppon the Stylliarde to write to Cullen (Cologne) to discharge the impost set upon our merchants for the clothes they carye between Empden and Frankeforde, orelles (or else) some remedy must be taken here. And for the present shippeng of woolles yt is thought good the same were staied for a month untill upon furder conference with the King of Spaines Embassadour resident here, yt might be more fully understanded to what ende we shall grow for the differences in the Low Cuntreyes," &c. Here, then, is the reply to both Germany and Flanders : the Steelyard is threatened with reprisals, and the Flemish clothmakers are threatened with the loss of English wool.

And now let us watch this wonderful game of chess developing. The Merchant Adventurers, with their cloth on board ship " for five months together " in the Thames and the Scheldt, are refused permission to unload at Antwerp, the Regent's prohibitions being issued in November and December 1563. By 22nd February 1564 " Anne Countess of East Friesland, and Erdtzard, Christopher, and John, Earls and Lords of the same," have given to the Merchant Adventurers " full passport, free abiding and safe conduct in Emden." [1] No time is lost, it will be seen, and no time could be lost. " Their merchants break every day," writes Mason to Challoner on March 23rd, of the Netherlands merchants ; and probably the English were also in a bad way.[2] Earl John is promised a pension of 3000 crowns

---

[1] *Cal. S. P.* (Foreign), 1564, p. 58.   [2] *Ibid.*, pp. 84–85.

by the Queen and taken into her service, and the Emden market is advertised all over Germany.[1]

On May 6th Fitzwilliams writes to Cecil from Antwerp that the merchants of the Netherlands have been forbidden to go to Emden to traffic with the merchants of England. He adds that " they of this town (Antwerp) would spend a good piece of money to have the traffic between both countries in the old order again."[2] By May 9th Philip is trying to get English wool into Bruges.[3] By May 27th Antwerp is pressing its Governor hard for a peace, and is also writing to Cecil desiring his assistance in restoring matters to their former footing.[4] By June 17th there is " good hope " of the English market in Emden prospering.[5] By June 24th, however, Thomas Aldersey reports from Emden that " the practices are marvellous to keep merchants from them. . . . Certain Easterlings persuade others that are willing to buy that they should forbear . . . the Commissioners of Cologne hinder other men from giving aid and showing friendship. By these means and others the writers are so straitened that unless the Queen and her Council provide that her restraint be kept they shall sustain loss and shame."[6] Evidently it is a close thing. By July 25th, Challoner from Madrid fears Emden will be frozen in the winter, and wonders if there is a chance of peace. By August 1st Cecil gives instructions to treat with the Spanish Ambassador for the opening of trade on both sides. By August 21st the Hanse have decided on the banishment of English cloth for six years.[7] By August 24th there is news that " many hundreds of men are gone out of Antwerp to Emden."[8]

---

[1] *Cal. S. P.* (Foreign), 1564, p. 105.   [2] *Ibid.*, p. 125.
[3] *Ibid.*, p. 129.   [4] *Ibid.*, p. 142.
[5] *Ibid.*, p. 158.   [6] *Ibid.*, p. 164.
[7] *Ibid.*, p. 191.   [8] *Ibid.*, p. 192.

It is a near thing, but the Queen wins. "At length," says Wheeler, "when the King of Spain, for all the instigation of his Netherlanders and Popish Ministers, saw that hee could not prevaile, and were at a stand, he and they were glad, and fayne to come to a provisional agreement, and to accept of such privileges and liberties as the said Netherlanders enjoyed in England in the last year of Queen Marie's reigne . . . and to call in all those aforesaid placates, edicts and prohibitions made against the Englishe, and bringing in of English wares." The fight lasted about a year : it was fought without bloodshed, but it was none the less a great and glorious victory.

In 1568 this strange war broke out again. The immediate cause was that a Biscayan ship had been chased into Plymouth by the French, and that there was some little dispute between Elizabeth and Philip over the ownership of the treasure it contained. The Duke of Alva seized all the goods and ships of the English merchants at Antwerp. The Queen replied by arresting the Netherlanders and their goods in England. The trade between the two countries was stopped, and English cloth was once more "without a vent." But Cecil had foreseen the rupture, and had been busy detaching Hamburg. Even in the previous fight that city had displayed a "coming-on" attitude, which encouraged the English to hope more from her than from Emden. The Ems was inconveniently close to the Netherlands border : Philip acted there as if he were Emperor. The Drossart of Emden, Ocko Freeze by name, was "very much inclined to the Spanish Party," and even the Earl—possibly because his "pension" was in arrears—had not been altogether satisfactory. On the other hand, Richard Clough, Gresham's agent, reported unfavourably of the Prussian character. " The Hamburgers," he said, " are a kind of people rude and nothing inclined to our nature, envious and beggarly both of goods and wits, incivil in manners and without all mercy where they are masters." But any port in a storm. And just as the Germans in the present war had prepared beforehand their position on the Marne, so Cecil and Gresham had prepared their position at Hamburg. In 1566 John Gilpin, the secretary of the Company, was sent to arrange the matter. On 19th July 1567 three English envoys signed a contract for ten years with the Senate of Hamburg. So that, when the war broke out in the following year, the English cloth trade had a snug Hamburg roof over its head. In April 1569 a great English fleet of twenty-eight well-equipped ships, laden with cloth and wool to the value of 700,000 thalers, left the Thames for Hamburg. The goods sold so well that the merchants declared they could do without Antwerp ; and on August 25th of the same year a second great fleet, convoyed by two men-o'-war, sailed for the same port. The sum total of the export to Hamburg in 1569 was estimated at 2,500,000 thalers.[1]

This was a terrible blow to Spain and to Antwerp. Philip saw the wealth on which he depended departing from the Netherlands, and, what was even worse, he had a shrewd suspicion that Cecil was using this commercial opening to push the Protestant cause in the North, and to supply the Protestant Princes with the means for revolt.[2] Antwerp, which had been created by English trade, which for English cloth had betrayed the looms of the Netherlands, and had become by Eng-

---

[1] Bertrand de Salignac, *Correspondance diplomatique*, vol. i. pp. 154–238.
[2] *Ibid.*

lish enterprise " the pack-house of Europe," the rival
and successor of Bruges, now saw her chief source of
wealth withdrawn. But to the Hanse the blow was
even more deadly. For years it had been falling into
a slow decay, and living mainly on the hopes dangled
before the Steelyard by the English Government.
Its trade now rested, not on the secure rock of unques-
tioned privileges and the favour of kings, but upon
yearly licences served out grudgingly, as charity is
given to strangers. Thus, in 1550–1555, the loading
of 50,000 pieces of cloth was permitted every Easter ;
in 1560–1562, 40,000 ; and in 1570–1575, only 30,000
pieces. As the English merchant service grew in
capacity to deal with English trade, so the licences to
German shippers were decreased. Cecil had told Denmark that he would never restore the Hanseatic privileges, because they were injurious to the trade of
England ; but the Hanse continued to scold and to
complain. " They do not seem to comprehend at all,"
says Sartorius, " the spirit which lived in this Queen,
nor the totally altered conditions of Europe, but continued to babble of their ancient priveleges "[1]—" their
olde antiquated and obsolete privileges," as Wheeler
calls them. But decay is a slow and disregarded process in empires as in persons : it needs the shock of a
great event to teach a man or a country that he is no
longer what he was. And this great event came to
the Hanse when Hamburg, its chief North Sea port,
made a separate contract with England.

The Hanse Day of 1572 at Lübeck was a day of
recrimination and bitterness. Hamburg had betrayed
Germany : she was false to the Hanse. The contract

---

[1] Georg Sartorius (*Geschichte des Hanseatischen Bundes*, vol. iii. pp. 360 *et
seq.*) is my chief authority for the following pages.

must be annulled.   It is easy to imagine lean and half-
starved virtue clamouring against the fat and prosperous
traitor.   They were all hungry : Hamburg was full of
bread—or, rather, cloth—and she justified herself with
a most irritating complacency.   If she had not received
the Merchant Adventurers, they would have gone again
to an outside town, like Emden, and dealt there with
strangers and Hanse merchants alike.   By her contract
she had obtained for the whole Hanse a somewhat
larger licence for the export of cloth from London, and
she had also secured protection against the English
pirates.   That, surely, was better than nothing.   But
if the Hanse insisted on Hamburg revoking her contract,
let them well consider the consequences, for in that
case, however reluctantly, she would withdraw her
representatives from the Common Council.

It was a terrible moment, and the Hanse was helpless.   Everywhere their domination had crumbled ;
everywhere the Queen was prepared.   In 1572, the
very year of this painful scene, Elizabeth had concluded
a treaty with Charles IX of France for joint action to
protect their commerce in the Netherlands, Germany,
Prussia, and Sweden.   Friendly negotiations had long
been proceeding between Denmark and England for
a treaty of defence against the League.   As for the
Emperor, he no longer counted : the glory of the
Empire had departed with Charles V.   Philip was the
real head of the imperial family, and the towns never
trusted Philip after his dismal failure to protect their
interests in England.

Still steps must be taken, and there were three things
which might be done—force Hamburg back into the
fold, excommunicate English trade, and supply Philip
with the means to conquer England.   Upon this pro-

gramme they set themselves to work, while Queen Elizabeth on her side continued the process of slow strangu-
lation. By 1576 it was declared at a meeting of the
towns that their annual export of undressed white cloth
had fallen from eight to five thousand pieces per annum,
and licences even for that amount were difficult to obtain. It was also reported by George Usemann, the
secretary of the Steelyard, that Elizabeth's relations
with other Powers made the time for striking opportune.
A strong policy would bring her to reason. In 1576
Lübeck decreed that the English must leave Hamburg.
The Privy Council tried to avert the blow by promising
more licences : they might go so far as 12,000 pieces.
The Steelyard was all for accepting a compromise, but
Lübeck stood firm : a strong policy, said the chief of
the League, is the only way to bring England to reason.
Then Elizabeth begins to strike hard. All licences for
the export of cloth are revoked ; the Mayor of London
begins proceedings against the Steelyard ; and on 7th
April 1579 all their remaining privileges, except their
freehold rights in the Steelyard and in other ports, are
revoked. At the same time the Queen gives a royal
charter to a company of Merchant Adventurers trading
to Eastland—the very land of the Easterlings.

Queen Elizabeth, it will be noticed, always keeps
something in reserve : the Steelyard itself, the symbol
of Hanseatic power, is left to the Hanse, although the
reality is taken away. For the Queen knows with whom
she is dealing. And the shrewdness of her calculations
is shown by a letter from Hamburg to Bremen of 21st
April 1580—a nervous, quavering letter : " One ought
not to enrage the Queen—the Steelyard may—which
God forbid—fall into the hands of the Merchant Adventurers ! "

In this same letter a reference is made to the " three towns chiefly concerned "—a phrase which opens out a deep conspiracy against the peace of England. In 1579 it is laid down that, in case the Queen should not give in, Lübeck, Hamburg, and Bremen are to sit in permanent committee on English affairs. According to this resolution, the first measure to be taken is a counter-vailing duty levied on English ships and wares, equal to the amount levied on the Germans in England ; the second step is to treat the English in the Hanse towns as hostages, and sequestrate part of their goods : these proceedings are called caution and contra-caution. If these do not succeed, the quarrel is to be made the business of the Empire. And, lastly, the three cities are to treat with Spain, whose enmity against England is notorious.[1]

The enforcement of caution and counter-caution found the Hanse divided and inefficient. Lübeck, the brain of the League, is all for severe measures ; Cologne is won over to the Lübeck view by the Hanseatic Syndicus ; Dantzig, Brunswick, and the masters of the *Kontors* all vote for severity ; but Hamburg is against all sharp measures, and in practice the towns are too much interested in the English cloth trade to enforce the measures.

The towns appeal to the Emperor, and the Electors assemble at Prague on 8th January 1580. The Hanse demands the expulsion of the Merchant Adventurers from the Empire ; they had raised the price of cloth by about 100 per cent., and they were disgraceful monopolists, who deserved no mercy. Above all, they must be expelled from Emden.

---

[1] Sartorius adds that this programme was first sketched out in 1557 and elaborated in 1579.

As a result of these representations the plenipotentiary of the Hanse, Calixt Schein, Syndicus of Lübeck, receives a letter from the Emperor to the Counts of East Friesland, commanding them to expel the English from Emden. Rudolf II also writes strongly to the Queen, and King Stephen of Poland backs him up with another letter to her Majesty. The Queen's reply gives no comfort. As for the Count of East Friesland, he is impenitent, and applies for help to the Queen. She hastens to send Ambassadors to Denmark, Poland, Prussia, and the Emperor.[1]

Lübeck makes much of the charge that the Merchant Adventurers are a monopoly, because monopolies are forbidden by the laws of the Empire. And a great controversy is started—Is, or is not, the English Company a monopolist? The town of Frankfort, asked for its impartial opinion, replies in a sense favourable to the Hanse—the Company is a monopoly. The town of Lübeck is absolutely certain on the point, and submits to the Emperor a report of such length that the Imperial Councillors refuse to read it until it is compressed into reasonable dimensions. Longston reports to Walsingham of the " lewd, untrue, and most unhonest libels blown and scattered abroad by the Hanse, stede of Lübeck, and others. . . . A man can now come almost in no company where any talk is had in these parts of general traffic and merchants, but one piece is of the English merchants monypolion."[2] The controversy travels to England, and is taken up by certain disgruntled " stragglers " and " outports," well-primed, as Wheeler insinuates, with stockfish and Rhenish wine.

[1] I still depend mainly on Sartorius; but see also Acts of the Privy Council and *Cal. S. P.* (Foreign) for this period.
[2] *Cal. S. P.* (Foreign), 1582, p. 442 ; see also *ibid.*, p. 550, a "Petition of the Merchant Adventurers touching the Slander of Monopoly their Traffic is charged withal."

In the meantime George Gilpin is sent to the Emperor's Court at Augsburg to prepare against the Diet. On 27th July 1581 he writes to Walsingham : " Great want generally amongst them of money, many debts and divers suitors for payment ; credit very small, charge great and least provision . . . almost all the Court hispaniolated ; such force have the King of Spain's pensions whereof most of those belonging to the House of Austria are provided." He also reports that the Hanse is making great and continual complaints against the Adventurers and the Earl of Emden. On 1st or 2nd September 1582, Herle writes that " the Free Towns will condescend to no contributions before their griefs are remedied." According to the Venetian Ambassador in Germany, the Hanse represented that forty millions of gold a year was involved in the trade with England, and that this was imperilled by the Tudor policy of raising the duty from 5 to 20 per cent. On 28th October 1582, Thomas Longston wrote to Walsingham that the Princes had resolved to send ambassadors to England before taking further steps—some at least of these Princes being in receipt of English " pensions "—but after the departure of the Princes, " through the lewd and unhonest dealing of the Hanse," [1] the Diet had passed a decree prohibiting the Merchant Adventurers in Germany.

The Emperor seems rather to have used this decree as a threat than enforced it. But the Queen remained undaunted : she replied haughtily that, if the Hanse merchants had grievances in England, the English Courts were the only place in which they could be

[1] *Cal. S. P.* (Foreign), May–Dec. 1582, pp. 418–419. Wheeler, however, says that the decree was obtained " by favour and assistance of the Spanish Ministers and of the princes and prelates of the Roman religion (the most part whereof were at the devotion of the House of Austrich)."

redressed. The Merchant Adventurers have learnt by experience that Germany cannot do without their cloth, and cheerfully continue their trade. Driven out of Hamburg in 1579, they again appear at Emden. This East Frisian town, having been refused entrance into the League, is a thorn in the side of the Hanse. Spain and the Emperor making things too hot in Emden, they are welcomed by Elbing, a Hanse city. The Merchant Adventurers negotiate for entrance into Livland, and English cloth is somehow sold in Nuremberg. When the King of Poland, at the instigation of Dantzig, drives them out of Elbing, they begin negotiations all over again with Hamburg. Sir Richard Saltonstall, Governor of the Merchant Adventurers, and Dr. Giles Fletcher, go to Hamburg to negotiate, but the City Fathers " held themselves very nice and coy." The truth is that they have been visited by Dr. Westendorpe of Gröningen, who brought glad tidings from Spain—" of the great preparation in hand and the invasion intended by the King of Spain against England, of which the Hamburgers (it would seem) conceived no small hope." They therefore excuse themselves, sometimes by " the unwillingness of their Commons, otherwhiles by want of authority from the rest of the Hanse, without whose privity and liking they might not conclude any such thing."

The decayed, old, down-at-heel town of Stade sees its opportunity, offers the Merchant Adventurers all the privileges they can desire, and is at once transformed into a flourishing city, to the utter disgust and chagrin of Hamburg and the rest of the Hanse. The cities, in fact, are beaten at every move, and there now remains nothing but Philip and his Armada.

CHAPTER XIX

CHECKMATE

THE reader will have noted how power has moved in Europe, in the course of our story, from north-east to south-west. The Grand-Master of Prussia has disappeared from the stage. He had sunk, in his latter years, under the suspicion of taking a pension from the Merchant Adventurers, and Dantzig had thereupon transferred her allegiance to the King of Poland. His territories were divided up between the King of Poland and the Electoral House of Brandenburg. The Teutonic Order of Livonia lasted a little longer, but in 1561 Gottard Ketler surrendered to the Poles. " The resigning of the records, the great cross of the order, the archives, the keys of the gates and castle of Riga and all other prerogatives into the hands of the Poles by the said Grand-Master was a sad spectacle, and could not be seen by any lovers of the German name without tears."[1] A year or two earlier the Russians had driven the German merchants out of Novgorod : the Hanse *Kontor* was shifted to Reval, and the Czar replied by seizing Narva and opening the Baltic to English, French, and Dutch commerce. The removal of the staple to Narva gave a pretext to Sweden, and Eric XIV seized the fleet of Lübeck as it was returning from that port, and carried it to Reval and Stockholm. The war which followed lasted eight years, to the further weakening of the League.[2] Denmark, too, had grown independent. In

---

[1] Thannus, lib. 28 ; Anderson, vol. ii. p. 116.   [2] Anderson, vol. ii. p. 104.

1553 Christian III raised the toll of the Sound so much that the great *Kontor* of Bergen became unprofitable to Hanseatic commerce, and the Danes took over a large slice of Hanseatic commerce in the Baltic.[1] By 1579 the Danish fleet was disputing the sovereignty of the Elbe and blockading Hamburg, and the Hanseatic city was fain to purchase peace with a great indemnity. The " upstart towns " of Holland, which, like Emden, had been denied entrance to the League, boldly went to war with the Hanse. In 1511 a Dutch fleet was attacked in the Baltic by the fleet of Lübeck, and was partly rescued by the fleet of Denmark. In 1532 Holland was again at war with the Hanse on account of assistance the Dutch had given to King Christian ; and their wars against the League being a revolt from the Empire, they gradually formed themselves into a political federation in alliance with Denmark and England against Germany and Spain.

All these things could hardly have happened but for the discovery of the New World by Spain and the Cape route by Portugal. Vasco da Gama took the Turk on his undefended rear, and so relieved the pressure on the Empire ; and the Empire, which had been kept together mainly by fear of the Crescent, lost the chief reason for its existence. Spain being unable to finance its vast new trade in America, applied to Antwerp for assistance, and Flanders financed the Spanish trade. The Spaniards lived on Flemish credit,[2] and possibly the natural desire of the debtor to burn the creditor's books may account for the otherwise unaccountable Fury of Antwerp. However that may be, it is probable that the financial dependence of Spain on Flanders led Charles V to make that fatal division of the Empire

---

[1] Anderson, vol. ii. p. 104.   [2] *Cf.* Wheeler, *Treatise of Commerce.*

which united Flanders and Spain under Philip. If Philip had been a man of genius like his father, he might with difficulty have reconciled the interests of Germany and Spain ; being only a man of talent, he was never supported in his world policy by a united Empire.

In 1579 Queen Elizabeth sent William Harborne to Constantinople, and completed the destruction of the Imperial trade system.

In the Middle Ages we saw two great trade routes from Asia to the West. One had its depot at Novgorod, the other at Venice ; the one came by way of Turkestan, the other by way of the Persian Gulf and the Red Sea. Both ended at Hanseatic *Kontors*. But when Anthony Jenkinson is sailing down the Volga with cargoes of English cloth to Astrakhan and the Caspian, when the Turkey Company is doing good business with Constantinople, and Dutch and English ships are competing with Spain and Portugal for the trade of the East and West Indies, it is obvious that the trade routes from Novgorod to the Baltic, and from Venice to Flanders, are no longer in their old position of predominance.

Thus everywhere the German trade system is falling to pieces ; the Court of the Empire subsists on Philip's bounty, and the Hanse, which once looked to Prussia for protection, now looks to Spain. Philip was eager to help. According to Sartorius, he had long pressed the Cities to join with him in an attack on England, and the Cities hesitated, not because they loved the Queen, but because they distrusted the King. But with the failure of " caution and contra-caution," and the miserable fiasco of the Imperial Bull, all hesitation is thrown to the winds, and the Hanse plunges with zeal into the great project of the Spanish Armada.

We have seen the date at which this secret alliance began, and it is easy to trace its progress through the archives of Venice, Simancas, and England. Thus, in 1586, Hieronomo Lipomano, Venetian Ambassador in Spain, reports to the Doge and Senate :

" The City of Hamburg, which governs itself as a Republic, and is hostile to the Queen of England on commercial and other grounds, has sent a letter to the King of Spain offering him the port of Hamburg, which is capable of sheltering a large fleet. The King is also in treaty for the use of another port near Hamburg. Both will be of service to Flanders and for putting some check on the Queen of England."

Poland, as we have seen, is now, owing to its connection with Dantzig, the close ally and protector of the Baltic cities. The King of Poland, as we have also seen, and will see again, is the obedient tool of the League. With this knowledge we are able to understand the significance of a report from the Venetian Ambassador at Madrid : [1]

" The King of Poland recommends the King of Spain if he makes an attack on England to do it seriously, first seizing Ireland and the Isle of Wight, as both of them will afford ports for the fleet. He adds that it would be better to take no steps at all than to take them insufficient to secure a victory. And such great preparations would have the additional advantage of destroying all hope that the Queen of England might indulge in her power to defend herself."

Probably it is to this advice that the Marquis of Santa Cruz refers in the letter he writes to Philip on 4th November 1587 : " If it be really decided to go to England itself I would only observe that this Armada,

---

[1] *Cal. S. P.* (Ven.), vol. viii, 24th August 1586.

even when united with the troops of the Duke of Parma . . . does not seem to me sufficient to attempt this enterprise in the very heart of winter. . . . Nor in my opinion would it be such an easy matter to take the Isle of Wight, or any other harbour, for the shelter of our fleet, *as is represented to your Majesty by those who stake nothing on the risk,* and have not been taught the difference between victory and defeat." [1]

Burghley is well informed on the secret understanding, as we gather from a note in his own handwriting to his friend, the King of Denmark, dated December 1585 : [2]

" To send to the King of Denmark to declare to him how cunningly the merchants of Dantzig, Lübeck, and other ports on the east side of the Sound have this summer-time made great provision of grain and other victual, and of all things belonging to shipping, and carried the same to Spain by passing the north of Scotland and west of Ireland. To require him to consider how hereby the King of Spain hath been furnished for his Navy which he hasteneth to lend all his forces to annoy us," &c.

Six months later, on 17th June 1586, Matheo Zane, Venetian Ambassador in Germany, reports that " a fleet of twenty-five vessels laden with pitch, sails, and shrouds for a large armament sailed from the German ports. To avoid the Breton and English cruisers the route was laid outside England. The fleet sails for Portugal, where these supplies are eagerly desired by the Marquis of Santa Cruz, whose absolute want of such necessaries makes it doubtful if he would be able

[1] *Cal. S. P.* (Ven.), vol. viii. p. 322.
[2] *Navy Records,* Spanish War, 1585–1587, pp. 53–54.

to man his fleet this year and to attack Drake." In 1588, the year of the Armada, we hear from the same source of "twenty Hamburg ships for Lisbon," and the abundant references in the archives show the enormous extent of these supplies.

Again, in 1586, the Venetian Ambassador in Madrid secured a copy of an estimate of supplies and ships for the Armada prepared by the Marquis of Santa Cruz—who but for his timely death was to have taken command. The reader who derives his knowledge of the Armada from James Anthony Froude will rub his eyes when I say that this estimate includes thirty German ships and 12,000 Germans. Did these ships actually form a part of the Armada?

There is no means of finding out that I know; but it is noteworthy that in the squadron of twenty-three " hulks " commanded by Juan Gomes de Medina two have obviously Hanseatic names, the *Barca de Amburg* (600 tons) and the *Barca de Anzic* (450 tons). Two others, the *El Gran Grifon* (650 tons) and the *Falcon Blanco Mayor* (500 tons), which were lost, are called German.[1] I am aware that Van Meteran, who should have known, calls these in his summary of forces " Flemish hulks "; but in the course of his narrative he says : " Sir Francis Drake was giving of chase unto five great hulkes which had separated themselves from the Spanish fleete ; but finding them to be Easterlings (Hanseatics) he dismissed them."[2] The contradiction is rather apparent than real, for the Hanse merchants

---

[1] *Navy Records*, vol. ii, Appendix G. The squadron was of the following strength : 23 ships ; 10,271 tons ; 384 guns ; 3121 soldiers ; 608 marines.

[2] An act of policy on Drake's part, for Burghley was still trying to detach the German cities from the Catholic interest. On 12th June 1587, for example, the Venetian Ambassador in Spain reports that Drake had found two Hamburg ships sailing for Lisbon, but he merely took their powder and some provisions and let them go on their way, " declaring that they were friends, and charging them to tell the Marquis that he was waiting for them."

or Easterlings were sometimes called Flemish, as we have frequently seen in the course of this story.

We may take it, then, as proved that there were Hanseatic ships in the Armada itself, just as there were Flemish, Venetian, Italian, Sicilian, and Levantine ships. For the Spanish Armada was not merely Spanish : it was the total naval power which King Philip's dominions and King Philip's friends, including the Pope and Venice on the one side, and the Hanse on the other, could put on the sea for the purpose.

But the Spanish fleet is chiefly intended to cover the invading army, which the Duke of Parma is preparing in Flanders. Our "joylly" friend, Count Mansfeld, who had so cunningly tried to lure Gresham into the financial meshes of the League, is, by the way, the Duke's second in command. The Duke's plan is elaborate. "He deepened," says Van Meteran, "the channel of Yper, commonly called Yperlee, employing some thousands of workmen in order to transport ships from Antwerp and Ghendt to Bruges, where he had assembled about a hundred ships called hoyes, being well stored with victuals, which hoyes he was determined to have brought into the sea by way of Sluys, or else to have conveyed them by the said Yperlee . . . into any part of Flanders whatsoever." In the river of Waten he caused seventy ships with flat bottoms to be built to carry thirty horses each ; 200 were built at Nieuport and forty-eight ships of war were concentrated at Dunkirk. "And," Van Meteran adds, " (the Duke) *caused a sufficient number of mariners to be levied at Hamburg, Bremen, Embden, and at other places.*" The Duke of Parma's army is partly Italian, partly Walloon, partly Scotch, partly Bur-gundian, partly Dutch, partly Spanish, partly High

German, and partly English (no doubt Catholics and Irish).

Almost needless to say, King Philip is also getting his financial support from Germany. Thus Hieronomo Lippomano writes to his Government, on 29th September 1586 : " The King is negotiating another loan in Germany for two millions of gold at the rate of 200,000 crowns a month in Flanders. There is no difficulty in the way, except the demand for 8 or 10 per cent., as the Fuggers have recently lent at 7." [1]

And again, on 18th October 1586 : " The King has raised another loan from the Fuggers of 500,000 ducats, to be paid in Frankfort, half now and half in March, and a similar loan from Genoese bankers, payable half on December 10 in Milan, and half on the same date in Flanders."

The King and the Duke had neglected nothing. Wheeler asserts that one of the objects of the exclusion of English cloth from the Netherlands was to create unemployment and foment labour troubles among the English cloth-workers. A peace conference at Borborch had been arranged on the very eve of the attack. " The Duke of Parma," says Van Meteran, " by these wiles enchanted and dazzled the eyes of many English and Dutchmen that were desirous of peace, whereupon it came to pass that England and the United Provinces prepared indeed some defence to withstand that dreadful expedition and huge armada, but nothing in comparison of the great danger which was to be feared." [2] But despite all these precautions and preparations the Armada failed, and the German-Spanish hopes were

---

[1] The Fuggers were the Rothschilds of the Middle Ages and the Renaissance. With the increase of wealth rates of interest had sunk since 1560.

[2] Just so our Government was " enchanted and dazzled " by the wiles of Baron Marschal von Bieberstein at the Hague Peace Conference.

broken into pieces by the guns of our ships and the iron-bound coasts of the Hebrides.

Even then the King and the Hanse did not quite despair. On 19th August 1589, the Venetian Ambassador in Spain reports : " At the Escurial there is an agent from Hamburg who has instructions from Dantzig to inform the King that many ships from those parts have been seized by the Queen of England, and to complain of her action. This agent is about to return home by way of Italy ; he is the bearer of a dispatch whose contents I cannot discover, owing to the secrecy in which the whole matter is kept." At this time Philip was preparing his second Armada, and the Hanse towns were busy supplying him with a new outfit. In 1588 William Harborne, our first and greatest Ambassador at Constantinople, returned overland to England. At Elbing, Dantzig, Wismar, Lübeck, and Hamburg he received flattering attentions, and was congratulated " on her Majesty's victory over the Spaniard." " Yet," he says, " the Dantzigs after my departure thence caused the merchants to pay custom for the goods they brought with them in my company, which none other town, neither infidels nor Christians, on the way ever demanded. And notwithstanding the premises, I was most certainly informed of sundry of our nation there resident that most of the Hanse towns upon the sea coast, especially Dantzig, Lübeck, and Hamburg, have laden, and were shipping for Spain, great provisions of corn, cables, ropes, powder, saltpetre, harquebusses, armour, iron, lead, copper, and all other munitions serving for the war. Whereupon I gather their feigned courtesy proceeded rather from fear than of any good affection unto her Majesty's service, Elbing and Stoad only excepted, which of duty for their commodities (*i.e.* English cloth) I esteemed well affected."[1]

Queen Elizabeth replied with a blow more crushing than anything the Hanse had so far suffered. On 30th June 1589, near the mouth of the Tagus, a fleet of about sixty Hanseatic ships were seized by Drake, and were held by the Queen despite every effort of the Hanse to procure their release. " Single members of the Hanse may have suffered before," says Sartorius, " but such a blow crushed them all completely."

The position of the Germans was now, in fact, desperate. One last tremendous coup was tried. In 1597 a great embassy rather Flemish than Spanish—for it consisted of the Earl of Barlamont, Dr. George Westendorpe, and John Van Nickerchen—was sent to Lübeck, as chief of the Hanse towns, and to Denmark to implore them to stop all trade with England and offering instead free trade with Calais, Graveburgh, Dunkirk, Sluys, and Antwerp, and the ports of Spain and Portugal. If the Hanse would only confine themselves strictly to these towns, the Ambassadors promised them that England would be brought to her knees and the Hanse privileges restored. The Decree of the Imperial Diet at Augsburg forbidding all English trade within the German Empire was at the same time to be enforced, and all English merchants ejected from Germany. And Ambassadors from Denmark and Poland were to be sent to England to frighten Queen Elizabeth into submission. It was a magnificent project, and a touch of sanctity was not wanting, for a new peace of Christendom and a new Crusade against the Turk were to be preached (the Queen of England being suspected of inciting the Turk against the Empire).

[1] Hakluyt, vol. vi. pp. 58–59.

On this complicated mission what Mr. Algernon Cecil calls " the gorgeous figure of Paul Dialyn " crosses our horizon.[1] He was the King of Poland's Ambassador, and his main purpose was to seek the restoration of the privileges of the Hanse towns and compensation for the loss of Hanse ships. Cecil gives Essex a lively account of the audience :

" There arrived here three days since in the city an Ambassador out of Poland, a gentleman of excellent fashion, wit, discourse, language, and person. . . . He was brought in attired in a long robe of black velvet, well jewelled and buttoned, and came to kiss her Majesty's hand, where she stood under the State ; from whence he straight retired ten yards off, and then began his oration aloud in Latin, with such a countenance as in my life I never beheld."

The speech was, in fact, a violent tirade on the injuries done to Hanse shipping by Elizabeth's Navy and by the Merchant Adventurers, a demand for the restoration of Hanseatic privileges, and a threat from the King of Poland, " conjoined," as he was, " with the illustrious House of Austria," that " if her Majesty would not reform it, he would."

" To this, I swear by the Living God," continues Cecil, " that her Majesty made one of the best answers extempore in Latin that ever I heard, being much moved to be so challenged in public, especially so much against her expectation. The words of her beginning were these :

" ' *Exspectavi orationem, mihi vero querelam adduxisti.* Is this the business your King hath sent you about ?

---

[1] *A Life of Robert Cecil, First Earl of Salisbury* (London, 1915), p. 108. See also Lansdowne MSS., No. 85, vol. xix., the account by Speed in his Chronicle and Wheeler.

Surely I can hardly believe that if the King himself were present he would have used such a language, for, if he should, I must have thought that being a King not of many years and that *non de jure sanguinis sed jure electionis, immo noviter electus,* may haply be uninformed of that course which his father and ancestors have taken with us and which peradventure shall be observed by those that shall live to come after us. And as for you,' saith she to the Ambassador, ' although I perceive you have read many books to fortify your arguments in this case, yet am I apt to believe that you have not lighted upon the chapter that prescribeth the form to be used between Kings and Princes ; but, were it not for the place you hold, to have an imputation so publicly thrown upon our justice, which as yet never failed, we would answer this audacity of yours in another style.' . . .

" I assure your Lordship," continues Cecil to Essex, " that I am not apt to wonder, I must confess before the Living Lord that I never heard her, when I knew her spirits were in passion, speak with better moderation in my life."

The formal reply to this remarkable embassy is given by Wheeler, who tells us that it was prepared by a Privy Council consisting of Lord Burghley, the Treasurer ; Sir John Fortescue, the Lord High Admiral ; and Sir Robert Cecil, the Secretary.

It begins by scoring a point against Poland. The Hanse privileges were given to cities not under Poland, but under Prussia, and if these cities were not confined to one kingdom they had no status. But it proceeds to a stronger position : " Whereas therefore it is plain that this King of Spain, being an enemy to this realm, is furnished, armed, and strengthened to continue this unjust war with ships, victual, and other warlike provisions out of certain cities under Polone and' other maritime cities of Germany," &c. As to Hanseatic privileges, they could not possibly be renewed.

" If the Hanses should have better conditions than the proper subjects of the kingdom, it would plainly follow that the prince of this realm should do his own natural subjects very great injury contrary to the law of Nature and Man's law, for by this means his subjects should become poor or rather destitute of all honest and profitable traffic and navigation, and the Hanses should grow opulent and possess the whole trade of the realm as monopolists of the whole kingdom."

And now I come to the very last card in the Hanseatic pack—the Augsburg Decree. It had not been seriously enforced in 1582, and was now (1597) launched upon the world anew. With all the ponderous volubility of which German lawyers are capable,[1] it recited the Hanseatic privileges, received partly by the " favour " of English kings, and partly " with great sums of money "; it recounted the enormities and " intolerable innovations " of that " monopolish Company," the Merchant Adventurers ; and it banned all English merchants from the Empire. Elizabeth's answer was as might have been expected :

" Elizabeth by the grace of God Queen of England, France and Ireland, Defender of the Faith, &c., to our right trusty and well-beloved the Mayor and Sheriffs of our City of London, greeting, whereas there hath been directed a commandment . . . from the Roman Emperor to all electors, Prelates, Earls and all other officers and subjects of the Empire reciting sundry complaints made to him by the Allied towns of the Dutch Hanse

[1] See Appendix IV.

in Germany . . . the English Merchants, namely the MM. Adventurers are forbidden to use any traffic of merchandise within the Empire . . . we have thought it agreeable to our honour in the meantime to command all such as are here within our realm, appertaining to the said Hanse towns, situate in the Empire . . . to depart out of our Dominions . . . charging them by the four and twentieth day of this month . . . they do depart out of this realm . . . witness our self at Westminster, the thirteenth of January in the fortieth year of our reign."

This was the end of the Germans in England at that time. For a few months negotiations dragged on, but on 25th July 1598 the Privy Council orders the Lord Mayor and Sheriffs of London to take possession of the Steelyard in the name of the Queen, and to evict the Germans from their houses. Ten days later, still protesting, the Germans left. "On the 4th August," says their report, "we at last, because it could never be otherwise, with gloom in our hearts, the Alderman Henry Langermann in front and we others after him, went out of the door, and the door was shut behind us ; also (we) did not want there to pass the night. May God have compassion."

CONCLUSION

We have now come to the end of our allotted task, which was to trace the German power in England from its rise in the time of Henry III to its fall in the time of Elizabeth. Here we push our little shallop ashore, for the currents of the stream of European history grow confused and tumultuous, and already in our ears there is the faint but ominous roar of that great and shattering cataract, the Thirty Years War. Into that dark abyss fell what remained of the first German Empire and the Hanseatic League, to be churned and broken to pieces. Some have called it a war of religion : I would call it rather the agony of dissolution. The Empire and the German cities fell together because their means of life had been drawn from them. Germany, as we have seen, depended upon certain great streams and fountains of wealth, the overland trade routes of Europe and the manufacturing centre of Flanders. When the roads from Venice to Bruges, from Novgorod to Dantzig, and from the Black Sea to Cracow were the highways of world commerce, Germany flourished and grew great. When England was the wool-farm of Flanders, and Germany carried English wool to be made into Flemish cloth, and Flemish cloth to be sold for more English wool, sea-power was added to land-power, and her monopoly was complete. But when Portugal found the way round the Cape of Good Hope to India, Venice and Constantinople lost in importance, since they depended on the Persian Gulf and Red Sea routes, which the Portuguese blockaded. Germany, forced to resort to the less secure depot of Lisbon, had to run the gauntlet of the English Channel. Germany suffered no less when England turned from wool-producing to cloth-producing, and organised her trade and her customs for national ends. And when the Merchant Adventurers of England, under the protection of Tudor power, carried English trade even into the markets of Germany, gaining for England the profits of the whole cycle of English trade, the end was within sight. Moreover, England in her struggle with Spain for the carrying trade of a wider ocean, cut that vital line of communications which linked Spain with Germany and the Netherlands.

> " For Spain and Flanders is as eche other brother,
> And neither may well live without other."

The merchants of Germany, as we know from Wheeler, financed the sailors of Spain. Even the Reformation would not have sufficed by itself to sever the mutual dependence. Thus George Nedham, in a marginal note to his *Tract on English Trade*,[1] says that " no English shipps maye lade in Spayne, if any Spanyshe shippe will take in the same lading, besyde the great trouble, spoyle and injuries don to your subjectes, their factours and servants for religion, *and for marchants of Estland and Germany who be likewyse of our religion they seldome trouble or medle with them.*" Where there was a community of interest, religion was not allowed to interfere with the practical business of life. Only

---

[1] Add. MS. 35207, *A Tract on English Trade*, addressed to Queen Elizabeth by George Nedham (about 1562), setting forth the advantage of transferring it from the House of Burgundy (viz. in the Spanish Netherlands) to the Port of Emden.

when the religious difference coincided with a conflict of material interest did it become the pretext for war.

Foreign policy springs naturally from interest, and the traditional foreign policy of England, laid down in the time of the Tudors, may be traced to the conflict with the Empire and the Hanseatic League. The alliances between England and Holland, England and Denmark, England and Russia, the change of the old hostile relations with France into a friendly understanding, such were the main lines of a policy designed to free England from German political and commercial domination. Since the outbreak of the present war I do not recollect that any of our politicians have explained to our people the meaning of the "scrap of paper" on the existence of which they raised their parrot cries. Burghley, who was more statesman than politician, illuminated the whole position in a phrase when he described the Netherlands as "the counterscarp of your Majesty's Dominions." A statesman, being a trustee, is false to his duty if he founds his policy on anything but the interest of his country—a truth better understood in those times than in these. That nation is in a dangerous case which begins to prefer ideas over realities. Honour demands the fulfilment, but only interest should dictate the acceptance of our obligations, and it is neither honest nor wholesome to suggest that action which is founded on necessity is prompted by altruism. This book is not written in vain if it explains to my countrymen the forgotten springs and hidden sources of our foreign policy.

When the main roads of European commerce passed through the centre of Europe, Germany was supreme;

when they passed along the Channel, England gained the mastery. The cities of the Hanseatic League, which had linked together the overland routes of Europe, fell apart. We have seen the League disintegrating in the reign of Elizabeth. Dr. Parkins, one of our agents in Germany, gave Sir Robert Cecil a vivid picture of their desolate state in a letter of 17th October 1595.[1] " The Hanses," he says, " are a society of cities, some in the Low Countries, some in the Empire, some in Poland. Lübeck is their mother-city, where they were wont to have their Parliaments every two years, till anno 91, since which year divers of their cities refusing the charge of a Parliament, which used to prove nothing profitable to their purses, there have been none ; others have separated from the society, and others are staggering and falling from them." Here we see the crumbling process well advanced : both cities and Empire are " staggering and falling " towards the abyss of the Thirty Years War.

In the last years of Elizabeth, even before its end, the Hanse is becoming a memory and a tradition : it is like a toothless old man who babbles of his ancient powers, his " obsolete priveleges." The enterprise of the Merchant Adventurers and the protective policy of the Tudors, working in happy unison, had made England independent. " As our Commonwealth now stands they can well be done without," writes an Englishman about the year 1580,[2] " for our own merchants are able to furnish the realm with the same commodities, and that in English bottoms, and the merchants of Russia from St. Nicholas (Archangel) and the Narwa would bring the same and more plentifully,

---

[1] Cotton MS., Nero, B ix, fo. 178.
[2] *A Discourse of the Trade of the Merchants of the Dutch Guild called the Hanse.*—Cotton MS., Faustina, c. ii, fo. 85–86.

and that too in English bottoms, if the Easterlings did not." Those cities, once so powerful, sit now in their neglected chimney-corner, peevish and querulous ; they complain, but they are not heeded, for " they can well be done without."

And it was said of them with truth, when they were established in England : " Also the Navy of the realm is by them much hindered, for they only carry commodities in their own ships." [1] So it was appropriate that when they left the Steelyard should be used for the English Navy. [2]

For it was the English Navy that broke the German power : it blockaded Flanders ; it cut off Germany from Spain ; it convoyed the merchant fleets of the Merchant Adventurers to Emden, Stade, and the Narwa ; it sailed to the Indies, East and West ; it even gathered up the crumbs and broken remnants of the caravan trade at Constantinople, and brought them also by sea to their ports of destination. The sea-

---

[1] *A Discourse of the Trade of the Merchants of the Dutch Guild called the Hanse.*—Cotton MS., Faustina, o. ii, fo. 85–86.

[2] Letter of the Privy Council to the Lord Mayor of London (30th January 1599), about the handing over of the Steelyard to the Royal Navy : " Lettre to the L. Majore of London. Whereas it was founde needfull after the avoydinge and departinge of the strangers, that did possesse the *howse of the Stilliarde,* that the said howse should be used and employed for her Majesty's service for the better bestowinge and safe custodie of divers prouisions of her Navie, which might very conueniently be kept there ; and thereupon order has bin giuen heretofore for the storinge and laynge up of diuers of here Majesty's said prouisions of that place : Now for as much as the Officers of the Navie do finde continuallie wante of more stoage, and no place more fitt for it then that howse ; And your Lordship by a lettre written to us of late has made some doubt, howe the rente shalbe answered to the Citty for that howse, if it be deliuered out of your possession into the handes of others ; to satisfie your Lordship therein, you shall understande, that the Officers of the Navie shall giue your Lordship and the Citty sufficient assurance for payement of the rent dew for the same. And therefore wee doe praie and requier you, without any further scruple or controuersie to cause the possession of the said howse of the Stilliarde to be deliuered to the Officers of here Majesty's Navie or such of them as shall attende you for that cause, to be used and employed for here Majesty's seruice aboue mentioned, upon assurance given by them for payment of the rente. Which wee doubte not but your Lordship will see perfourmed. And so wee etc."—MS. Harley 4182, *Register of Council Causes from 30th July* 1598 *until 10th April* 1599, fo. 152.

power of England—it broke Germany once, it can break Germany twice.

But it must be intelligently used, and it must be supported by a national trade policy. We see Queen Elizabeth protecting English cloth and English hardware ; she builds powder-mills ; she smuggles in German metal experts to teach her subjects the arts of smelting, and Italian alum-workers to make England independent of Florence in a commodity then essential to cloth-finishing. Contrast this policy with the recent and present policy of England. We had allowed Germany to renew her supremacy in the metal trade. In all things connected with arms and high explosives she had again become supreme. And so in the cloth trade. She was gradually securing control of the dyes and even the finishing processes of our English cloth : we were again becoming the journeyman of the German cities.

Before the war Germany was regaining the position she had once held in the days of the Hanseatic League. Her financiers and her bankers were in the counsels of our Government, and financed our politicians. We might find the prototypes of Sir Edgar Speyer and Baron Schröder in the days of the Plantagenets. We might compare the policy of the late Government with the policy of Henry III and Henry VI. Joseph Chamberlain, like Warwick, died in a vain attempt to fortify England against the German danger ; and Lord Roberts fell, like De Montfort, in the field against the German power. The Hague Conventions and the Declaration of London were a betrayal of the sea-power of England no less shameful than the Treaty of Utrecht. Like Richard II, the late Government drifted into war with Germany without knowing the German power ; and as in the time of Richard II there are two forces in England, one working for national ends, the other for German interests. "If England," says List, "had clung to *laissez faire*, she would still be the wool-farm of the Hansa." And I gather this lesson from our history, that if we are to defeat the German power again, as we defeated it before, we must have a national policy: a policy of Britain for the British, with protection for the workman against German labour and for his produce against German imports. "Cherish marchandise," that is, found ourselves on the sale of our own manufactures, and "keep the Admiralty." "As your tweyne eyne, so keepe the narrow see"—so the old nameless poet of the Yorkist cause advised, and so our English story teaches.

APPENDICES

APPENDIX I

THE ANGEVINS AND GERMANY

THE following extracts from German authorities may help to elucidate the relations between Germany and England in Angevin times :

By giving one of his daughters in marriage to Henry the Lion, Henry II of England had outlined a Guelph policy for his dynasty. To this principle, which is, in an immeasurable degree, at the root of the destruction of German unity, the Italian towns, as well as those of Southern and Northern Germany, have to thank for their wonderfully quick growth into almost autonomous communities. The election of the Emperor Otto IV, the Guelph who for the first time had pushed aside the Hohenstaufen, had been carried through by aid of his uncle, Richard Cœur de Lion, and the English money paid by him.

The Cologners stuck to Otto to the last ; even after the battle of Bouvines, where Otto and John were beaten by French arms and Hohenstaufen policy, they clung to him.

When the great Emperor Frederic II died, after a long reign full of changes, and soon after him his successors had found their tragic end, there appears among the aspirants to the throne of the divided empire a Prince from the House of Plantagenet as representative of the Guelph idea—Richard of Cornwall, the brother of Henry III of England. To him the Hanse is indebted for its recognition in England. Already King John had endowed the Bremeners with the same rights as the Cologners possessed—now soon afterwards there follow the Hamburgers, the people of Lübeck, and the outposts of the Hanse : Rostock, Wismar, Stralsund, and Greifswald. Jealous of the pushing North Germans, the Cologners grumbled—but, grumble as they would, in 1260 Henry III issued the great privilege to *all* the merchants of Almain who possess at London the house which is called the Teutonic Guildhall, the Aula Teutonicorum.[1]

Eleanor, the wife of King Henry II of England, heiress to the county of Poitou and the duchy of Guyenne, which was combined with Gascogne and Navarre, had enriched the crown of England, to which already belonged the duchies of Normandy and Anjou, by certain important possessions held as " Lehen " from the King of France. In the last years of the twelfth century, Otto, soon afterwards Emperor Otto IV, appears as Duke of Guyenne and Count of Poitou.

Richard Cœur de Lion, invited by an embassy of the Archbishops of Cologne and Mayence and other German princes to assist at the election of a Roman King, had scruples about going in person, and preferred to send his ambassadors. He intended that the Imperial Crown should go to his nephew, the Palatine Henry. Henry not having returned from a Crusade, and the election being a most pressing business, he induced the princes to elect the Duke Otto, Henry's brother. An embassy was sent to the Duke at Poitou with the news of his election, and from there, enriched by presents from his uncle, the new King travelled to Germany. Meanwhile Richard furthered the affairs of his nephew at the Court of Rome, where his munificence was most useful to Otto. From merchants at Placentia he borrowed 2125 marks, which amount he sent to the Pope, through the Bishops of Anjou and Bangor.

Besides the gifts from Richard, a petition by the German princes, dated the 29th December 1198, was presented to the Pope. In this petition they applied for the Pope's confirmation of the election.

Innocent III thereupon was delighted to declare Otto to be the worthiest of the princes to bear the Roman Crown.[2]

Dr. Sudendorf gives information as to the value of money

---

[1] Reinhold Pauli, *Der Hansische Stahlhof in London*, p. 5.
[2] *Die Wilfen Urkunden*, &c., by Dr. H. Sudendorf, pp. 1–4.

at that time, which will enable the reader to judge the true amount of Richard's ransom :

ENGLISH MONEY, 1066–1300, AND ITS RELATIVE VALUE.

3 marks = 2 libera (lb.) (pounds).
1 liber (pound) = 20 shillings.
1 shilling = 12 pfennig.

	1 bushel oats	1 horse	1 ox	1 cow	1 sheep
1 the year 1150	4½ pfennig	12 shillings 5 pfennig	4 shillings 8¼ pfennig		1 shilling 8 pfennig
1 the year 1250	1 shilling 7¾ pfennig	1 pound 11 shillings	1 pound 7 pfennig	17 shillings	1 shilling 7 pfennig

	1 pig	1 goose	1 hen	1 cock	Daily Wag
1 the year 1150	3 shillings		3 pfennig		2 pfennig
1 the year 1250		1 shilling	3 pfennig	4½ pfennig	

The " noble," which appears in England in the middle of the fourteenth century, is worth 80 pfennig or 6 shillings 8 pfennig.[1]

APPENDIX II

THE HANSE TOWNS

THAT the Hanse was a German institution is not disputed : how thoroughly German it was is made clear by the following

[1] *Die Wilfen Urkunden*, &c., by Dr. H. Sudendorf, pp. xii, xiii (Preface) ; H. Knyghton, *Chronic*, 1344.

list from the *Hansische Geschichtsblätter* (1871–3), vii. p. xxxi :

ALPHABETICAL LIST OF HANSE TOWNS as compiled by the Hansischer Geschichtsverein and published at the Meeting, Lübeck, May 30 and 31, 1871.

Amsterdam [1]	Gardelegen	Krakau(Cracow)	Soest
Anklam	Gollnow	Kulm	Soltbomel
Arnheim	Goshar	Lemgo	Stade
Berlin	Göttingen	Lippstadt	Stargard
Bielefeld	Greifswald	Lübeck	Staveren
Bolsward	Gröningen	Lüneburg	Stendal
Brandenburg	Halberstadt	Magdeburg	Stettin
Braunsberg	Halle	Minden	Stolpe
Braunschweig	Hamburg	Münster	Stralsund
Bremen	Hameln	Nordheim	Tangermünde
Breslau	Hamm	Nymwegen	Thiel
Briel	Hannover	Oschersleben	Thorn
Buxtehude	Harderwyk	Osnabrück	Uelzen
Dantzig	Hasselt	Osterburg	Unna
Deventer	Helmstedt	Paderborn	Utrecht
Dordrecht	Herford	Pernau	Venlo
Dorpat	Hildesheim	Quedlinburg	Warburg
Dortmund	Kampen	Reval	Watershagen
Duisburg	Kiel	Riga	Wesel
Erinbeck	Koesfeld	Roermonde	Wisby
Elbing	Köln (Cologne)	Rostock	Wismar
Elburg	Köln-on-the-Spree	Rügenwalde	Zierixee
Emmerich	Königsberg	Salzwedel	Zütphen
Frankfurt a. Oder	Kolberg	Seehansen	Zwolle

Bergen, Bruges, Novgorod were not Hanse towns, but *Kontors ;* the Eastern (Polish) Hanse towns were German colonies. The only possible exception is the strange case of Dinant.

Amongst the towns which temporarily belonged to the German Hanse, there is none of which the conditions and relations to the League would appear more mysterious than this town, situated on the rivers Meuse and Sambre, in the bishopric of Liège. The merchants of Liège appear already in Anglo-Saxon times among the privileged, like those of Hogge and Vivelle ; but Dinant is never mentioned. This town obtained

---

[1] Anderson (vol. i. pp. 356–9), following Werdenhagen, does not reagrd Amsterdam as Hanseatic.

for itself from King Edward III in 1329, May 15, a special recognition for an unlimited period of the privileges granted by King Edward I to the Spanish and other foreign merchants, and confirmed by himself (Edward III) on July 8, 1328, for a term of three years.[1] In this document the town is referred to as the town Dynant in Almayn, the bishopric of Liège having always belonged to Germany. It is, therefore, remarkable that this town considered it necessary to obtain for itself a special privilege while other Hanseatic towns had ceased to bother about individual privileges. The citizens of Dinant, however, seem soon to have attached themselves to the German confederation, at least as far as London was concerned, as we find it proved, fifteen years later, in 1344, at the Royal Court of Chancery, that they were members of the German Guildhall, and as such entitled to share in the enjoyment of the privileges granted to the merchants belonging to the same. This document already proves clearly that under the designation "Dynanters" are meant not only German merchants living there. But we cannot find Dinant mentioned at any Hanseday nor in any list of the federated towns. Its merchants seem, from this, to have incorporated themselves only with the London "factory." Yet King Edward III gives again, 1359, to the Dynanters a separate safe conduct.[2] In the London statute from 1437 Dinant appears in our MS. after Cologne, while it is not mentioned in others. Also, it is missing from the statutes of the *Kontor* from 1554.

The number of Dinanters or the importance of their commerce must, nevertheless, have been for some time great, as they had a separate hall, and perhaps other buildings in or next to the Steelyard. When in 1369 the town of London paid to the King an extraordinary war contribution, it demanded from the foreign merchants residing at London the sum of £62 sterling— from which sum the Germans ought to have paid £40, and the Dinanters £22.

Sept. 8, 1369 : "dat geld scholde denne vorgadderen van den husen, de in der warde stunden, . . . so eskeden se vns lxii ℔

---

[1] Lappenberg, *Urkundliche Geschichte der deutschen Hanse*, Part II, p. 742.
[2] *Calendarium rotulorum patent.*, p. 170, No. 10.

sterl. dat is tho vorstande den Dutschen xl ℔, vnd den Dynanters xxii ℔ van welkem eskene wy nicht schuldich en weren noch en synt hir tho gevene, by vreyheyden, de uns de Konynk gesegelt heft. Vnd vmme des willen dat wy disse vorseiede eskynge nicht geuen noch betalen en wolden na erem willen, so kamen se vnd beselgeden (besegelden) vns vnse boden vnd kammern na der tidt vnde apenden eyn del boden vnd nemen guder daruth vnd fordertent in the Engelsche gylthalle, dar wart dat gud geprised und vorkoft. Des worden gesellen ordyneret, de tho dem konynge reden vnd en (vm) disse sake tho vorstande. Do antwerde en (enen) de konynk : men scholde vns holden vnse vryheit. Vnd darup vorfolgenden wy disse sake vor den meyger, rekorder vnd olderluden van Lunden. . . ." [1]

" . . . this money should be gathered in from the houses which stood in the ward. . . . so they asked from us 60 ℔ sterl., this is to be understood from the Germans 40 ℔, and from the Dynanters 22 ℔, from which demand we did not owe anything nor need we give, by freedom which the king has sealed us. And because we did not want to pay or give this aforesaid demand after their will, so they came and sealed up our store-rooms and chambers after the time and opened up the store-rooms and took goods out and carried them to the English Guildhall, there the goods were priced and sold. So members were ordered to talk to the king and make him understand this matter. The king answered : let us beware our freedom. And thereupon we followed up this matter before the Mayor, Recorder, and Alderman of London. . . ."

The MS. ends by saying that they agreed to pay half of the amount asked for, and this not by force or by their right, but by their free will.

This unequal proportion seems explicable only by the size of the buildings occupied by the Dinanters. The name of the Dynanter Hall was preserved among the Steelyard buildings till they were burnt down in 1666.

Of the Hanseatic relations of Dinant we hear only o nce more. The town, which had become very wealthy through its commerce and its copperworkers—the pots and other goods

---

[1] MS. *Hamburger Commerz Bibliothek*, fo. 73.

were commonly called " Dynanterie "—had particularly inflamed the ire of the enemy in the war waged by Duke Philip the Good of Burgundy against the Liègers. Dinant, in 1466, was completely destroyed by the besiegers and by fire.[1] Its merchants took flight to the friendly town of Huy. Being now inhabitants of this town, they could no more claim their privileges in England. The Bishop of Liège, however, by negotiations with the *Kontor* of Bruges, and later with the Hanse towns, succeeded in obtaining for them from the Hanse, under the 4th April 1471, permission to enjoy their privileges for another twenty years.[2] After this time the name of Dynant vanishes from the history of the Hanse, and we come across her in only one other case : on 9th November 1471, Edward IV permitted the merchants and smiths (*officium bateriæ*) of the town of Middleburg, although they were not included in the German Hanse, all the prerogatives and exemptions which they from Dinant had enjoyed in the whole kingdom before their town was destroyed. Here we have, then, another quite unexpected recognition of the position of Dinant in the German Hanse and its prerogatives in England. Middleburg, however, is not counted among the Hanse towns, not even in London, as shown in the statute of 1554.

APPENDIX III

THE GERMAN SHARE IN ENGLISH TRADE

THE Hanseatic share in English trade is difficult to estimate, and must have varied with times and events. Two circumstances serve to show its extent : (1) that the Hanseatic decree of trade excommunication brought England to her knees in the time of Richard II and Henry IV, and (2) that Edward III could decree that Englishmen should take no share in the staple export trade. The Germans had at one time a substantial monopoly in the Baltic, which supplied England with corn, wax,

---

[1] *Memoires de Ph. de Commynes, Magnum Chronicon Belgicum, etc.,* part III, p. 426.
[2] MS. *Hamburger Commerz Bibliothek,* p. 82 *sq.*

pitch, hemp, timber, steel, furs, copper. They also carried a large part of the English wool to Flanders. As to the cloth trade, their favourable position is clearly shown by the subjoined table, by Gresham's letter to Queen Elizabeth, and by the statement of Wheeler : "Among the privileges, one was to carry out and bring in wares for an old custom of one and a quarter upon the hundred, and were thereby exempt from all personal or real contribution, which all other merchants are subject to." [1] Macpherson speaks as if they had an entire monopoly of the English carrying trade ; but this is probably an exaggeration. Schanz says, of the reign of Henry VII, that the German share was not so large as is generally supposed, although "important enough to make the English Government reflect." The Hanse, according to his figures, had then 97 per cent. of the wax import, 23 per cent. of the English cloth export, and not quite 7 per cent. of the remaining movement of goods. He adds, however, that it was at that time rapidly growing. The Merchant Adventurers, in their great Privy Council Case against the Hanse in 1551, stated that in the third year of Edward VI the Easterlings shipped from London alone " in strange bottoms " 42,897 cloths, whereas other strangers trafficking from the same ports only 1080 cloths." Lappenberg misquotes this passage, and makes it read that all other foreigners and Englishmen shipped only 1100 pieces. Possibly he had never seen the original documents of the case to which I refer elsewhere. It is amusing to trace this little error back to its source. Rapin has it that " all the English merchants together exported 1100 pieces." Sir John Heyward, in his *Life and Reign of Edward VI* (1552), has the figures right, " not above 1100 by all strangers besides." So that Rapin must have begun the mistake which has misled nearly every writer on the subject since his time. Smith, in his *Memoirs of Wool*, shrewdly discovers the blunder, though he does not know the source of the statement, and he shows that the Merchant Adventurers exported about 40,000 pieces of cloth in one year. Now at this time the English Merchant Adventurers had a practical monopoly of such English cloth trade as was in English hands, so that

---

[1] Wheeler's *Treatise of Commerce.*

the German merchants carried at least as much English cloth as the English merchants. Schanz, then, is perfectly right when he says that the Hanseatic share was rapidly increasing in the time of Henry VII. It not only increased in bulk, but it increased in proportion to the total. In the reign of Edward VI we might say, upon this evidence, that the Hanseatic League had roughly an equal share with the Merchant Adventurers of the English cloth-carrying trade.

EXPORT OF ENGLISH CLOTH by the Germans and by all foreign merchants in England. MS. dated 1552.[1]

Shipped by the Merchauntes of the German Stillyard, from the first yeare of King Edward the second unto Michaels last past, as by the Kinges recordes of his Grace's Exchequer it dothe plainely appeare, as hereafter followeth. The first yeare of King Edward the second (1307) owt of this realme of England but . vi clothes

Brought into this realme by the said Marchauntes in the same first yeare in all other wares and marchaundyse, but to the valew of m^l ii^c xix^{li} vi^s xi^d whereof the kinges Matie had for his custome after the rate of iii^d the pound . . . . . . Summa xv^{li} iiii^s x^d

The second yeare of the same king Edward the second the said Marchauntes of the Styllyard shipped owt of this realme but . . . . . . vii clothes

In all other wares and merchandize to the valew of so moch as paied the king in custome . . . . xxxv^{li} xii^s x^d

The first yeare of King Henry the sixt (1422) the said Marchauntes of the Styllyard shipped owt of this realme the nomber of . . iiii^{ml} iiii^c lxiii clothes xxii yeardes

,, first yeare of King Edward the fourthe (1461) vi^{ml} i^c lix clothes

,, fifteenth yeare of King Henry the seaventhe (1500) xxi^{ml} iii^c iiii^{xx} ix clothes

,, iiiith yeare of King Henry the Eight (1513) . xxi^{ml} v^c lvi clothes

,, xxviiith yeare of King Henry the Eight (1537) xxxiiii^{ml} vi^c iiii^{xx} xiii clothes and xi yeardes

,, xxixth yeare of King Henry the Eight . xxxiii^{ml} vii^c lxxviii clothes

,, xxxth yeare of King Henry the Eight . xxxiiii^{ml} i^c xlii clothes

,, xxxith yeare of King Henry the Eight, which was the first whole year that Merchaunt straungers paied but English Custome . . . . . xxvii^{ml} ii^c lx clothes

,, xxxiith yeare of King Henry the Eight xxvii^{ml} vi^c xix clothes

---

[1] MS. in the British Museum. MS. Cotton, Claudius E. VII, fo. 99.

The xxxiiith yeare of King Henry the Eight xxiii^{ml} iiii^{c} xii clothes vi yeardes
  „   xxxivth „   „   xxiiii^{ml} ii^{c} xxi clothes ix yeardes
  „   xxxvth „   „   xxvii^{ml} lii clothes vi yeardes
  „   xxxvith „   „   xxxiii^{ml} ix^{c} lxiii clothes
  „   xxxviith „   „   xxxi^{ml} l clothes iii yeardes
  „   xxxviiith yeare of King Henry theight
      and the first yeare of King Edward
      the sixt (1547) . . . . xxix^{ml} vi^{c} iiii^{xx} ix clothes
  „   second yeare of King Edward the sixt xliiii^{ml} v^{c} iiii^{xx} iii clothes
  „   third   „   „   xliiii^{ml} iiii^{c} ii clothes
  „   fourthe   „   „   xxxix^{ml} viii^{c} liiii clothes
Shipped by the Merchauntes straungers from the xiiiith yeare of King
    Henry the VIIth unto Michaels in the xxxviiith yeare of King Henry
    the Eight, as hereafter followeth.
The xiiiith yeare of King Henry the
    Seaventhe (1523) . . . . iii^{ml} i^{c} iiii^{xx} i clothes
  „   iiiith yeare of King Henry the Eight
    (1513) . . . . . . iiii^{ml} xxxi clothes
  „   xxviiith yeare of King Henry the Eight
    (1537) . . . . . . v^{ml} ii^{c} lxxiii clothes
  „   xxixth yeare of King Henry the Eight iiii^{ml} vi^{c} viii clothes viii yeardes
  „   xxxth yeare of King Henry the Eight.
    This yeare straungers paied Englishe
    custome and vii yeares after . . xxviii^{ml} iii^{c} xviii clothes
  „   xxxith yeare of King Henry the Eight xxiiii^{ml} v^{c} lxvi clothes
  „   xxxiith „   „   xxix^{ml} vii^{c} xxxii clothes
  „   xxxiiith „   „   xxix^{ml} ii^{c} lxvii clothes et viii
                            yeardes
  „   xxxiiiith „   „   xiiii^{ml} vi^{c} lxxix clothes
  „   xxxvth „   „   xxiiii^{ml} ii^{c} iiii^{xx} xiiii clothes
  „   xxxvith „   „   l^{ml} iii^{c} lix clothes
  „   xxxviith „   „   lxii^{ml} viii clothes
Ended the said 7 yeares, and since they paied straungers custome to
    the King.
The xxxviiith yeare of King Henry the Eight
    and the first yeare of King Edward
    the sixt. . . . . . xiiii^{ml} vii^{c} iiii^{xx} xiii clothes
  „   first yeare of King Edward the sixt
    from Michaels to the vith of July next viii^{c} iiii^{xx} x clothes
  „   second yeare of King Edward the sixt xiii^{c} lxi clothes
    third   „   „   xi^{c} iiii^{xx} iii clothes

GERMAN PREFERENCE IN ENGLISH CUSTOMS

TARIFF OF CUSTOMS from the time of Henry VII and Henry VIII, compiled by Schanz, *Eng. Hand.*, ii. p. 6, after sources in Public Record Office, London : Enrolled Accounts of Customs, Packets 20, 21, and 22, in the Pipe Office.

Kind of Merchandise.	Merchants.	Custom.	Subsidium.	Total D‹ as Perce age of R Value
ʼool, 1 sack or 240 skins	Staple merchants	6*sh*. 8*d*.	33*sh*. 4*d*.	33, ₃
	Non-staple	10*sh*.	66*sh*. 8*d*. and 8*d*. Cales	70, ₀
oth, undyed, per piece	Natives	1*sh*. 2*d*.	—	1, ₉
	German	1*sh*.	—	1, ₇
	Foreigners	2*sh*. 9*d*.	1*sh*. in the £ value	7, ₉
,, dyed, ,,	Natives	2*sh*. 4*d*.	—	
	German	2*sh*.	—	
	Foreigners	5*sh*. 6*d*.	1*sh*. in the £ value	
,, half dyed, ,,	Natives	1*sh*. 9*d*.	—	
	German	1*sh*. 6*d*.	—	
	Foreigners	4*sh*. 1*d*.	1*sh*. in the £ value	
, Panni Cornub, per piece so-called dozens	}Natives	{ from £1 value	} 9*d*.	
	Foreigners	{ from £1 value	}1*sh*.	
ngle worsted, per piece	Natives	1*d*.	(1*d*. in the £ value)	
	German	1*d*.	(1*d*. ,, ,,)	
	Foreigners	1½*d*.	1*sh*. ,, ,,)	
›uble ,, ,,	Natives	2‹*d*.	(1*d*.) }	0, ₆
	German	3*d*.	(1*d*.) }	
	Foreigners	3*d*.	1*sh*. in the £ value	3, ₁
ax, per ctr.	Natives	1*sh*.	—	1, ₈
	German	1*sh*.	—	1, ₈
	Foreigners	1*sh*.	1*sh*. in the £ value	5, ₄
l other goods	Natives	—	1*sh*. in the £ value	(5)
	German	{ 3*d*. in the £ value }	—	(1, ₂₅)
	Foreigners	{ 3*d*. in the £ value }	1*sh*. in the £ value	(6, ₂₅)

I have omitted from this list those goods which show no preferential treatment of the Germans, and where they are on the same footing with other strangers.

About non-sweetened wine there seems to have been a difference in customs, but no satisfactory evidence is to hand.

APPENDIX IV

THE AUGSBURG DECREE

WE Rudolph the Second by the grace of God elect Roman Emperor etc. . . . heretofore as also in the time of our reign over the Empire, the Confederate Dutch Hanse towns, and some others thereby interested . . . especially at Augsburgh in the year 1582 and at Regensburgh in the year 1594 last past have in complaining wise declared and showed that they three hundred years ago and above had obtained and gotten notable privileges immunities freedoms and exemptions within the realm of England partly by the special grace and favour of the kings of that land, and partly with great sums of money for the good and commodity of the holy Empire . . . granted approved and confirmed by fourteen kings of England successively and in the year 1470 by foreknowledge and consent of the States of the Land both spiritual and temporal made of the force and nature of a perpetual and irrevocable contract : whereupon they held their residence and officers within the city of London in an house or counter called the Dutch Guildhall (*Gildhalla Teutonicorum*) whereby they used to buy cloth of the subjects of the Crown of England and carried the same from thence into Dutcheland . . . which notwithstanding certain covetous companies of merchants whereof some call themselves Merchant Adventurers seeking their own private gain . . . are sprung up in the said realm who by bad means have wrought and practised to the great and notorious hurt and damage of the foresaid Hanses, and have taken upon them to bring in many intolerable innovations, contrary to the abovesaid old customs privileges and perpetual contract obtained . . . so that . . . the Queen of England . . . will not any longer endure or confirm the said Hanse's privileges, and now finally the last year to the farther and more intolerable grievance of the foresaid Hanse towns (specially for that they found it not reasonable or fit to yield unto the said MM. Adventurers a residence according to their desire at Hamburg) hath wholly forbidden and cut off all privileged trade both within and without the said realm of England, thereby the better to strengthen the trade of the foresaid Adventurers Company, and to bring their monopolish traffic to a full course . . . in that the Hanse cannot enjoy their privileges whereas on the English side the English Adventurers Company increaseth in numbers to wit in Dutcheland first at Emden, and afterwards in other places more and now presently at Stade . . . finally through the drift and dealing of these Adventurers the Dutch Merchants hath the best of his trade taken from him . . . and the Queen of England hath presumed with armed hand to be convoyed . . . by means whereof the Hanse towns . . . are forced to forsake . . . the foresaid free navigation throughout the whole Western Sea and in the Ems stream for as much as . . . the Merchant Adventurers used a hurtful monopoly (here follow ponderous pages of repetition) we prohibit banish out and proscribe all the forenamed English Merchants, to wit the whole company of the Merchant Adventurers, together with their hurtful dealings traffics and contractings out of all the holy Empire . . . specially out of the town of Stade and out of all other parts and places (several pages of prohibitions follow) given in our royal castle at Prague, 1st August 1597.—From Wheeler's *Treatise of Commerce.*

APPENDIX V

SEBASTIAN CABOT

IN 1521,[1] when Cardinal Wolsey was trying to organise a voyage to Newfoundland, the merchants were asked to contribute, but the Drapers' Company protested that they would prefer to be guided by " mariners born within the realm," rather than by Sebastian Cabot. Perhaps they were right, for Cabot was at that time in the employment of the Emperor. " I wrote to the Emperor," he afterwards told Contarini, " by no means to give me leave to serve the King of England (in Wolsey's voyage), and that on the contrary he should recall me forthwith." But in 1547 the Privy Council paid £100 " for the transporting of one Shabot, a pilot, to come out of Hispain to serve and inhabit

---

[1] See also *Cabot Bibliography*, by G. P. Winship.

in England " (Acts of the P.C. 9th October 1547); and in 1549 one Henry Oystryge also got £100 " for conducting of Sebastian Cabot." The Emperor earnestly wanted him back. " Secondly, he (the Emperor) desired that whereas one Sebastian Gabote, or Cabot, grand pilot of the Emperor's Indies, was then in England, forasmuch as he could not stand the King in any great stead, seeing that he had but small practice in these seas and was a very necessary man for the Emperor, whose servant he was and had a pension of him, that some order might be taken for his sending over." [1]   But the Privy Council had its own views on the subject : " as for Sebastian Cabot he of himself refused to go either into Spain or to the Emperor, and that he being of that mind, and the King of England's subject, no reason or equity would that he should be forced or compelled to go against his will." [2]   On 21st June 1550 Sebastian " Cabotto " receives a warrant to the Exchequer for £200, " by waie of the King's Majestie's rewarde." Strype gives the date of this grant as March 1551, possibly payment may have been delayed until that date, or Strype may have mistaken the date. Upon this the legend has grown that Sebastian Cabot was granted this money as a reward for managing the case against the Germans. Thus Mr. Coote : " Important work was soon found for Cabot, in addition to a general supervision of the maritime affairs of the country. He was called upon to settle the long-growing disputes that had almost reached their height between the merchants of the Steelyard, a colony of German traders of the Hanseatic League, and the merchants of London, who, for a long period, had suffered from the monopolies exercised by the former." But this story, as Harrisse [3] shows, has no better authority than Campbell's *Lives of the Admirals*. Moreover, Mr. Coote is again wrong when he says that " the Company of Merchant Adventurers was formed and incorporated on 18th December 1551 with Cabot as Governor for life." M. Harrisse makes it clear that Cabot was not Governor of the Company at least until after 1552. M. Harrisse, however, thinks it proved that Sebastian Cabot was Governor of the Merchant

---

[1] Strype, E. M., vol. ii. pt. i. p. 296.
[2] Harl. MS. 523, fo. 6, quoted by Coote on "Sebastian Cabot " in *D.N.B.*
[3] *John Cabot and Sebastian his Son*, by Henry Harrisse (1896), p. 331.

Adventurers' Company, depending on Willoughby's statement that his sailing instructions were "compiled, made, and delivered by the right worshipfull Sebastian Cabota, Esquier, Governor of the Mysterie and Companie of the Merchants Adventurers," and again that the document is signed "I Sebastian Cabota, Governour." Therefore, says Harrisse, "there can be no doubt that in May 1553 he was already in possession of the office."

But for my part I find it hard to believe that Cabot, a mariner and map-maker by profession, should ever have filled such an office. The Merchant Adventurers had been for generations the great national Guild of the wholesale cloth-merchants, regulating the price and the sale of cloth in England and in Flanders. It had subsidiary guilds in all the great towns of England connected with the cloth export trade, Bristol included. What did Cabot know about the sale of cloth ? The fact is that M. Harrisse falls into the same error as all his predecessors. Sebastian Cabot was not Governor of the Merchant Adventurers, but " Governour of the Mysterie and Companie of the Marchants Adventurers for the discoverie of Regions, Dominions, Islands and Places Unknowen." [1] The geographical limits of the Merchant Adventurers' Company proper would not have covered such a voyage : it was necessary to promote a subsidiary company. This subsidiary company became, in due course, the Russia Company, and is called " The Merchants of Russia " in the Royal Charter of 1555. It is of this company that Sebastian Cabot is here and elsewhere styled Governor.

APPENDIX VI

THE "BAYE" IN HANSEATIC DOCUMENTS

The " Baie " and the " Browasie " belong evidently to the most important commercial places of the West, from the middle of the fourteenth to the end of the sixteenth centuries.

---

[1] Hakluyt, vol. ii. p. 195 (1903 ed.).

All the Easterlings had intercourse with these places.[1] Besides other products (wine, oil), particularly the "Baiensalz" (salt from the sea, brine) was exported from there to the East.

Browase, Browasie, also Borwasie, and Latin Burwongia, is the modern Brouage, south of Rochefort, north of Bourdeaux. The *Spiegel der Seefahrt* (1589) (Mirror of Navigation), which still uses the French name Brouage (in the Index) beside the German Brovagien, says that in its (chart) map it shows the counties "Poictou" and "Xantoigne," &c.—"Here are situated the islands St. Martin and Oleron, *which produce salt in abundance.* On the first is *Brouage* . . . and the whole of France, the Netherlands, Norway, *and every place on the Baltic*, also Lithunia and Russia, are furnished with this salt." Merian, *Topographia Galliæ* (1654), vol. vii. p. 16: "Brouage . . . has a good harbour, *and salt is being made there.*" *Missive of the Council of Dantzig to the King of France* (1491) mentions a naval engagement which had taken place "sub oris Brittanniæ ante Bayas"—the author must have taken "Baye" as a certain place in the Bretagne. Indeed, such a place is to be found in the *Spiegel der Seefahrt:* Baye in the (modern) Bai of Bourgneuf. A document[2] in the *Archives of Dantzig* supports this view. It says, that a number of Prussian and English "Admirals," Captains and Skippers handed over to the "Komthur" of Dantzig (a dignitary of the "Teutonic Knights," governor) a report about a brawl which had taken place, in 1443, between Hollandish and English seamen "in the Baye," and in which the Prussians had intervened. The drunken affair ends with the Hollanders being sent to *Bunde* (on the old map called Bonges) and the English to *Bourgneuf.* There cannot be any doubt that "*the Baye*" means the small harbour in front of Bourgneuf. "Bayensalt" is the coarse sea-salt found in great quantities on the islands and the shore in the Bai of Bourgneuf, as distinguished from the "Travensalt" gained by boiling, at Lüneburg and exported via Lübeck. The name has deceived some writers, who take it to be the Bay of Biscay.[3]

---

[1] Chronicles of Weinreich, Detmar, and Kantzow.
[2] No. 2462, *Dantz. Arch.*, LXIX.
[3] See Theodor Hirsch and F. A. Vossberg, *Explanations to Caspar Weinreich's Dantziger Chronicle.*

Although I have generally given my sources for points of consequence at the foot of the page, the following list of the more important authorities may be found of service :

Geschichte der Stadt Köln, aus den Quellen des Kölner Stadt-Archives.— Von Dr. Leonard Ennen. Köln and Neuss, 1869.

Dr. Georg Schanz, A.O., Professor der Staatswissenschaften in Erlangen.— Englische Handelspolitik gegen Ende des Mittelalters mit besonderer Berücksichtigung des Zeitalters der beiden ersten Tudors Heinrich VII und Heinrich VIII. Leipzig, 1881.

Dr. Leonard Ennen und Dr. Gottfried Eckertz.—Quellen zur Geschichte der Stadt Köln. Köln, 1863–79.

J. M. Lappenberg.—G. F. Sartorius Freyherrn von Waltershausen, Urkundliche Geschichte des Ursprunges der deutschen Hanse. Edited by J. M. Lappenberg. Hamburg, 1830.

J. M. Lappenberg, Dr.—Urkundliche Geschichte des Hansischen Stahlhofes zu London. Hamburg, 1851.

Georg Sartorius, Professor at Göttingen.—Geschichte des Hanseatischen Bundes. Göttingen, 1802.

Die Welfen-Urkunden des Tower zu London und des Exchequer zu Westminster.—Edited by Dr. H. Sudendorf. Hannover, 1844.

Hanse Recesse from 1431–1476.—Verein für hansische Geschichte, Lübeck.

Hanse Recesse.—Königliche Akademie der Wissenschaften, Munich.

Bertrand de Salignac de la Mothe Fénélon.—Correspondance diplomatique de 1568 à 1575. Ed. Edinburgh, Bannatyne Club, 1838.

Urkundenbuch der Stadt Braunschweig, 1227–1499.—Edited by the Archiv-Verein zu Braunschweig. Braunschweig, 1862.

Hansisches Urkundenbuch.—Edited by Konstantin Höhlbaum. Published by the Verein für Hansische Geschichte.

Der Hansische Stahlhof in London.—Ein Vortrag, gehalten im Saale des goldenen Sterns zu Bonn am 11ten März, 1856, von Reinhold Pauli. Bremen, 1856.

Abhandlungen zur Verkehrs- und Seegeschichte, im Auftrage des Hansischen Geschichtsvereins, herausgegeben von Dietrich Schäfer. Band V. Die Hanse und England von Eduards III bis auf Heinrichs VIII Zeit, von Dr. Friedrich Schulz. Berlin, 1911.

Friedrich Rauers.—Zur Geschichte der alten Handelsstrassen in Deutschland, Gotha. Justus Perthes, 1907. (Herausgegeben vom Verein für Hansische Geschichte.)

Hansische Chronik, aus beglaubigten Nachrichten zusammen getragen von D. Johann Peter Willebrandt. Lübeck, 1748.

Chronik des Franciscaner Lesemeisters Detmar, nach der Urschrift, etc., herausgegeben von Dr. F. H. Grautoff, Professor und Bibliothekar in Lübeck. Hamburg, 1830.

Caspar Weinreich's Dantziger Chronik. Herausgegeben von Theodor Hirsch und F. A. Vossberg. Berlin, 1855.

Die wirtschaftlichen Grundlagen der deutschen Hanse und die Handels-
stellung Hamburgs bis in die zweite Hälfte des 14ten Jahrhunderts.
Von Dr. jur. G. Arnold Kiesselbach, Secretär der Handelskammer
in Hamburg. Berlin, 1907.

Die Beziehungen der Hanse zu England im letzten Drittel des 14ten Jahrhunderts.—Von Dr. F. Keutgen. Giessen, 1890.

Beiträge zur Geschichte der deutschen Hanse bis um die Mitte des 15ten
Jahrhunderts.—Von Walther Stein. Giessen, 1900.

Hansisch-Venetianische Handelsbeziehungen im 15ten Jahrhundert.—Von
Wilhelm Stieda. Rostock, 1894.

Die Hanse.—Von Prof. Dr. Dietrich Schäfer. Biebfeld, Leipzig, 1903.

Die Haltung der Hansestädte in den Rosenkriegen.—Von Reinhold
Pauli. Hansische Geschichtsblätter, 1874–76, herausgegeben vom
Verein für Hansische Geschichte. Leipzig, 1878.

Hanseakten aus England, 1275–1412.—Edited by Karl Kunze. Verein
für Hansische Geshichte. Hansische Geschichtsquellen, vol. vi.
Halle, 1891.

Professor Georg Waitz.—Lübeck unter Jürgen Wullenweber und die
europäisches Politik. Berlin, 1855.

Constantin Höhlbaum.—Mittenlungen aus dem Stadtarchiv von Köln.
Cologne, 1882.

Walther Stein.—Die Genossenschaft der deutschen Kaufleute zu Brügge
in Flandern. Berlin, 1890.

Paul de Rapin-Thoyras.—Acta Regia, or an Account of the Treaties,
Letters and Instruments . . . published in Mr. Rhymer's Fœdera,
1726.

Thomas Rymer, Fœdera, conventiones, &c. London, 1816.

Adam Anderson.—An Historical and Chronological Deduction of the
Origin of Commerce. 4 vols. London, 1787.

Richard Hakluyt.—The Principal Navigations, Voyages, Traffiques and
Discoveries of the English Nation. 12 vols. Glasgow, 1903–04.

John Wheeler, Secretary to the Society of Merchant Adventurers.—A
Treatise of Commerce, wherein are shewed the commodies [sic]
arising by a wel ordered . . . Trade . . . such as that of Mer-
chantes Adventurers is proved to bee, &c. London, 1601.

Calendar of State Papers, Foreign, Venetian, Simancas, Domestic
Chronicles and Memorials, &c. (Rolls Series).

INDEX

THE END

Printed by BALLANTYNE, HANSON & CO.
Edinburgh & London

THE NATIONAL REVIEW

THOSE who are acquainted with the policy of the *National Review*, edited by L. J. Maxse, will never forget the supreme and ceaseless efforts made in its pages for the past 20 years to arouse the British Nation to a lively sense of the dangers threatening its existence and to the necessity of preparing to meet them.

The purpose of the *Review* to be National in thought, scope and sentiment has never been lost sight of for a moment, and those who have consulted the editorial Episodes of the Month— a leading feature of the *National Review*—have secured invaluable information not obtainable anywhere else in which fearless and brilliant criticism and a fine fighting spirit for the highest cause are predominant characteristics.

The present demand for it is a gratifying testimonial from that section of the Public who have learnt how effectively its purpose has been fulfilled.

The Annual Subscription rate is 30/– post free. Single copies, 2/6 net.

14 TAVISTOCK STREET, COVENT GARDEN, LONDON, W.C.

PLEASE DO NOT REMOVE
CARDS OR SLIPS FROM THIS POCKET

UNIVERSITY OF TORONTO LIBRARY

ImTheStory.com

Personalized Classic Books in many genre's

Unique gift for kids, partners, friends, colleagues

Customize:

- Character Names

- Upload your own front/back cover images (optional)

- Inscribe a personal message/dedication on the

    inside page (optional)

Customize many titles Including
- Alice in Wonderland
- Romeo and Juliet
- The Wizard of Oz
- A Christmas Carol
- Dracula
- Dr. Jekyll & Mr. Hyde
- And more...

Lightning Source UK Ltd.
Milton Keynes UK
UKHW021518090919
349456UK00015B/4318/P